Speaking with God

 McMaster Divinity College Press
**McMaster Biblical Studies Series,
Volume 8**

Speaking with God
Probing Old Testament Prayers for Contemporary Significance

Edited by
PHILLIP G. CAMP and ELAINE A. PHILLIPS

☙PICKWICK *Publications* • Eugene, Oregon

SPEAKING WITH GOD
Probing Old Testament Prayers for Contemporary Significance

McMaster Biblical Studies Series, Volume 8
McMaster Divinity College Press

Copyright © 2021 Wipf and Stock Publishers. All rights reserved. Except for brief quotations in critical publications or reviews, no part of this book may be reproduced in any manner without prior written permission from the publisher. Write: Permissions, Wipf and Stock Publishers, 199 W. 8th Ave., Suite 3, Eugene, OR 97401.

Pickwick Publications
An Imprint of Wipf and Stock Publishers
199 W. 8th Ave., Suite 3
Eugene, OR 97401

McMaster Divinity College Press
1280 Main Street West
Hamilton, Ontario, Canada
L8S 4K1

www.wipfandstock.com

PAPERBACK ISBN: 978-1-7252-8351-0
HARDCOVER ISBN: 978-1-7252-8349-7
EBOOK ISBN: 978-1-7252-8352-7

Cataloguing-in-Publication data:

Names: Camp, Phillip G., editor | Phillips, Elaine A., editor

Title: Speaking with god : probing old testament prayers for contemporary significance / Phillip G. Camp and Elaine A. Phillips.

Description: Eugene, OR: Pickwick Publications, 2021 | McMaster Biblical Studies Series | Includes bibliographical references and indexes.

Identifiers: ISBN 978-1-7252-8351-0 (paperback) | ISBN 978-1-7252-8349-7 (hardcover) | ISBN 978-1-7252-8352-7 (ebook)

Subjects: LCSH: Bible. Old Testament—Prayers—History and criticism | Prayer—Biblical teaching.

Classification: BS1199.P68 C36 2021 (paperback) | BS1199.P68 (ebook)

09/20/21

A previously published version of Daniel I. Block's "Wrestling with God: A Study on Prayer in Deuteronomy" appeared in *The Triumph of Grace: Literary and Theological Studies in Deuteronomy and Deuteronomic Themes*. Eugene, OR: Cascade, 2017, 240–63. It is used here by permission.

A previously published version of Steven Mann's, "Ask and You Shall Intercede: The Peculiar Perlocutionary Power of Asking God Questions," appeared in *BBR* 29 (2019) 208–24. Copyright © 2019. The revised article is used by permission of the Pennsylvania State University Press.

Contents

Preface / vii
Abbreviations / ix

Introduction: Setting the Stage

1. Prayers in the Hebrew Bible: Boundaries, Intentions, and Theological Interfaces / 3
   —Elaine A. Phillips

Section 1: Moses' Prayers

2. Wrestling with God: A Study on Prayer in Deuteronomy / 23
   —Daniel I. Block

Section 2: Prayers of Kings

3. The Temple Prayer of Solomon (1 Kings 8:1—9:9) / 51
   —Ted Hildebrandt

4. Changing the Mind of God: The Prayer and Tears of King Hezekiah (2 Kings 20:1–6) / 66
   —David T. Lamb

5. "We Do Not Know What We Should Do, but Our Eyes Are on You": The Prayer of King Jehoshaphat in 2 Chronicles 20:6–12 / 81
   —Brittany Kim

Section 3: Prayers of Prophets

6 A Prophet like Fire, Burned Out, and Rekindled: Exploring the Significance of Elijah's Prayers (1 Kgs 17–19) / 101
—MICHAEL WIDMER

7 Joyously Drawing Water from the Springs of Salvation: Praise as Structure and Goal of the Book of Isaiah / 119
—MARK J. BODA

8 "Do Not Pray, Plead, or Pester Me Because No One is Listening" (Jeremiah 7:16) / 138
—ELAINE A. PHILLIPS

9 Ask and You Shall Intercede: The Power of a Prayerful Imagination / 154
—STEVEN T. MANN

Section 4: Prayers of Others

10 Prayers of Women in the Old Testament Narratives: A Theological Exploration / 175
—PHILLIP G. CAMP

11 Getting It Right While Getting It Wrong: Joshua's Prayer in Joshua 7 / 192
—DAVID G. FIRTH

12 A House of Prayer for All Nations? Temple, Prayer, and Xenophobia in Ezra 9 and 1 Kings 8 / 207
—KEVIN J. YOUNGBLOOD

13 Recycled and Reclaimed: God's Words as Echoed in Nehemiah's Prayer (1:5–11) / 225
—SHERI L. KLOUDA SHARP

14 Agur's Prayer (Proverbs 30:7–9): An Everyday Response to Extraordinary Revelation / 238
—JOANNA GREENLEE KLINE

Postscript: Reflections after Seven Years of Studying Prayer in the Old Testament / 253
—PHILLIP G. CAMP

Index of Modern Authors / 261
Index of Ancient Sources / 265

Preface

THE CHAPTERS IN THIS book, with just a few exceptions, began as presentations in the "Theology of Prayer in the Old Testament" research group at the annual meetings of the Institute for Biblical Research (IBR) from 2015 to 2018. We, the book's editors, served as co-chairs of the group, which was formed at the suggestion of Tremper Longman III, president of the IBR during that time. At that point, he and Phillip Camp had just co-edited an initial volume on the topic, *Praying with Ancient Israel: Exploring the Theology of Prayer in the Old Testament* (Abilene Christian University Press, 2015). This was a collection of presentations on the theology of prayer for the Thomas H. Olbricht Christian Scholars' Conference at Lipscomb University from 2012 to 2014. It was clear, however, that the topic was far from exhausted!

Whereas the earlier volume focused broadly on the theologies of prayer in the different parts of the OT canon, this current collection explores the prayers of particular individuals within the framework of their role(s) in the covenant community. These range from prayers of Israel's leaders and prophets to those of women and a seemingly obscure contributor to the Wisdom corpus, Agur.

The contributing authors are all scholars who do their work not only to contribute to the academy but also to serve the church. To this end, every chapter includes reflections on how these studies can help individual believers better understand prayer and more meaningfully engage in practices of communication with God. It is our own prayer that readers will discover anew the joy of their deepening relationships with God.

Preface

To make book more accessible to readers who are not specialists in biblical and theological studies, we have tried to reduce the academic jargon, and Hebrew has been transliterated following *The SBL Handbook of Style*'s general-purpose transliteration.[1] Also, where the English versions' versification differs from the Hebrew, the English verses are cited with the Hebrew in brackets (e.g., Ps 44:9 [10]). With respect to the use of YHWH or Yahweh for the Divine Name, we retained the individual authors' preferences.

In addition to the contributors, we want to thank the following for their support and encouragement: our institutions, Lipscomb University and Gordon College, McMaster Divinity College Press, Wipf & Stock Publishers, and the Institute for Biblical Research. Our spouses, Amy and Perry, deserve special and loving acknowledgement for their unswerving devotion to the God of the Scriptures and to each of us. In the latter case, that is nearing on half a century! To God be the glory!

---

1. For the transliteration guide, see section 5.1.2 in *SBLHS*, 58–59. The one exception to the transliteration guide is that we distinguish the *aleph* and *ayin*, using a single close-quotation mark (') for the former and a single open-quotation (') mark for the latter.

Abbreviations

AB	Anchor Bible
ACCS	Ancient Christian Commentary on Scripture
ANET	Pritchard, James B., ed. *Ancient Near Eastern Texts Relating to the Old Testament*. 3rd ed. Princeton: Princeton University Press, 1969.
ANEM	Ancient Near Eastern Monographs
ApOTC	Apollos Old Testament Commentary
BBR	*Bulletin for Biblical Research*
BBRSup	Bulletin for Biblical Research Supplement Series
BCOTWP	Baker Commentary on the Old Testament Wisdom and Psalms
BDB	Brown, Francis, S. R. Driver, and Charles A. Briggs. *A Hebrew and English Lexicon of the Old Testament*. Oxford: Clarendon, 1907.
BECNT	Baker Exegetical Commentary on the New Testament
BETL	Bibliotheca Ephemeridum theologicarum Lovaniensium
Bib	*Biblica*
BibInt	*Biblical Interpretation*
BKAT	Biblischer Kommentar Altes Testament
BO	Berit Olam
BSac	*Bibliotheca Sacra*
BZAW	Beihefte zur Zeitschrift für die alttestamentliche Wissenschaft

Abbreviations

BZNW	Beihefte zur Zeitschrift für die neutestamentliche Wissenschaft
CATR	*Canadian-American Theological Review*
CBQ	*Catholic Biblical Quarterly*
CBQMS	Catholic Biblical Quarterly Monograph Series
COS	Hallo, William W., and K. Lawson Younger Jr., eds. *The Context of Scripture*. 4 vols. Leiden: Brill, 1997–2016.
DCH	Clines, D. J. A., ed. *Dictionary of Classical Hebrew*. 9 vols. Sheffield, 1993–2014.
FAT	Forschungen zum Alten Testament
FOTL	Forms of Old Testament Literature
GKC	Gesenius, Wilhelm. *Gesenius' Hebrew Grammar*, edited by Emil Kautzsch. Translated by Arthur E. Cowley. 2nd ed. Oxford: Clarendon, 1910.
HALOT	Koehler, Ludwig, Walter Baumgartner, and Johann J. Stamm. *The Hebrew and Aramaic Lexicon of the Old Testament*. Translated and edited under the supervision of Mervyn E. J. Richardson. 2 vols. Leiden: Brill, 2001.
HBM	Hebrew Bible Monographs
HvTSt	*Hervormde Teologiese Studies*
IBC	Interpretation: A Bible Commentary for Teaching and Preaching
ICC	International Critical Commentary
Int	*Interpretation: A Journal of Bible and Theology*
JBL	*Journal of Biblical Literature*
JSOT	*Journal for the Study of the Old Testament*
JSOTSup	Journal for the Study of the Old Testament Supplement Series
LHBOTS	The Library of Hebrew Bible/Old Testament Studies
NAC	New American Commentary
NCBC	New Century Bible Commentary
NIBC	New International Biblical Commentary
NICNT	New International Commentary on the New Testament

Abbreviations

NICOT	New International Commentary on the Old Testament
NIDOTTE	VanGemeren, Willem A., ed. *New International Dictionary of Old Testament Theology and Exegesis.* 5 vols. Grand Rapids: Zondervan, 1997.
NIVAC	New International Version Application Commentary
NSBT	New Studies in Biblical Theology
OBT	Overtures to Biblical Theology
OTG	Old Testament Guides
OTL	Old Testament Library
PBM	Paternoster Biblical Monographs
SBLHS	*Society of Biblical Literature Handbook of Style.* 2nd ed. Atlanta, GA: SBL Press, 2014
SBLWAW	Society of Biblical Literature Writings from the Ancient World
SBS	Stuttgarter Bibelstudien
SHBC	Smyth & Helwys Bible Commentary
SJOT	*Scandinavian Journal of the Old Testament*
SSN	Studia Semitica Neerlandica
SymS	Symposium Series
TOTC	Tyndale Old Testament Commentaries
TynBul	*Tyndale Bulletin*
VT	*Vetus Testamentum*
VTSup	Supplements to Vetus Testamentum
WBC	Word Biblical Commentary
ZAW	*Zeitschrift für die alttestamentliche Wissenschaft*

Introduction

Setting the Stage

1

Prayers in the Hebrew Bible

Boundaries, Intentions, and Theological Interfaces

ELAINE A. PHILLIPS

INTRODUCTION

WE ARE EMBARKING ON an exploration of individuals' prayers as we encounter them in the Hebrew Bible. This venture invites us to pause with familiar biblical figures and listen again. As we do, our initial questions will be: what actually constitutes prayer? Does all second-person address to the God of heaven qualify as prayer, even if there is no perceived response? In addition, in the wealth of biblical narrative and poetry, we find a number of what we might label as failed attempts to communicate with God. What about those? Interwoven with these questions is the rich literary and theological fabric that lies inside whatever boundaries we draw.

DEFINITION AND BOUNDARIES—"ARE WE EVER NOT PRAYING?"

Even with the matter of definition, a number of interrelated issues must be sorted through. The distinctions below are not intended to create

Introduction: Setting the Stage

discrete categories. They are simply a means of formulating with some degree of order the components of a possible definition.

Verbal

We turn first to the matter of Hebrew prayer vocabulary. In addition to the noun, *tefillah* (prayer), and its related cognates, we encounter *darash* (seek, inquire), *'atar* (entreat), *sha'al* (ask), *yadah* (thank), and *barakh* (bless). "Calling upon the Name of the Lord" and "X said to God . . . " are also signals in narrative portions of Scripture.[1] These are not, however, entirely sufficient to cover what happens in conjunction with wide-ranging conversations with God. Often lodged deeply in the brokenness of human experience, prayer bursts forth in emotionally charged circumstances that prompt crying out, summoning, pleading, and seeking God's face. The supplicant often asked for favor or grace (*tekhinnah* and cognate forms). Some of these reach a desperation level well beyond "conversation."

Prayer may also include accusatory questions that emerge from doubt and fear in one's wretched straits. "How long, O Lord?" is a familiar one, and it demanded a response. The divine Partner was occasionally called upon to "wake up" (Isa 51:9–10) followed by pleas to "protect, keep, guard, or deliver" (Ps 7:1–6 [2–7]). In dire circumstances, oaths and even curses might be uttered. Should these terms be caught in our vocabulary net or do they remain outside?

Beyond Verbal

To the verbal indicators of prayer, add physical involvement—tears, loud inarticulate cries, kneeling, lifting up hands, and falling prostrate to the ground. Those who prayed sometimes turned to music, because music has the capacity to transport the human soul when the vocabulary fails (2 Kgs 3:9–20). There are "sung prayers" beyond the boundaries of the recorded psalms. This foray into prayer vocabulary has already drawn us toward matters of form and motivation.

---

1. Balentine, *Prayer in the Hebrew Bible*, 31.

Form

In the psalms, we find praise and thanksgiving, confession and petition, pleas for deliverance and blessing, complaints, and laments, all of which have recognizable formal features. Does each of these shape our deeper understanding of the sovereign God to whom Israel directed its liturgy? At the least, having liturgical structures, especially for thanksgiving and blessing, is necessary to keep our prayers from being primarily in response to crises.

Among the characteristic forms, laments are worthy of special consideration because they juxtapose two apparently irreconcilable truths—the presumed utter trustworthiness of God alongside the devastating experience(s) of the one grieving. Further, there are those laments that say precious little about God's faithfulness, and instead describe the heavy hand of God. The classic example is Ps 88, which is a microcosm of Job. The tragedy of human loss resonates through David's lament over Jonathan (2 Sam 1:17–27). These anguished expressions prompted Goldingay to redefine the prayer of lament as outright protest.[2] From there, it is a very short step to the uncertainty, fear, and anger that often underlie vows, oaths, and imprecations. Are these likewise lodged under the umbrella of prayer?

A further matter of form merits our consideration before turning to intentions and motives underlying biblical prayers. Our own prayers do not always arrive fully formulated. In fact, they are often feeble attempts bereft of substantial focus and shape other than self-centered grumbling. This is likewise true of the saints of the Hebrew Bible as they appealed to God in their straits. In sum, we might make a case for a rather wide range of vocabularies and forms.

Just as the section on "vocabulary" included non-verbal expressions, the accoutrements for prayer are noteworthy. Wearing sackcloth is sometimes associated with prayer (e.g., 1 Chr 21:16–17; Ps 35:13; Dan 9:3; Jonah 3:5–8). Prayer and fasting were occasionally conjoined (1 Sam 7:6; Ezra 9:3—10:6). What did these accomplish toward the efficacy of that prayer? Rituals such as pouring out water (1 Sam 7:6)

---

2. Goldingay, *Theology: Volume Three*, 209–22.

Introduction: Setting the Stage

were also part of the solemn gathering. Could it be that more serious circumstances required more liturgical "vestment"?

Intention: Call and Response

God's people prayed because they were invited, in fact, commanded to do so. Even though the Israelites would be scattered because of their idolatry, God promised that when they returned to God, seeking him with all their heart, they would find him (Deut 4:29). The prophet Jeremiah echoed these words: "Then you will call (*qara'*) upon me and come and pray (*hitpallel*) to me, and I will hear you. You will seek (*darash*) me and find me, when you seek me with all your heart" (Jer 29:12–13, ESV). God repeatedly commanded his radically disobedient children to *seek* him (Amos 5; see also Zeph 2:3). Isaiah prodded the people who call upon the Lord to give him no rest as they continued to pray (62:6–7). The motive above all was to restore and maintain relationship with God.

God's people prayed that God would hear, see, remember, forgive, deliver, and bring justice. These prayers arose from front-line needs as enemies threatened, famine struck, leaders made errors, individual suffering and uncertainty loomed. Fear was a prominent part of the emotional landscape surrounding many of the prayers; the circumstances were sufficiently horrifying to rupture the fragile trust God's people had in his faithfulness. In those contexts, afflicted people and individuals tried to sort through the meaning of their experiences, accompanied by the apparent silence from the heavenly realms.

In addition to praying through the crises of their lives, other situations motivated prayer. God's people offered thanks to God for his manifold blessings and expressed their trust in him with prayers that were songs (Isa 25:1–5; 26:1–3). Jacob boldly asked for blessing (Gen 32:24–32), and Jabez requested both blessing and freedom from harm (1 Chr 4:9–10). Does the frequency and fervency of prayer change in the flush of good circumstances? Proverbs 30:7–9 suggests an unsettling tendency to forget about God when all seems to be going well (see also Deut 6:10–15; 8:11–20).

Additional motivating factors for prayer appear in the Hebrew Bible. Samson's father asked for specific knowledge as to how to rear the promised son as a Nazirite (1 Sam 13). Elijah implored God that the people would know that the God of the covenant with Abraham, Isaac, and Israel is indeed God (1 Kgs 18:36–37). God's triumph over Baal and Asherah at Mount Carmel was followed by Elijah's conversation with the LORD at Horeb, expressing his despair at being the only one left who did not bow the knee to Baal (1 Kgs 19:9–14).

This exchange between God and Elijah raises another question for our investigation. There are occasions when God commissioned his servants to engage a particular task, and they talked back. We might think of Moses's commissioning (Exod 3:1—4:17) or that of Jeremiah (Jer 1:4–10). In Elijah's case, his complaint to the effect that he was the only one left and that his enemies were out to get him was the catalyst for God's giving him three more tasks (1 Kgs 19:15–17). Did these dialogues constitute prayer on the part of the human participant?

A further question arises: is there a distinct marker on the route between self-focused lament and fledgling attempts to call on an apparently *silent* God? Job would be our test case here, but there may be others as well. When God was to all intents and purposes silent, did that prayer fail to be prayer? In that regard, the notion that prayer is primarily a means of self-help surfaces occasionally; the one praying is refined through the process of articulating the concerns, and that is what really counts. That is, however, an insidiously anemic view of prayer—and of God. In fact, prayer as it was practiced in the Hebrew Bible was intended to move God to action.[3]

THEOLOGICAL CONNECTIONS: COVENANT AND KINGDOM

God's covenant with his people has everything to do with relationship; so does prayer. On the basis of the covenant, they appealed for mercy, even in the face of deserved judgment. "For the LORD is good and his unfailing covenant love (*khesed*) endures forever" is a repeated refrain. The Israelites affirmed that God was their transcendent majestic and glorious King; all of reality is his Kingdom. At the same time, God's

---

3. Goldingay, *Theology: Volume Three*, 230–31.

Introduction: Setting the Stage

people directed their appeals to the "eyes" and "ears" of God, emphasizing his immanence and presence with them.

Under the Kingdom and covenant umbrella, the roles and character of those who prayed are also significant. In many cases, they were leaders of God's people. Nevertheless, there are a number of prayers from "ordinary folks."

Theocratic Offices

The prayers of theocratic leaders are those most often recorded. These prayers reflect prophetic voices, royal figures, and the office of the priest. Within that configuration, we might expect to read more prayers from priests because they, after all, were to serve as mediators. Nevertheless, they are actually the least represented among leaders' recorded prayers.

Prayers of the Prophets[4]

This is a large and potentially unwieldy category. For now, we will simply summarize the intercessory roles of significant prophetic figures to see what patterns might emerge, what unique features pique our curiosity, and how these continuities and discontinuities might be focal points for further study. Whether or not miraculous activity accompanied the prophets' messages also requires our attention.

In the remarkable exchange between the Lord and Moses after the golden calf incident (Exod 32–34), that premier prophet (Deut 18:15–22; 34:10–12) interceded on behalf of God's flagrantly disobedient people. Well before that, however, Moses had been in the unusual position of praying for the oppressive pharaoh and his people when they felt the heavy force of God's judgments (Exod 8:28–32; 9:27–35; 10:16–20).

In the historical books, the most significant prophetic voices who also uttered prayers on behalf of God's people include Samuel, Elijah, and Elisha. Each of them appeared at critical points in Israel's history, and, while they appealed to the Lord, the recorded contents of their

---

4. Widmer, *Standing in the Breach*, explores at length the major prophetic and intercessory figures in the Hebrew Bible, from Abraham through the towering figures of Moses, Samuel, Solomon, and Jeremiah to the prayers of Amos and Joel. The bottom line—intercessory prayer is the heart of theology.

prayers are relatively abbreviated—sometimes non-existent. We simply know that they prayed and God responded.

At the outset, Samuel was assured of his calling in a conversation that God initiated (1 Sam 3:1–14). Subsequently, while serving as judge, prophet, and priest, Samuel interceded on behalf of the people at Mizpah and God answered (7:5–9). Likewise, Samuel prayed regarding the king they requested, and God answered (8:6–9; 12:18–25). He later cried out to the Lord all night regarding Saul's catastrophic disobedience (15:11). After the Lord removed his spirit from Saul, Samuel asked the Lord, "How can I go to Bethlehem to anoint David?" and received specific instructions so as to avoid the paranoid wrath of Saul (16:1–3). This was an anxious question to which God provided an answer. Was it prayer? Did it fall into the category of intercession in the covenant context? It certainly continued the process toward enthroning the man after God's own heart even though that came to pass much later.

By the time Elijah burst onto the scene, the kingdom had split, and the north was awash in Baal worship that had been imported from Phoenicia as the state religion by Ahab and Jezebel. Elijah's initial prayer engaged that menace directly as he pleaded with God for the life of the deceased son of the widow of Zarephath in Phoenician territory (1 Kgs 17:19–24). Elijah invoked the name of the Lord God of Abraham, Isaac, and Jacob against the prophets of Baal and Asherah on Mount Carmel (1 Kgs 18:36–37). In other words, he called God to remember God's covenant relationship and turn the hearts of the people back. God responded mightily, but Elijah was sufficiently frightened by the royal power of the house of Ahab that, even after this apparent triumph, he fled directly to Horeb, the source of the covenant. Elijah expressed his deep despair at the turn of events and God responded again (1 Kgs 19:9–18). One of his appointed tasks was to anoint Elisha.

Surrounded by enemies at Dothan and apparently gravely threatened (2 Kgs 6:17–20), Elisha's prayers had to do with seeing—or not. He first requested that the eyes of his terrified servant be opened to see the heavenly hosts surrounding them. Immediately thereafter, he asked that the enemy forces be struck with blindness; they were led directly to Samaria and, once there, their eyes were opened!

Introduction: Setting the Stage

Fear and anxiety are common factors in these narratives of prayer, launched into geo-political and religious contexts that were overwhelming from the human perspective. It is important that we not overlook the drama of God's responses: ongoing oracular guidance for Samuel, pyrotechnics as well as a profound silence[5] for Elijah, and a vision of the heavenly host for Elisha's servant.

A vision into the heavenly realms is a good segue to Isaiah, whose call in the temple involved both an extraordinary vision and a conversation (Isa 6). At the prospect of his forthcoming task, Isaiah first expressed his dismay at being unworthy, next said "send me," and finally inquired as to "how long?," to which he received a rather disheartening response.

Additional prayers in Isaiah are woven together with his prophetic and advisory roles. They reflect pleas of the people as well as his own petitions (see Isa 12; 25:1–5; 26:1–3, 7–15; 33:2–4). Isaiah promised that the LORD would be gracious when Israel cried for help, and would hear and answer (30:19; see also 55:6–7 and 58:9). With a sense of urgency, he summoned the arm of the LORD to wake up and act as in the days of old (51:9–10). In keeping with the universal focus of the book of Isaiah, the temple is called the "house of prayer for all nations" (56:7). In spite of these encouraging references, there are allusions to God's hiding his face (e.g., 54:8; 57:17), and to the fact that he would not hear (59:2).

Jeremiah's prayers are studies in lament and protest, arising from the horror of the fall of Jerusalem. More than once he accused God of deceiving both the people (4:10) and Jeremiah himself (20:7–18). In response to his complaint regarding God's ill treatment of him (15:15–18), God called him to repent, challenging him not to cave in (15:19–21). Threading its way through Jeremiah's prophetic utterances is a steady admonition from God back to Jeremiah: "Do not pray for this people . . . I will not listen" (7:16–28; 11:11–14; 14:11–12). This is frightening; the prophet whose task it was to call the people back to

---

5. The Hebrew is *kol demamah dakkah* (1 Kgs 19:12), suggesting an overwhelming and inexplicable experience of both sound and silence in the Presence of the LORD God of Israel.

covenant obedience was informed that the situation was too far gone.[6] The interwoven fabric of covenant and prayer had been torn apart.

We hear the same echoes in Ezekiel, a figure profoundly affected by the exile. God asked Ezekiel if he should allow the wicked elders of Israel to seek him (14:1–8; see also 20:1–3, 30–31). The implicit answer was no; they were no longer fit to engage in prayer. On a more personal note, after his difficult commission from God, the prophet went "with a bitter and angry spirit with the LORD's heavy hand upon him" (3:14). Although this was not a formulated prayer, it was a response to God's forceful spirit! Ezekiel also protested against God's command that he defile himself by cooking with human excrement (4:14). Ezekiel's title for God is "Sovereign LORD." "Will you, Sovereign LORD, destroy the entire remnant in wrath?" (9:8; see also 11:13), a prayer from the crucible of destruction and exile.

With Daniel, we encounter a wider range of prayer language, forms, persons, and circumstances. Daniel's first recorded prayer extolled the nature and wisdom of God as God made known the interpretation of the king's dream to Daniel (2:20–23). Daniel transgressed three times a day king Darius's edict against praying by offering thanks and petition (6:10–13). After the apocalyptic visions of chs. 7 and 8, Daniel engaged in full-fledged confession and pleading on behalf of the people (9:1–19), complete with fasting, sackcloth, and ashes. The prayer vocabulary is extensive—*tefillah*, *takhnunah*, and cognate forms are laced throughout the prayer. God's covenant relationship with his people was the theological backdrop, starting with the deliverance from Egypt. Daniel identified fully with his people's sins of rebellion against their righteous God, noting that the curses and judgments written in the Torah of Moses, now poured out against them, had been "earned." Daniel asked God to listen, forgive, hear, and act. While he was still praying, Gabriel came to give him understanding (9:20–23).

The Minor Prophets likewise hold a range of possibilities. In the dire circumstances represented by the locust plague, Joel issued a call to corporate prayer (1:13–14), followed by further exhortations to call on the LORD (2:12–17, 32). Amos repeatedly appealed to the northern kingdom to seek God and live (ch. 5). Their recalcitrance meant God's

---

6. See Widmer, *Standing in the Breach*, 346–55.

Introduction: Setting the Stage

impending judgment. Even so, Amos begged the LORD to forgive Jacob because Jacob was so small. Twice God relented (*nikham*), but then forestalled Amos's further plea, saying judgment was due (7:1–9).

Awash in the sea and fearing the depths of *she'ol*, disobedient Jonah called for help and followed that plea with a prayer of thanksgiving from the belly of the great fish (2:1–9 [2–10]). His prayer was efficacious and God rescued him, just as God chose to rescue the people of Nineveh, all of whom, from the king to the domestic animals, donned sackcloth, fasted, and called upon God (3:6–9). Jonah could not fathom this development, and his next prayer revealed both his understanding of God's *khesed* as well as his own perturbation that God would think to show that faithful, forgiving love to the Ninevites. A conversation ensued at this point as well. God questioned: "Do you have any right to be angry?" Jonah: "I do; it's better to die than be in these circumstances" (see 4:1–11).

The references to prayer in Micah are fleeting. Micah was a contemporary of Isaiah but lived "outside the Jerusalem beltway," and apparently did not hobnob with kings and leaders. He only briefly warned that unjust leaders would cry out but God would not answer (3:4), and closed his message with a doxology addressed to God: "Who is a God like you? . . . faithful to forgive sins, not holding on to anger forever, delighting in *khesed*, casting sins into the depths of the sea and being true to the covenant relationship with the forefathers" (7:18–20). By way of contrast, Habakkuk protested vigorously about the injustice that God apparently tolerated, asking "How long?" and pressing God further after God's initial response (chs. 1–2). Even though God's second response was disheartening in the short term, Habakkuk nevertheless sang a prayer (*tefillah*), rejoicing in God and his majestic power (ch. 3). Echoing Amos, Zephaniah admonished the people three times to seek God (2:3) even as the horrors of the Day of the LORD loomed (1:14–18). On the other side of those judgments, God would purify the lips of peoples so they could call upon the LORD and serve him (3:9).

In Zechariah, the *angel of the* LORD responded to the LORD (1:12–13), asking how long he would withhold mercy. That prompted the LORD's messages via both the angel and Zechariah whose visions warranted angelic interpretation. The message of Malachi is couched in a dispute form between the people and God as mediated by Malachi. Both Zechariah and Malachi introduce mediating voices in the "conversations," making the prospect of distinguishing elements of prayer more complicated.

Because the prophets were mediators of the covenant, kings were often their immediate audiences. We turn that direction next.

Prayers from the Throne

Even prior to the transition to the monarchy, Israel's leaders appealed to God. Joshua addressed the commander of the army of the Lord regarding the forthcoming battle for the land (Josh 5:13–15), and he pleaded with God regarding the loss at Ai (7:6–13). As a contrast, when the Gibeonites concocted their deceptive scheme, the narrative pointedly says that the Israelites neglected to inquire of the Lord (9:14). Nevertheless, Joshua prayed that the sun "be silent" over Gibeon during the battle to defend Israel's new Gibeonite allies, and the text indicates that "God listened to a man" (10:12–14).

The book of Judges commences with Israel as a whole inquiring of the Lord (1:1) and crying out for help (4:3; 6:6–7), a pattern that continued when they descended into bitter straits (10:10–15). At the same time, individual judges conversed with God. Gideon's initial call was accompanied by an exchange with the Lord (6:11–23), a good part of it intended to bolster his confidence. His request regarding the "fleece" is memorable (6:36–40). Jephthah's vow was also a prayer of sorts, sobering as its results were (11:30–31). Notably, Samson did not pray until the very end of his life when he was in the temple of Dagon in Gaza, calling out for vengeance on his enemies (16:28). Each of these individual instances seems on the margins of prayer as we commonly construe it, and yet the communication is vital.

The debacle at the end of the book of Judges compelled Israel to plead with God. Who should go first against Benjamin (20:18–28)? They took an oath at Mizpah (21:1–3) and cursed anyone who would give his daughter to a Benjamite man (21:18). It was a dismal close to that period and laid the ground for the transition to the monarchy. More to our pursuit, where on the fringes of prayer lie oaths and curses?

Introduction: Setting the Stage

En route to the monarchy, we are reminded of Samuel's role as he anointed both Saul and David, and agonized before the Lord when the former forfeited the kingdom by his disobedience. As king, Saul's attempts to communicate with the Lord were dubious at best. He put his army under an oath not to eat, with nearly disastrous results in regard to Jonathan. His inquiry of the Lord presumably utilized the Urim and Thummim, although they are not specified (1 Sam 14:24–45). When Saul tried again to inquire of the Lord just prior to the disastrous battle on Mount Gilboa, he encountered only silence, driving him to the witch at En-Dor (28:6). How do we understand attempts at prayer by those who have been cut off from God?

Because Abiathar escaped the purge of the priests by Saul (1 Sam 22:6-23) and brought the ephod with him to David, David was able to inquire on a regular basis for specific direction in regard to his next moves (1 Sam 23:1–12; 2 Sam 2:1; 5:19–25). Seeking the Lord and his guidance seemed to involve oracular equipment, manipulated in some way by the priest. Sometime during the reign of David, a severe famine afflicted Israel. David asked why the famine was happening, and God said it was on account of Saul's mistreatment of the Gibeonites (2 Sam 21:1). David gave seven descendants of Saul over to the Gibeonites who hanged them and left them exposed until the rains fell after the barley harvest (21:2–14). These were not instructions from the Lord but after it was all over, God did respond to their pleas for the land, perhaps because the end of the matter involved their proper treatment of the deceased. Nevertheless, this whole incident gives us pause.

David also uttered oaths, cementing his covenant with Jonathan (1 Sam 20:3) and his mourning for Abner (2 Sam 3:35). When he learned that a son of his would build the temple, he spoke to the Lord about the promises regarding David's "house" (2 Sam 7:18–29). After his transgressions with Bathsheba and Uriah, he pleaded with God and fasted until the child died, after which he worshiped God (2 Sam 12:16–20). Realizing the enormity of his sin of numbering the fighting men of Israel (2 Sam 24:10; 1 Chr 22:8), he accepted the plague at the hand of the Lord, and then offered a sacrifice on the site that would become the temple (2 Sam 24:14–25; 1 Chr 13–26; 2 Chr 3:1).

The prayer with which Solomon initiated his reign and his temple dedication prayer make him a high-profile figure for this study (1 Kgs 3–8). Among the many important covenant concerns articulated in his dedicatory prayer is Solomon's inclusion of foreigners who would have the privilege of praying to the God of heaven and earth in the context of the place where God had chosen to establish his Name (8:41–43). Solomon's prayer demonstrated that he knew the covenant sanctions for good and ill. God responded at length in 1 Kgs 9 (see also 2 Chr 6–7).

Starting with Rehoboam and Jeroboam, Israel's leaders characteristically depended on human wisdom rather than seeking God's direction, an ominous turn accompanying the downward spirals of both northern and southern kingdoms. In those cases, God delivered prophetic words to challenge their decisions. Examples that come to mind are Hanani's rebuke of Asa (2 Chr 16:7–9) and Micaiah's severe message to Ahab and Jehoshaphat (1 Kgs 22).

The exception to that observation is Hezekiah. Both the historical narrative and Isaiah's description indicate that, under the threat of Sennacherib, Hezekiah tore his clothes, put on sackcloth, went to the temple, and sent leaders to Isaiah for counsel (2 Kgs 19:1–14; Isa 37:1–14). He then prayed, pleading with God to incline his ear, open his eyes, see, and hear what Sennacherib had said, and save so that all would know God was God alone (2 Kgs 19:15–19; Isa 37:15–20). God's response came via Isaiah (2 Kgs 19:20–34; Isa 37:21–35).

Under quite different circumstances, Hezekiah prayed when he was ill, asking God to remember the good he had done (2 Kgs 20:2–3; Isa 38:2–3). God again responded through the words of Isaiah, granting him fifteen additional years and a sign (2 Kgs 20:4–11; Isa 38:4–8; see also 2 Chr 32:24). Notably, Manasseh was born during that added fifteen-year period; he was twelve years old when he became king upon Hezekiah's death. Manasseh's fifty-five year reign of terror was disastrous for Judah, but remarkably he sought the LORD from captivity in Assyria, and was restored to Jerusalem (2 Chr 33:1–20).[7]

---

7. The passing reference to Manasseh's prayer being "written" prompted what we know as the extra-canonical "Prayer of Manasseh."

Even though Josiah's reforms were notable, and he inquired of the prophet Huldah regarding the rediscovered book of the Torah (2 Kgs 22:13–20; 2 Chr 34:21–28), we have no record of his prayers.

At the news of Jerusalem's dismal state, Nehemiah fasted and prayed, asking that God keep his ears and eyes open to hear the prayer of his servant (Neh 1:4–5). Appointed governor of Judah, he was paradigmatic in integrating defensive prayers with defensive actions. He was not shy about praying against those who would destroy God's people (4:4–5 [3:36–37]; see also 6:14). He and the people prayed and set guard (4:9 [4:3]). He entreated God to strengthen his hand (6:9). The people entered into a curse and oath to obey the covenant stipulations, particularly those that had to do with Sabbath and temple-related procedures (10:28–39). Finally, Nehemiah frankly asked God to "remember him for the good he had done" (5:19; 13:14, 31).

Priestly prayers

While we might expect to read an abundance of priestly mediating prayers, there are precious few of them. The high priest was entrusted with the Urim and Thummim, the means for ascertaining God's will in difficult circumstances (Exod 28:30). In addition, the offerings, the blood, and the incense were the comprehensive means of intercession; Ps 141:2 likens the incense to prayers ascending to God. Aaron's benediction (Num 6:24–26) is a timeless invocation for God's presence, blessing, and protection.

Several generations after the return from exile, God's people succumbed to the temptation to intermarry with their neighbors. Into this context stepped Ezra, the priest and teacher of the Torah. His intercession on behalf of the people was intense; he prayed, tore his clothes, plucked out his beard, fell to his knees with his hands spread out, and fasted, not eating or drinking (Ezra 9:3—10:6). The penitential prayer of the people (Neh 9) was an echo of Ezra's model intercession. The longstanding covenant relationship and prayer continued to be intertwined.

Prayers of God's People

Isaiah 12 records prayers that include both singular and plural participants who would sing and shout their praise for salvation, for refuge, and for God's mighty deeds. The same themes appear in Isa 25:1–5, a song of praise for God's powerful provision of shelter and refuge. And "in that day," a song of trust would be sung in Judah (26:1–3; 17–19). Isaiah continued the themes of God's gracious response to the *cries of his people* (30:19; 33:2–4).

In contrast to Isaiah's affirmations of joy-filled prayers of God's people, detestable offerings were made to the queen of heaven (Jer 7:18; 44:17–19, 25), indicating that amidst the popular understanding of piety was the ubiquitous temptation to try out the local gods. The text does not specify prayer language, but it is implicit in the indictment. A further disheartening incident occurred in the aftermath of the exile when the people asked Jeremiah to pray to the LORD as to what they should do, and then they did precisely what God commanded them not to do (Jer 42:1—43:7).

Along with Israel at large and the major figures in the theocratic corporate environment, we have a steady drumbeat of "ordinary folks" praying. Isaac prayed on behalf of his barren wife. When the long-awaited twins were jostling about in her womb, Rebekah inquired of the LORD, and God answered her (Gen 25:21–23).

Hannah brought her despair to the tabernacle at Shiloh, praying, weeping, and making a significant vow in Eli's presence (1 Sam 1:10–16). God heard her prayer as well. Notably, we do not read a specific indication that the priest prayed on her behalf, although he did send her on her way saying, "may the God of Israel grant you what you have asked of him" (1 Sam 1:17). Eli seems to have been unaware of the details of her request. When she returned to the tabernacle with Samuel, she prayed with gratitude and joy, a song profoundly focused on the character of the LORD (1 Sam 2:1–10).

Samson's father, Manoah, wanted to hear a clearer message than his wife heard in regard to the care and nurturing of their Nazirite-to-be-son (Judg 13:8), so he prayed. While the answer made it evident that she already had all the information they needed, God did answer. In fact, the text says "and God listened to the voice of Manoah" (13:9).

Introduction: Setting the Stage

LOCATIONS—CONTEXTUALIZATION

There are spatial components to prayer. For one thing, prayer is at the intersection of heaven and earth;[8] God in heaven hears the prayers of his people from our earth-bound locations. Narrowing the focus, although praying was not limited to the temple, that place did represent God's dwelling with his people and became the focal point for prayers of confession (1 Kgs 8). There are tender references to Zion and Jerusalem—her dust, her stones (Ps 102:14 [15]), and her peace (Ps 122). The location of Zion engendered grief in the people's lament from "a land far away" (Jer 8:19, NIV). On several occasions, individual prayers were offered outside the land; Moses, Ezekiel, Daniel, Ezra, and Nehemiah were in that company. While the narrative of Esther in the Hebrew Bible includes no prayers, the Greek version embellishes the tense parts of the story with prayers of Mordecai and Esther.

WHEN AND HOW GOD ANSWERED—OR NOT

God's answers were multi-faceted demonstrations of his commitment to his people. Many were verbal and immediate; we think again of Elijah on Mount Horeb. Some had a visionary component. Some responses appeared to be long overdue; Daniel lived through a good number of ambiguous situations as the world empire transitioned from Babylonian rule to Persian domination before his prayer referencing Jeremiah's seventy weeks was answered (Dan 9). God asked his own questions of Jonah and his parting shot in that context likely did not sit well with Jonah. The book of Job combines both the "long-overdue" element as well as the later barrage of questions in response to Job's pleas and accusations.

Long before God's responses, Job's anguished expressions challenged God's unbearable silence; this was prayer in its most raw form. Habakkuk's prayers for justice confronted the God who seemed hidden. Imprecations against those who had brutally broken the covenant fundamentally implored God to bring the situation to rights. One of the most extensive of these is Ps 109; it is not easy to read.

---

8. Balentine, *Prayer in the Hebrew Bible*, 38–39.

Finally, there are more numinous experiences. Abraham asked "how can I know?" in the night time. God answered with a covenant-cutting event that was an adumbration of God's unfailing, sacrificial faithfulness (Gen 15). Jacob wrestled in the dark; the being with whom he wrestled left at daybreak but not before leaving his mark (Gen 32:22–32). Job's darkness continued well beyond day and night sequences.

VENTURING FORWARD

Needless to say, this modest volume cannot explore all of these avenues. Instead, these suggestions are intended to direct us into rich and ongoing engagement with the Scriptures. Most of all, let us be mindful that this must never become a dry or inapplicable study. On the contrary, we will be probing a most vital aspect of our relationship with our loving and responsive God and Father. May each endeavor be transformative and enriching.

BIBLIOGRAPHY

Balentine, Samuel E. *Prayer in the Hebrew Bible: The Drama of Divine-Human Dialogue*. OBT. Minneapolis: Fortress, 1993.

Goldingay, John. *Old Testament Theology: Volume Three: Israel's Life*. Downers Grove, IL: IVP Academic, 2009.

Widmer, Michael. *Standing in the Breach: An Old Testament Theology and Spirituality of Intercessory Prayer*. Siphrut 13. Winona Lake, IN: Eisenbrauns, 2015.

Section 1

Moses' Prayers

2

Wrestling with God

A Study on Prayer in Deuteronomy[1]

Daniel I. Block

INTRODUCTION

UNTIL RECENTLY, HUMAN BEINGS generally have had an intense sense of alienation from the divine. Many modern Westerners dismiss the notion of divinity itself as fiction, a mythical construction of unenlightened minds. However, the desperate need for contact with the gods in the ancient Near East is expressed poignantly in prayers, as in King Mursili II's desperate plea for divine rescue from a plague that had struck the Hittites (1321–1295 BC)[2] and in the "Prayer to Every God," recovered from Ashurbanipal's library.[3] The latter is a pathetic plea to get relief from suffering, which the supplicant is convinced he has experienced because he has violated some divine law. However, it

---

1. This is an abbreviated version of an essay previously published in Block, *The Triumph of Grace*, 240–63. It is republished here with permission.

2. For translation, see Singer, in *Hittite Prayers*, 58–59.

3. For the text in translation, see *ANET* 391–92; Foster, *Before the Muses*, 763–65.

Section 1: Moses' Prayers

is also an implicit protest that he should not be singled out for divine wrath because he does not know which god he has offended, what the crime is that he has committed, and what it will take to appease the god's fury.

The book of Deuteronomy asserts that on all three counts the ancient Israelites were a privileged people, the objects of remarkable divine grace. First, their God had introduced himself to them by name: "I am YHWH your God who brought you out of the land of Egypt" (Deut 5:6). Second, he had clearly revealed himself and his will to his people (4:9–13; 6:20–25; 30:11–14). Third, he heard them when they prayed (4:7–8).

Moses highlighted the problem posed by pagan deities in 4:28: these gods of wood and stone are "the work of human hands; they neither see, nor hear, nor eat, nor smell." In Ps 115:2–8, a later psalmist was even more specific. Moses captured Israel's unique privilege in having a God who actually hears human supplicants in Deut 4:6–7: "'Surely, that great nation is a wise and discerning people.' *For what great nation is there that has a god so close at hand as is YHWH our God whenever we call upon Him?*"[4] In 15:9 and 24:1–15, Moses concretized the notion declared generally in 4:7, observing that YHWH not only hears the prayers of priests, and kings, and other social elites; even the socially marginalized have access to his ears.

MOSES: THE PROPHETIC MAN OF PRAYER

Although Moses was involved in priestly, judicial, administrative, and legislative activities, neither the narrator nor Moses himself ever applies to him epithets like "priest" (*kohen*), judge (*shofet*), or "lawgiver/legislator (*khoqeq*). Judging by the speech act verbs used of him, in Deuteronomy Moses is primarily the mediator and teacher of divine revelation,[5] an observation reinforced by the paraenetic tone and style of his addresses.

Remarkably the only professional title that Deuteronomy applies to Moses is *navi'*, "prophet" (18:15–22 [esp. v. 15]; 34:10). However, this

---

4. Unless otherwise indicated, all translations in this essay are my own.

5. For detailed discussion of Moses' role in Deuteronomy and the pedagogical/paraenetic genre of his addresses, see Block, *Gospel According to Moses*, 68–103.

epithet is appropriate because fundamentally prophets were officials who had access to the divine presence (Jer 23:18, 21–22) and were authorized to speak for God to his intended audience. While most agree that Exod 3–4 represents Moses' call to divine service, fragments of his call to prophetic service are preserved in Exod 19:3, 6, 9, 19–21 and 20:18–21. However, although the narrator portrays him entering the presence of YHWH, he avoids the term *nabi'* (prophet),[6] as did Moses himself when he recalled this event four decades later (Deut 5:22–33). Having granted open access to his presence and commissioned Moses to speak for him to the people, apparently YHWH had formally inducted Moses into the prophetic office. Moses reinforced this impression in Deut 18:9–22. Unfortunately, in their preoccupation with the identity of "the prophet like Moses,"[7] commentators regularly miss the primary foci of the passage: the response of the people to future authorized messengers (vv. 9–19) and the integrity of the prophetic office (vv. 20–22).

To this point, the discussion of Moses as prophet has focused on his role as conduit and authorized interpreter of divine revelation. But prophets were more than transmitters of revelation from the deity to the people; they could also relay messages from and concerning the people to the deity (cf. Exod 19:3–25, esp. vv. 8–9), or present their own private issues before him, as we see in the case of Abraham (Gen 18:16–33; 20:7).

MOSES' INTERCESSORY PRAYER (9:18–19, 25–29)

Moses embedded two remarkable prayers in his speeches before the assembly of Israel on the Plains of Moab: a personal prayer in the first address (3:23–29), and an intercessory prayer in the second address (9:18–19, 25–29). Although the personal prayer precedes the intercessory prayer within Deuteronomy, Moses' prayer on behalf of his people occurred almost forty years prior to his private prayer (cf. 2:7; 8:2, 4; 29:5).

---

6. For detailed discussion of this portrayal of Moses, see Kibbe, *Godly Fear*, 31–39.

7. For discussion, see Block, *Triumph of Grace*, 349–73; Block, "A Prophet Like Moses? Who or Why?," 19–37.

Section 1: Moses' Prayers

The Context of Moses' Intercessory Prayer (Deut 9:18–19)

Before considering the prayer of Moses itself, it is instructive to observe how YHWH invited his intervention. "Release from me [your hand]" (*heref mimmenni*, v. 14) is a virtual command, but it reflects the extraordinary bond between YHWH and Moses. In "begging" Moses to leave him alone that he might destroy Israel, paradoxically YHWH opened the door for his intercession.[8]

Moses' response to the people's sin, YHWH's threat, and his charge to leave him alone involved four elements: (1) a symbolic gesture of smashing the tablets (vv. 15–17); (2) a symbolic gesture of intercession before YHWH (vv. 18–19); (3) an intercessory gesture on behalf of his brother Aaron (v. 20); and (4) a symbolic gesture of disposing of the calf (v. 21). The brief reference to his prayer for Aaron contributes to the present discussion, but I shall focus on Moses' intercession for the people, which is the focus of vv. 18–19 and 25–29.

In vv. 18–19, Moses describes his symbolic gesture of intercession before YHWH. Moses' non-verbal response to the divine threat consisted of prostration before YHWH and fasting. The former, prostration (*hithnappel*), refers to the act of supplicants falling to the ground before a superior (in this case YHWH) as a gesture of submission and urgent entreaty. Moses' forty-day-and-night fast reinforced his urgency. Whereas previously he had fasted to concentrate on his official role as recipient of communication *from* YHWH for the people (v. 9), now this action highlighted his concentration on his intercessory role *before* YHWH on behalf of the people.[9]

Moses' explanation of the intensity of his intercession involved two motive clauses (v. 18b). He summarized the grievous nature of the people's crime, speaking of "the sin that you have sinned by doing the evil in the sight of YHWH," and thereby provoking him to anger (*hikh'is*). This statement recalls 4:25, where Moses anticipated a similar future crisis in the land, involving the manufacture of images (*pesel*), which he interpreted as "doing the evil in the sight of YHWH" and

---

8. Cf. Moberly, *At the Mountain of God*, 50; Balentine, *Prayer in the Hebrew Bible*, 136.

9. Exodus 32:11–13 does not mention a forty-day struggle with YHWH.

resulting in his vexation/provocation (*hikh'is*).¹⁰ Moses reinforced the intensity of his response to the prospect of YHWH destroying Israel in v. 19 by using the rare word *yaghar*, "to be terrified," to express his own emotion, followed by his three-fold reference to YHWH's fury: *'aph* (anger), *khemah* (heat), and *qatsaf* (to provoke).

Moses' present report of YHWH's response lacks the drama of "and YHWH relented (*nikham*) concerning the harm with which he had threatened his people," in Exod 32:14. Nevertheless, "And YHWH listened to me at that time as well," expresses his relief even as he reported this event thirty-eight years later.¹¹ The note reflects YHWH's extraordinary relationship with his representative, and declares that the prayer of this righteous man was indeed powerful and effective (Jas 5:16).

The Content of Moses' Intercessory Prayer (Deut 9:25–29)

Hearers recognize that the recollection of Moses' actual prayer in vv. 25–29 belongs immediately after his report of his physical gestures of intercession in vv. 18–19. However, between the framework represented by vv. 7–8 and 22–24, Moses' singular rhetorical goal has been to demonstrate that, far from being morally worthy to receive the land of Canaan from YHWH, the Israelites had disqualified themselves. Naming additional places associated with rebellion in rapid-fire succession in vv. 22–24, Moses spoke directly about YHWH's fury in response to the peoples' sin and the punishment they deserved. Even in recalling his own frightful reaction, he knew that YHWH's pronouncement of death on his people was just. Inserting the prayer in its natural location would have disrupted the flow and shifted attention away from the sinful people to God himself.

Displaying significant stylistic and substantive connections with the narrator's reports of Moses' prayers in Exod 32:11–13 and Num

---

10. As in this text, the definite form (*hara'*), "the evil," suggests a specific crime, that is, violation of the Supreme Command by worshiping divine rivals.

11. It seems most logical to link the added particle (*gam*), "also, as well," to *kari'shonah*, "as at first, previously," in v. 18 (cf. Exod 32:11–14). However, Moses may have had in mind other crises during the desert wanderings in which his intercession resulted in sparing the people. Cf. Exod 14:15; 15:25; Num 11:2; 12:13–14; 14:13–20; 21:7–9.

Section 1: Moses' Prayers

14:13–19, Moses' recollection of his intercession involved a masterful combination of pathos and argumentation, undergirded by a profound covenantal theology. We may highlight the distinctive argumentation of the prayer as recalled here by juxtaposing it with the argumentation found in the earlier narratives (Table 1):

Table 1: A Synopsis of Moses' Argumentation in His Intercessory Prayers

	Exodus 32:11–13	Numbers 14:13–19	Deuteronomy 9:26–29
1	Israel is YHWH's people, not his (v. 11a).		Israel is YHWH's people, not his (v. 26a).
2	YHWH has invested great effort in saving the Israelites from the bondage of Egypt: by implication, to destroy them would mean this effort was wasted (v. 11b).	YHWH has invested great effort in saving the Israelites from the bondage of Egypt; by implication, to destroy them would mean this effort was wasted (v. 13).	YHWH has invested great effort in saving the Israelites from the bondage of Egypt; by implication, to destroy them would mean this effort was wasted (v. 26b).
3	YHWH's reputation among the nations will be damaged if he destroys Israel; they will think his intent was malicious from the beginning—to destroy Israel in the desert (v. 12).	YHWH has been uniquely close to his people: he is in their midst and has been personally leading them; by implication, it makes no sense to destroy them (v. 14).	Hold back for the sake of the patriarchs; overlook the sin of their descendants (v. 27).
4	Hold back for the sake of the patriarchs; to them he promised to multiply their seed and give them the land of Canaan as their possession forever (v. 13).	YHWH's reputation among the nations will be damaged if he destroys Israel; they will think that he slaughtered them in the desert because he was unable to carry through on his promise to give them the land (vv. 15–16).	YHWH's reputation among the nations will be damaged if he destroys Israel; they will think that he brought them out to destroy them in the desert because he was unable to carry through on his promise to give them the land, and because he hated them (v. 28).

5		YHWH's gracious character is in question; he has proved himself merciful in the past—may he be gracious again and forgive his people (vv. 17–19).	Israel is YHWH's people, not his (v. 29a).
6			YHWH has invested great effort in saving the Israelites from the bondage of Egypt; by implication, to destroy them would mean this effort was wasted (v. 29b).

Moses' argumentation is obviously most complex in the Deuteronomic version of this prayer. The structure of the passage and the rhetorical devices Moses employed to move God are impressive.

Structurally, vv. 25–29 consist of a prose preamble (vv. 25–26a), followed by an extended quotation of Moses' prayer (vv. 26b–29).[12] Unlike Exod 32:11–14 and Num 14:13–19, here Moses did not follow up the report of his prayer with a notice of YHWH's answer. In Exod 32:14, the narrator announces explicitly, "Then YHWH relented (*nikham*) and did not bring on his people the disaster he had threatened" (v. 14). In Num 14:19 the narrator quotes YHWH's response: "Then YHWH said, 'I have forgiven (*salakh*), according to your word'" (Num 14:20; cf. Moses' use of *salakh* in 14:19). In the present self-effacing autobiographical account, instead of announcing his effectiveness as an intercessor, Moses moved immediately to reporting the replacement of the tablets of the covenant that he had smashed (10:1–5).

The preamble to the prayer (vv. 25–26a) involves several expressions encountered earlier in this context. Moses reminded his audience of his prostration (*hithnappel*) before YHWH (cf. v. 18a), his forty-day-and-night fast (cf. v. 18b), and his motivation: YHWH had said he would destroy (*hishmid*) Israel (cf. v. 19). This recapitulation was

---

12. Cf. the form and structure recognized by Miller, *They Cried to the Lord*, 342–43.

Section 1: Moses' Prayers

necessitated by the literary distance between Moses' first reference to his intercession in the face of YHWH's threat (vv. 18–19) and the actual words of the prayer (vv. 26b–29). The generic designation of his verbal response to God (v. 26) is the same as it had been with reference to his intercession for Aaron (v. 20); he "prayed to YHWH." The hithpael form, *hithpallel*, denotes intercession to gain a favorable decision from a superior. While it often involves intercession on behalf of someone else (Gen 20:7; Num 21:7; 1 Sam 7:5; Job 42:8), this is not always the case.[13]

As for the prayer itself, Moses began formally with the vocative, "O Lord YHWH" (*'adonay yhwh*), whereby he both acknowledged his own vassal status and addressed God by his personal name, "YHWH."[14] Unlike many other biblical prayers that follow the address with doxological descriptors concerning God, acknowledging either his recent action or his personal qualities,[15] Moses immediately launched into his demands. The prayer is dominated by three imperatives: (1) "Do not destroy your people" (v. 26); (2) "Remember your servants, the patriarchs" (v. 27a); and (3) "Do not look on the sin of your people" (v. 27b). We might compare Moses' present wrestling with YHWH with a comparable earlier event. Whereas at the time of Moses' call YHWH was determined to get Moses' will in line with his own (Exod 3–4), this time the man was determined to bend YHWH's will. Refusing to take "No" for an answer, he interceded urgently for his people, appealing to God's mercy, reputation, and fidelity to his promise. Each demand deserves brief comment.

1. "Do not destroy your people" (v. 26)

The language of Moses' first demand is striking on several counts. First, the verb *hishkhith* ("to destroy, exterminate") is the same word he had used earlier to reassure the Israelites that YHWH is a compassionate God; he will not fail his people, nor "destroy" them, nor forget his covenant with the ancestors (4:31).

---

13. Cf. 1 Sam 1:10; 2 Sam 7:27; 1 Kgs 8:30, 35, 42, 44, 48; 2 Chr 7:14; Dan 9:4.
14. Cf. Exod 32:11; Num 14:14.
15. See Gen 32:9–12 [10–13]; 1 Chr 29:10–19; 2 Kgs 19:15b–19; Dan 9:1–19.

Second, Moses personalized the object of the verb by adding the suffix, and then qualifying "your people" (*'ammekha*), with "your special possession" (*nakhalatekha*). With the former, he not only threw back into YHWH's court the ball he had been tossed in v. 12; he also highlighted Israel's status as YHWH's covenant people. Forty days earlier on Horeb, YHWH had established his covenant with them, taking Israel as his people and becoming their God, in fulfillment of his own declared aims in Gen 17:7 and Exod 6:7. If YHWH would destroy Israel, then he would eliminate his partner in covenant. Moses reinforced his appeal to YHWH's personal relationship with Israel by characterizing them as "your special possession."[16] Although *nakhalah* is usually translated with inheritance language, this is a feudal metaphor whereby YHWH claims Israel out of all the nations for his own direct prized possession (cf. 32:8–9).[17]

Moses' argumentation was deliberate, responding directly to YHWH's own statement in v. 12. On the one hand, his choice of verb in *'al tashkhet*, "Do not destroy," played on the root YHWH had used when he spoke of Israel becoming "corrupt" (*shikhet*). On the other hand, he also reacted directly to YHWH's disowning the Israelites by speaking of them as "your people, whom you brought out of Egypt." In appealing to YHWH's self-interest—surely, he would not destroy his prized possession—Moses also served notice, "Don't put this lot on me! They are your people, not mine."

Third, Moses reminded YHWH that Israel was the product of his own extraordinary saving efforts. The man would accept neither the credit (cf. the people's statement in Exod 32:1) nor the blame (cf. YHWH's statement in v. 12) for the people who had gathered at Horeb. On the contrary, YHWH had "redeemed" (*padah*) them himself "with his greatness," and brought them out of Egypt "with a strong hand." Moses probably had in mind YHWH's speech in Exod 6:2–7, where he had expressly declared that the purpose of the deliverance was to rescue the Israelites from their enslavement to Pharaoh, and to claim them

---

16. On Israel as YHWH's *nakhalah*, cf. 4:20; 9:29; 32:9.

17. This usage of *nakhalah* places it within the same semantic field as *kheleq*, "portion," and *segullah*, "treasured possession" (7:6; 14:2; 26:18).

Section 1: Moses' Prayers

for himself as his own covenant people.[18] Again appealing to divine self-interest, Moses suggested that if YHWH would destroy this people now, all this effort would have been wasted.

2. "Remember your servants, the patriarchs" (v. 27a)

Moses' second demand was cryptic: "Remember (*zakhar*)[19] your servants, Abraham, Isaac, and Jacob." A comparison of this statement with its counterpart in Exod 32:13 confirms that he had in mind specifically YHWH's covenant commitments to the ancestors. By raising this issue Moses reminded YHWH that if he would break the covenant he had ratified with Israel at Horeb, he would violate his irrevocable covenant with the ancestors. His characterization of Abraham, Isaac, and Jacob as "your servants/vassals" (*'avadekha*) appealed to YHWH's deep attachment to the ancestors. Moses had recognized this special relationship in 4:37, where he had declared that YHWH chose Israel as the object of his deliverance and beneficiary of his kindness because of his "love" (*'ahav*) for the ancestors.

3. "Do not look on the sin of this people" (v. 27b)

Moses expressed his third demand most fully and most daringly, calling upon YHWH to turn away (*'al tefen 'el*, lit., "Do not turn to") from the "stubbornness" (*qeshi ha'am*, cf. *qesheh 'oref*, "stiff of neck," in vv. 9, 13), "wickedness" (*resha'*, a stylistic variation of *rish'ah* in vv. 4–5), and "sin" (*khatta'th*) of "this people" (*ha'am hazzeh*). Moses' use of three words to describe the Israelites' spiritual and moral state expresses the superlative degree (i.e., "utter sinfulness"), and by charactering them as "stiffnecked" and referring to them as "this people," he assented to YHWH's contempt for them. Moses neither excused his people nor minimized their sin. He could only plead for mercy, that YHWH would turn the other way and overlook their fundamentally sinful condition.[20] Within the overall argument of ch. 9, this is extremely significant, undercutting

---

18. See also Lev 25:55.
19. *Zakhar* signifies, "to take into account, to act on the basis of."
20. See further Miller, *They Cried to the Lord*, 270–71.

any Israelite claims to the land based on moral superiority over the Canaanites.

Moses' rationale for this demand was daring. First as a warning to YHWH, he declared that if he would destroy this people his reputation among the nations would be damaged (v. 28b).[21] As Moses had noted in 4:6–8, 32–40, YHWH had chosen and rescued Israel to showcase to the world that he alone is God and that all his ways are righteous. As he frequently did in his valedictory addresses, Moses highlighted the public reaction by placing it on the lips of interlocutors, in this case the Egyptians. Egypt was an appropriate representative of hypothetical observers, since they had suffered the greatest loss when YHWH had "robbed" them of a significant portion of their population. Furthermore, Moses had told Pharaoh that the reason for the Israelites' journey into the desert was to serve YHWH[22] and to celebrate a feast in his honor.[23]

The first part of the Egyptians' quotation expresses two hypotheses that should have been intolerable to YHWH. First, having succeeded in freeing this people from the Egyptians, YHWH would realize that this mission was impossible. Unable to see the Israelites through to the promised land, as he had promised (cf. Exod 3:8; 6:6–8), he simply slaughtered them in the desert. The second hypothesis is even more sinister. Rather than being driven by love (*'ahav*) for the ancestors (Deut 4:37) and their descendants after them (7:6–9), as Moses had declared to the people, YHWH's removal of the Israelites from Egypt was driven by hatred (*sin'ah* from *sane'*). Before the eyes of both Israelites (cf. Exod 14:11–12) and Egyptians the scheme of Israel's salvation would be exposed as a cynical and diabolical plot. The Egyptians would scarcely have distinguished between immediate divine causation and ultimate human responsibility for the people's fate. Moses hereby argued that for the sake of his own reputation YHWH had to overlook the people's sin and resume his mission.

---

21. This argument occurs also in the Exodus version of the prayer (Exod 32:12) and in Moses' prayer at Kadesh-barnea (Num 14:14–16). See further Miller, *They Cried to the Lord*, 272–73.

22. Exod 3:12; 4:23; 7:16; 8:1, 20; 9:1, 13; 10:3, 7–8, 11, 24, 26; 12:31.

23. Exod 3:18; 5:1, 3, 17; 8:7 [4], 27–28 [23–24].

Section 1: Moses' Prayers

Concluding where he had begun, Moses reminded YHWH again that Israel was his people, his treasured possession, in whose rescue he had invested a great deal of energy (v. 29; cf. v. 26). He should therefore overlook their rebellion and carry on with his project.

YHWH's Response to Moses' Prayer (10:1–5)

In 9:19, Moses had noted in passing that YHWH listened to his prayer, but unlike the narrator of these events in Exod 32:14, he did not describe YHWH's response. Having left the issue hanging, in Deut 10:1–5 he resumed the unfinished business. If Moses' smashing of the original divinely inscribed tablets demonstrated symbolically that the worship of the golden calf had terminated YHWH's covenant with them, then the manufacture of new identical tablets demonstrated symbolically that YHWH had taken them back. Moses reinforced this conclusion by noting YHWH's appointment of the Levitical priests as guarantors and guardians of the covenant (10:8–9), and his order to move on from Horeb to claim the land that he had promised on oath to the ancestors (v. 11). By declaring again that YHWH listened to him (v. 10), Moses suggested that these actions proved that YHWH had retracted his intention to destroy his people.

Moses' reticence to speak of having moved YHWH to change his heart (*nikham*) reflects not only his modesty, but also his determination to keep the focus on YHWH and his grace. The narrator may praise the man (Deut 34:5–12), but the man would not praise himself. This episode was not about him; it was about God and his grace toward his people. When they would cross the Jordan, this would not happen because of their superior numbers (cf. 7:6–10), or strength (8:17–18), and certainly not because of their superior righteousness (9:1–24). Nor would it happen because of their leader, however fearless he had been in interceding on their behalf. It would be due entirely to the grace of God.

MOSES' PERSONAL PRAYER (3:23–29)

In contrast to Moses' downplaying of his own role in his intercessory prayer, his report of his personal prayer is candidly self-interested.

Whether or not his original audience was aware of the events described in 3:23–29 prior to his telling, the absence of a counterpart in the narratives of Numbers means this account catches hearers by surprise. Although Num 20:1–12 provides the historical background to this prayer, and Num 27:12–14 probably reflects the occasion, neither text alludes to Moses' impassioned personal plea. Because the latter involved a private encounter with YHWH on Mount Abarim, had Moses not divulged this information no one would have known of Moses' embarrassingly ineffectual conversation with YHWH.

In v. 23, Moses declares the genre and context of his prayer. The expression *hithkhannen*, from a root *khanan*, "to be gracious, to favor someone," followed by the preposition *ʾel*, "to," means "to implore the mercy/grace of" and signals a specific and pointed request.[24] If the cognate noun, *khen*, speaks of undeserved action by a superior toward an inferior, then *hithkhannen* involves seeking such a response from the superior. By definition, the superior is not obligated to respond as requested.[25]

The only clue Moses provides regarding the occasion of the prayer is vague; "at that time," apparently refers to events following the defeat of the two Amorite kings. Excited by those conquests, the 120-year-old man was desperate to see his dream of entering the promised land fulfilled; his sights were on "home" just across the Jordan. The prayer itself is short, consisting of twenty-nine words (not counting deictic *ʾet*) and taking up only vv. 24 and 25, but it contains several typical features of biblical prose prayers.

The Invocative Address: "O Adonay YHWH"

As in 9:26, the only other occurrence in Deuteronomy of this double invocation, with this opening Moses sought to establish contact with the invisible deity. In the address Moses made two significant points. First, by opening with *ʾadonay*, which means "lord, master," he acknowledges his own inferior status; YHWH is his Suzerain. Moses acknowledges his role in this relationship explicitly with his reference to himself as

---

24. Cf. Merrill, *Deuteronomy*, 111.

25. Cf. The expression is also used of prayers to God in 1 Kgs 8:33, 47, 59; 9:3; Ps 30:8 [9].

Section 1: Moses' Prayers

'*eved*, "your servant/vassal," in the following statement.[26] Although he often characterizes the Israelites' status as slaves in Egypt with the same word (e.g., 6:21; 28:68), the word actually bore a wide range of meanings from servile slave to royal government officials. In courtly circles the title '*eved hammelekh*, "servant of the king," identified a person with a high position (2 Sam 18:29; 2 Kgs 22:12 [= 2 Chr 34:20]; 25:8). This is confirmed by the plethora of ancient seals and bullae from Israel and its environs bearing epithets like '*bd hmlkh*, "servant of the king," or more specifically, "servant of *RN*," where RN represents a royal name. Only important officials had their own seals; slaves did not. Moses' self-identification as YHWH's servant declares both his subordinate status and his official role in the administration of YHWH's people.

Second, by adding the personal name "YHWH," Moses acknowledged the theological foundation for this prayer—YHWH's accessibility and his own personal relationship with God (cf. 4:7).[27] Whatever the etymology of the name, its significance was revealed through YHWH's election of Israel and his mighty acts of redemption, his covenant with Israel, and his gift of the promised land (cf. Exod 6:2–8) on one hand, and his gracious forgiveness and propositional utterance on the other (Exod 34:6–7).[28] Moses' plea for grace (cf. Deut 3:23) was based on his personal knowledge of and relationship with Israel's Suzerain.

> The Description: "You have begun to show to your servant your greatness and your strong hand. For what god is there in heaven or on earth who can do the deeds and mighty works you do?"

Many prayers embedded in biblical narratives follow the opening invocation with a description of God, proclaiming his attributes or celebrating his actions.[29] Moses' doxology consists of a declarative statement

---

26. In prayers '*avdekha*, "your servant," expresses humility and subjugation even as it reflects the hope that the '*eved* ("servant"), will receive a measure of goodwill from his '*adon* ("lord").

27. Contrast this with the plight of the author of the "Prayer to Every God," noted above.

28. For detailed discussion, see Surls, *Making Sense of the Divine Name in Exodus*.

29. Cf. Gen 32:9 [10]; 2 Sam 7:18–24; 1 Kgs 8:15; 2 Kgs 19:15; Dan 9:4. On the descriptions, see Miller, *They Cried to the Lord*, 63–68. On the form and structure of this prayer, see Miller, *They Cried to the Lord*, 342.

followed by a rhetorical question. The former hints at YHWH's victories over Sihon and Og; in these events Moses had witnessed the beginning demonstrations of YHWH's "greatness" (*godel*) and "strong hand" (*yadekha hakhazaqah*). However, the latter expression suggests that Moses was actually looking back to the Exodus as the beginning phase of YHWH's mighty acts. His reference to the beginning of YHWH's revelation, "you have begun to show," suggests that in his mind and as announced in Exod 3:6–10 and 6:2–9, the exodus was the first of a multi-phased project whose ultimate goal was the delivery of the land of Canaan into the Israelites' hands (cf. Deut 6:20–25; 26:5–9).

The second part of Moses' description of YHWH is cast as a rhetorical question: "Who is a god in heaven or earth whose actions can match the mighty acts of YHWH?" The question obviously demands a negative answer: "There is no god like YHWH!" Moses will elaborate fully on this notion at the end of this address (4:32–40).

The Petition: "Let me go over and see the good land beyond the Jordan—that fine hill country and the Lebanon."

Moses expressed his petition forthrightly and passionately. His singular desire now was to cross the Jordan and experience (Heb. *ra'ah*, literally "to see") the good land firsthand. The depth of his grief at being barred entry into the land would be even more apparent later in 8:7–10 and 11:9–12, where in idealized and Edenic detail he described the land. Whereas modern visitors to the land of Palestine perceive the land differently—as a land of rocks and hills—having spent forty years in the desert, to the Israelites any landscape with green would have seemed Edenic. But for Moses Canaan was more than a place on the map; it was a theological idea. The land was good because YHWH had promised it to the ancestors and reserved it for his people. Moses had never lived there, but he could see "home" across the Jordan; this was the destination toward which he and the people had been headed since they left Egypt (Exod 3:8).

Section 1: Moses' Prayers

The Divine Response (vv. 26–28)

As recounted here, YHWH's answer to Moses' plea consisted of three parts. First, he declared in no uncertain terms his refusal to grant his request. Apparently angered that Moses had not taken as final his earlier statement that neither he nor Aaron would enter the land (Num 20:12), YHWH cut Moses off;[30] he did not want to hear about the matter again.

Second, YHWH offered Moses a consolation prize. Reversing the order of the requests in v. 25, he invited Moses to climb to the top of Mount Pisgah and to look across the Dead Sea and over the Jordan River and take in the sight of the promised land in all directions. While technically, "See (*ra'ah*) it with your eyes" answers to Moses' second request—that he "see" the land—the level of "seeing" would not satisfy him. While for Moses merely "observing" (rather than "experiencing") the land meant an aborted dream, in YHWH's mind his mission was finished; he had brought the people to the brink of the Jordan.

Third, YHWH charged Moses to prepare Joshua to replace him and lead the people across the Jordan. For Moses, turning over the reins of authority to his apprentice, who would deliver Canaan into Israel's hands, undoubtedly heightened the anguish. But never mind; Moses was to prepare Joshua for the challenges ahead.

Moses' painful epilogic note concluded his recollections of this event with YHWH: they remained in the valley opposite Beth-Peor on the plains of Moab (34:1). His own personal journey was over.

REFLECTIONS ON MOSES' INABILITY TO MOVE YHWH

The self-portrait that Moses, the man of prayer, paints in Deuteronomy (a literary "selfie") sends an ambivalent message. On the one hand, ch. 9 casts him as a bold servant of the people and agent of God, who through prayer moved YHWH to withdraw his threat against his own people and preserve their role in redemptive history. By contrast, in terms of achieving personal goals, his last wrestling match with YHWH was a

---

30. The construction *rav le-* has been encountered earlier in 1:6 and 2:3, where it meant something like "long enough." Here the expression is strong, in effect, "Stop it!" or "Shut up!"

failure. Even before Moses had finished speaking, YHWH ordered him never again to express his desire to enter the promised land.

From our modern Western vantage, we marvel at YHWH's mercy at Horeb, but we question both his justice and his compassion toward Moses at the end of his life. Where was the grace that he had proclaimed so dramatically in Exod 34:6–7, after the golden calf affair? Was the offense that caused him to slam the door to the promised land in Moses' face such an egregious crime? If YHWH could overlook the people's violation of the Supreme Command at Horeb and reinstitute the covenant, could he not forgive Moses and reopen the door for him? Was his request unreasonable? After leading this people for YHWH's sake for forty years, did he not deserve a more sympathetic "Thank you"? Was it not a small thing that he was asking: just to cross the river, breathe the air, touch the land, and taste the fruit on the other side, and then return across the Jordan to die? For Moses the east side of the Jordon obviously did not represent the promised land.

Why was YHWH's answer here so different from what it had been forty years ago? We might begin to address the question by taking a synoptic look at both prayers (Table 2).

Table 2: A Synopsis of Moses' Prayers in Deuteronomy

Feature	Deuteronomy 3:23–29	Deuteronomy 9:18–19, 25—10:11
Location	Plains of Moab (1:1–5)	Mount Horeb (9:8)
Occasion	YHWH's prohibition of Moses from entering the promised land, in response to his professional and spiritual failure (32:48–52).	YHWH's fury and his threat to destroy Israel for their blatant apostasy (9:8–19).
Petitionary posture	---	Prostration before YHWH (*hithnappal*, 9:18a, 25a).
Genre of the Prayer	A plea for divine mercy (*hithkhannen*, 3:23).	Intercession for divine change of heart (*hithpallel*, 9:26).
Invocation	O Lord YHWH! (3:24a).	O Lord YHWH! (9:26b).
Description of Addressee	YHWH has begun to show his incomparable greatness and power in his mighty acts on behalf of Israel (3:24b).	---

Section 1: Moses' Prayers

The Request	Let me cross over and see the good land (3:25a).	Do not destroy your people. Remember your servants Abraham, Isaac and Jacob. Do not regard the stubbornness and sin of this people (9:27–28).
The Argument	The land is good (3:25b)	Israel is YHWH's people, not Moses' (9. 26a, 29a). To destroy Israel would mean YHWH's saving acts were wasted (9:26b, 29b). YHWH's loyalty to the ancestors is at issue (9:27). YHWH's reputation among the nations would be irreparably damaged (9:28).
YHWH's Immediate Response	YHWH was cross with Moses (3:26a). YHWH refused to listen to Moses (3:26a). YHWH ordered Moses to stop and never mention the subject again (3:26b).	YHWH listened to Moses (9:19b; 10:10b), and his will was changed—he was unwilling to destroy Israel (10:10b). YHWH renewed the covenant (10:1–5)
YHWH's Provision for the Future	Moses was to climb Mount Pisgah and view the land (3:27). Moses was to commission and encourage Joshua to succeed him (3:28).	YHWH commissioned the Levites for divine service (9:26a).
Result	Israel remained camped at Beth-Peor (3:29).	YHWH charged Moses to lead the people on to the promised land (10:11).

The most obvious differences involved the occasions and the goals of the prayers. Whereas Moses' earlier prayer was intended to stave off divine fury against others (his people), the goal of the later prayer was personal and private. Indeed, Moses appears embarrassingly self-absorbed. Whereas at Horeb he was willing to sacrifice ambition[31]

---

31. YHWH offered to start his project over with him, and in effect make him the patronymic ancestor of his (YHWH's) people (9:14). Had he accepted it we would be

and life itself to win the favor of YHWH on the people's behalf with extra-ordinary self-denial (Exod 32:30–34), his account of his personal prayer reveals a man focused on himself and the satisfaction of private wishes. This scarcely looks like the same man. Several factors account for this contrast.

First, while we may not make too much of arguments from silence, the absence of a reference to physical prostration before YHWH his superior (cf. 9:18, 25) may suggest he took access to the divine presence for granted.

Second, while his invocative address in 3:24 is identical to that in 9:26, and he explicitly acknowledged his status as "servant" (*'eved*, 3:24b), the latter could be construed as self-serving, claiming membership in YHWH's court as a ground for a favorable hearing.

Third, although divine descriptions following the invocative address are common in biblical prayers,[32] given the context and nature of Moses' plea one wonders if his characterization of YHWH in 3:24 reflected genuine respect or shallow flattery.

Fourth, whereas his prayer at Horeb consisted of profound theological arguments, the present request involved merely a personal desire. Moses could at least have declared his intention to celebrate YHWH's faithfulness to his promises, perhaps by setting up a memorial altar as Abraham had done at Shechem (Gen 12:7).

Fifth, and most telling of all, without a hint of acknowledgement of his own culpability for an offense that had precipitated YHWH's closing the door to the promised land to him (cf. 32:48–52), when YHWH rejected his request, he blamed the people. Moses' statement in 3:26 deserves a closer look. This is the middle of three variations of this clause in this first address:

> 1:37 But against me YHWH's fury burned because of you.
>
> 3:26 And YHWH was enraged against me because of you.
>
> 4:21 And YHWH's fury burned against me because of you.

---

talking about Mushites (i.e., Moses-ites), rather than Israelites.

32. See the prayers of Jacob (Gen 32:9 [10]), David (1 Chr 29:11–13), Hezekiah (2 Kgs 19:15b–19), and Daniel (Dan 9:4).

Section 1: Moses' Prayers

The first and third statements are awkwardly inserted in their respective contexts, suggesting that, as he spoke to the people, intense bitterness was boiling just below the surface. Technically Moses was correct. If the Israelites had entered the land from Kadesh-barnea, his offense against YHWH would never have occurred, and by now he would have been enjoying the blessings of the land for almost four decades. However, at another level, the words were patently false; as YHWH would emphasize in 32:49–52 (cf. Num 20:12), Moses had only himself to blame for his failure to enter Canaan. These were not the words of a "suffering servant,"[33] innocently bearing the judgment that rightly belonged to others; they were the laments of a bitter old man, frustrated with God and angry with his people.[34]

Although YHWH's reaction to Moses' personal prayer seems calloused, this episode is just one detail in the literary portrait of a remarkable if complex man. In assessing Moses, we need to consider the entire book. After this first address, the only person who spoke of Moses being barred from the land was YHWH himself, and that immediately prior to Moses' decease (32:48–52). In Moses' lengthy second address he never again alluded to this event. Instead he focused on the gospel represented by YHWH's electing and saving actions (4:32–40; 6:20–25; 7:6–11; 10:15; 11:2–4; 26:5–8), YHWH's care in the desert (8:1–5, 15–16), his provision of a homeland in fulfillment of his covenant promises (6:10–11, 23; 7:12–16; 8:7–14; 10:11; 11:9–12; 26:9), and his vision/promise of Israel's well-being in that land in the future (7:12–16; 8:12–13; 11:13–15; 28:1–14). Occasionally Moses expressed pessimism regarding Israel's spiritual future, but his disposition toward the present generation seems positive. He commended them for their fidelity to YHWH (4:3–4; cf. 5:2–5), and gladly acceded to desires that might surface once they have entered the land: as mundane as eating meat in their hometowns (12:15–16, 20–25) and as consequential as the establishment of a human monarchy (17:14–20). Having vented here, he seems to have moved on emotionally.

YHWH had obviously not dismissed him from his service because of his failure to his commission and his Commissioner by not

---

33. Contra Miller, "Moses My Servant," 253–54.
34. Cf. Moses' transparency about his feelings in 1:9–12.

treating YHWH as holy in the midst of the people (32:51). Indeed, after the Meribah-kadesh incident (cf. Num 20:1–13), for thirty-eight years he had faithfully administered and shepherded YHWH's people. In his recollections he acknowledged his privileged role as mediator and interpreter of divine revelation (5:23–33; 18:15–22), warned the people not to add to or subtract from the Torah he proclaimed (4:2; 12:32), and pronounced the curse (*kherem*) on anyone "who preaches another gospel" (12:28—13:18 [19]; 18:20; cf. Gal 1:6–9). Even though the boundaries of Moses' speech are coterminous with the boundaries of YHWH's speech in Deuteronomy, in the end he appeared resigned to his fate.

If hearers of Moses' addresses doubt his disposition toward YHWH, his biographer did not. YHWH's last recorded words reminded him that he would not cross the Jordan: "But you will not cross over there" (34:4). However, when Moses climbed Mount Pisgah for the last time, his standing with YHWH was intact, as ch. 34 indicates. First, whereas earlier YHWH had declared that Moses would see the land with his own eyes,[35] the narrator has *YHWH showing him all the land* (v. 1), and highlighting the totality of the exposition (vv. 1–3). In his final speech YHWH acknowledged his own involvement, literally, "I have caused you to see it with your own eyes." Second, having identified Moses earlier as "the man of God" (*'ish ha'elohim*, 33:1), the narrator now refers to him by a second honorific title, "servant (*'eved*) of YHWH" (v. 5). Third, he interprets Moses' death in Moab as the fulfillment of the divine word (v. 5). Fourth, in the burial notice, he describes Moses' unparalleled final privilege; he was buried in a secret place by YHWH himself (v. 6). Fifth, he highlights Moses' incomparable personal relationship with YHWH; since his death there has been no prophet like him, "whom YHWH knew face to face" (v. 10). Sixth, contrary to Moses' own statements,[36] and the entire Hebrew Bible, the narrator attributes all the "signs and wonders" performed in Egypt to Moses, though he adds that he did so as YHWH's "commissioned" (lit. "sent," *shalakh*) agent (v. 11).

---

35. 3:27; 32:49, 52.
36. Deut 4:34; 6:22; 7:19; 13:2, 3, etc.; Exod 7:3; Neh 9:10; Ps 78:43; 135:9.

Section 1: Moses' Prayers

In the end, the narrator has the last word; this idealized view of Moses should determine our reading of the entire book. Nevertheless, it is quite remarkable that in the first address the narrator refused to sanitize Moses' own comments that might have cast his character in a negative light. The biographer's earlier characterization of Moses as "a very humble man, more so than any other man on earth" (Num 12:3, NRSV) still stood (Deut 34:10–12).[37]

Whereas through Moses' intercession YHWH was willing to overlook much more serious crimes and take his people back, when Moses demanded this personal favor, YHWH refused, "because you did not treat me as holy in the midst of the descendants of Israel" (32:51). Obviously, YHWH took Moses' role as leader of the people extremely seriously. Like the king anticipated in 17:14–20, Moses' first responsibility was to embody righteousness as defined by the covenant. Presumably on the principle, "To those to whom much is given, of them much is required, and from those to whom much is entrusted, of them more will be demanded" (cf. Luke 12:48), at this critical moment in the nation's history YHWH could not tolerate leaders publicly violating his trust and misrepresenting his sanctity. Moses had transgressed the fundamental covenant principle: "You shall love YHWH your God," that is, "You shall be covenantally committed to him so that you always act in his interest."[38]

CONCLUDING REFLECTIONS ON A DEUTERONOMIC THEOLOGY OF PRAYER

Whether we examine these two episodes together or separately, Moses' frank conversations with God illuminate the nature and process of trusting prayer.

First, prayer is an act of worship. If "true worship involves reverential acts of submission and homage to the divine superior in response

---

37. This negative image argues for the authenticity of the first address. A biographer of the seventh century or later, when the image of Moses had been so idealized in the popular imagination, would not have created a speech like this.

38. The essential meaning of "You shall love YHWH your God." On which see Block, *Deuteronomy*, 144, 182–84, 189–90, *et passim*.

to his gracious revelation of himself and in accord with his will,"[39] then prayer represents the supreme expression of that. When Moses cast himself to the ground (Deut 9:18, 25), addressed God as "Adonay YHWH" (3:24, 9:26), and referred to himself as "your servant" (3:24), he illustrated physical, psychological, and spiritu[...] to gaining a hearing with God. YHWH is the divine [...]gs are his subjects.

Second, prayer must be grounded in correct th[...]nt Israel, high theology was demonstrated not so muc[...]e- cital of creeds or lofty recitation of divine attribute[...]i- mony to and celebration of YHWH's gracious concre[...]'s behalf. Through YHWH's saving acts at the time of t[...] demonstrated his supremacy over all so-called gods.[...] declared in 4:32–40, his "signs and wonders" on Israel's [...] were unprecedented in all of human history and demonstrated to all with open eyes of faith that he alone is God. Moses was eager to see the memory of these saving acts kept alive as the Israelites engaged the Canaanites. As they entered the land with its seductive fertility religions and illusory gods, their confidence would need to be in YHWH alone. He may be personally and physically invisible, but the very existence of Israel as a people represents the clearest proof of his existence. Confident prayer is based upon the relationship that God has established with his people.

Third, effectual intercessory prayer requires a "righteous" intercessor (Jas 5:16). As in the rest of the Hebrew Bible, in Deuteronomy the word "righteous" (*tsedeq/tsedaqah*) denotes behavior that conforms to an established standard, the standard in this instance being the covenant stipulations as revealed to the vassal by YHWH, the covenantal Suzerain.[40] Moses was a righteous man. In interceding for his people at Horeb he demonstrated his "covenant commitment" through actions in their interest. Fully acknowledging their sin, and thereby YHWH's justice in punishing them, when he appealed for YHWH to withdraw

---

39. For detailed development of this thesis, see Block, *For the Glory of God*, esp. 23–27.

40. The word means the same with reference to divine Suzerain, whom Deut 32:4 declares to operate justly (*kol derakhayv mishpat*) and to be faithful (*'emunah*), righteous (*tsaddiq*), upright (*yashar*), and lacking in caprice (*'en 'avel*). For further discussion, see Block, *How I Love Your Torah, O LORD!* 16–18.

his anger he could only plead for mercy. However, his personal prayer reflects a momentary lapse in his righteous conduct. Preoccupied with self-interest he overlooked the sin that had triggered YHWH's closing the door to the promised land for him in the first place. God is not obligated to answer such prayers in the petitioner's favor.

Fourth, even in prayer God remains the Sovereign, and he retains the right to say "Yes" or "No" to a human supplicant's requests. As Moses would assert in 4:6–8, of all the nations, only Israel had a God so near that he heard them whenever they called upon him. But "No" is an answer. When people pray several different outcomes are possible. (1) As Moses recounted in ch. 9 and the narrator described in Exod 32 and Num 14, through the effectual fervent prayer of a righteous person, God's disposition may be changed (cf. also Jonah 3–4). (2) God may indeed answer fervent prayer affirmatively and effect a change in one's external circumstances (cf. Acts 12:5–17). (3) Through prayer the persons praying may themselves be changed. Rather than bringing God's will into conformity with ours, sometimes through prayer God brings the petitioner's will into conformity with his own will. In such cases this is not a failure of faith, because true faith accepts God's "No." Sometimes that "No" is final.

BIBLIOGRAPHY

Balentine, Samuel E. *Prayer in the Hebrew Bible: The Drama of Divine-Human Dialogue*. OBT. Minneapolis: Augsburg, 1993.

Block, Daniel I. *Deuteronomy*. NIVAC. Grand Rapids: Zondervan. 2012.

———. *For the Glory of God: Recovering a Biblical Theology of Worship*. Grand Rapids: Baker, 2014.

———. *The Gospel According to Moses: Theological and Ethical Reflections on the Book of Deuteronomy*. Eugene, OR: Cascade, 2012.

———. *How I Love Your Torah O LORD! Studies in the Book of Deuteronomy*. Eugene, OR: Cascade, 2011.

———. "A Prophet Like Moses? Who or Why?" In *Distinctions with a Difference: Essays on Myth, History, and Scripture in Honor of John N. Oswalt*, edited by Bill T. Arnold and Lawson G. Stone, 19–38. Wilmore, KY: First Fruits, 2017.

———. *The Triumph of Grace: Literary and Theological Studies in Deuteronomy and Deuteronomic Themes*. Eugene, OR: Cascade, 2017.

Foster, Benjamin R. *Before the Muses: An Anthology of Akkadian Literature*. 2nd ed. Potomac, MD: CDL, 1996.

Kibbe, Michael. *Godly Fear or Ungodly Failure? Hebrews 12:18–29 and the Sinai Theophanies*. BZNW 216. Berlin: de Gruyter, 2016.

Merrill, Eugene H. *Deuteronomy*. NAC. Nashville: Broadman & Holman, 1994.

Miller, Patrick D. "'Moses My Servant': The Deuteronomic Portrait of Moses." *Int* 41 (1987) 245–55.

———. *They Cried to the Lord: The Form and Theology of Biblical Prayer*. Minneapolis: Fortress, 1994.

Moberly, R. W. L. *At the Mountain of God: Story and Theology in Exodus 32–34*. JSOTSup 22. Sheffield: JSOT, 1983.

Singer, Itamar. *Hittite Prayers*. SBLWAW 11. Atlanta: Society of Biblical Literature, 2002.

Surls, Austin. *Making Sense of the Divine Name in Exodus: From Etymology to Literary Onomastics*. BBRSup 17. Winona Lake, IN: Eisenbrauns, 2017.

Section 2

Prayers of Kings

3

The Temple Prayer of Solomon
(1 Kings 8:1—9:9)

Ted Hildebrandt

INTRODUCTION

THE TEMPLE PRAYER OF Solomon in 1 Kgs 8 and the divine response in 1 Kgs 9 make up one of the longest and most fascinating prayer narratives in the Old Testament. Together they prompt the following succession of questions that we will seek to explore. How does this prayer fit into the literary structure? What may be learned from ancient Near Eastern parallels concerning prayer and kings building/dedicating temples? What intertextual influences echo into and out of this prayer? How are Solomon and the suppliants portrayed in the prayer? How is God portrayed? Solomon articulated seven prayer occasions, that is, types of situations that might prompt prayer in Israel's future—justice, defeat, drought, disaster, pious foreigners, war, and exile. What do we learn from these for God's people then and now?

Section 2: Prayers of Kings

HOW DOES SOLOMON'S TEMPLE PRAYER FIT INTO THE LITERARY STRUCTURE?

Solomon's Temple Prayer is embedded in a brief chiastic structure, the segments of which correspond to the choreographed movements of Solomon himself (v. 14, turning; v. 22, standing; vv. 54–55, kneeling to standing).

> A. People summoned to sacrifices and cultic installation of the ark + theophany (1 Kgs 8:1–13)
>> B. Solomon blessed the people and praised the LORD (1 Kgs 8:14–21)
>>> C. Solomon's Temple Prayer (1 Kgs 8:22–53)
>>>> Opening (1 Kgs 8:22–30)
>>>>> Seven prayer occasions (1 Kgs 8:31–51)
>>>> Closing (1 Kgs 8:52–53)
>>> B.' Solomon rose, blessed the people and praised the LORD (1 Kgs 8:54–61)
> A.' Sacrifices and cultic activity, people dismissed + theophany (1 Kgs 8:62—9:9)[1]

HOW DOES THE PRAYER FIT WITH ANCIENT NEAR EASTERN TEMPLE BUILDING/DEDICATION CONTEXTS?

Victor Hurowitz has offered an important cultural background for temple building and dedication that can help us better understand the literary movements found in Solomon's Temple Prayer. After surveying Sumerian, Assyrian, Babylonian, and North-West Semitic parallels to temple/palace building projects, Hurowitz lays out the following standardized literary form, which closely parallels the Solomonic temple narrative in 1 Kgs 5–9: (1) a reason to build or restore a temple/palace along with the command from or consent of the gods to engage the project (1 Kgs 5:3–5); (2) preparing for the building—acquiring

---

1. The larger literary structure for the Solomon narrative of 1 Kgs 1–11 is elucidated in Parker, *Wisdom and Law*, and Williams, "Once Again," 49–66.

materials, drafting workers, laying the foundation (1 Kgs 5:6–18); (3) a description of the process of construction of the building and its furnishings (1 Kgs 6:1–38; 7:13–51); (4) dedication of the temple/palace with the appropriate festivities and rituals (1 Kgs 8:1–11, 62–66); (5) a prayer or blessing "meant to assure a good future for the building and builder" (1 Kgs 8:12–61); and (6) an optional addition of blessings and curses for those rebuilding or damaging the temple/palace in the future (1 Kgs 9:1–9).[2] With some variation, 1 Kgs 5–9 exemplifies this common literary flow found in the description of ancient Near East temple building projects.[3]

Michael Hundley also provides a conceptual framework for understanding temple narratives. He writes:

> In a dangerous and volatile world, the ancient Near Eastern temple was the primary point of intersection between human and divine. As a principal means of establishing security in an otherwise insecure world, it situated the deity in the midst of human habitation, so that humanity might offer service and gifts in exchange for divine protection and prosperity.[4]

Ritual also plays an important role in anchoring the ancient Near Eastern gods to their statues and to earth. Rituals, such as graduation ceremonies, pass the participant from one realm into another. "Similarly, in the ancient Near East, ritual activities in an installation ritual (in addition to being thought of as actually affecting divine presence) mark the transition from the crafting of the divine statue to its taking up its role as god on earth, without which the transition would be considered either incomplete or uncertain."[5] Elsewhere Hundley labels the presence of the deity in the cult object a "metonymy of presence" as one aspect of the full divine presence.[6] This "metonymy of presence" or, perhaps, "synecdoche of divine presence," fits well with YHWH's

---

2. Hurowitz, *I Have Built You an Exalted House*, 64, 109–10, 311–12. See also his *Keeping Heaven on Earth*.

3. Hurowitz, *I Have Built You an Exalted House*, 71–73.

4. Hundley, *Gods in Dwellings*, 3.

5. Hundley, *Gods in Dwellings*, 366

6. Hundley, *Gods in Dwellings*, 135, 150.

presence in the temple in which he would dwell on earth, although even the heavens cannot contain his full presence (1 Kgs 8:27).

Ritual played a key role in the ceremonial movement of the ark on this special annual fall Tabernacles festival in the seventh month (1 Kgs 8:2–4, 65), and it established continuity between the old tabernacle and the dedication of Solomon's new temple. The installation of the ark provided the backdrop for Solomon's Temple Prayer. This is similar to the "ceremony of the brick" in ancient Near Eastern cultures where a first brick of the old damaged temple was transferred to the new temple as a means of picturing the continuity between the old and the new.[7]

WHAT ARE THE INTERTEXTUAL ECHOES INTO AND OUT OF THIS PRAYER?

Within the broad framework of Israel's long worship experience, echoes may be heard in this prayer from the dedication of the tabernacle in Exod 40 (see Lev 8–9). Looking forward, similar motifs reverberate into the description of the post-exilic inauguration of the second temple (Ezra 1; 6; see also Haggai). The record of Solomon's prayer from the post-exilic time frame (2 Chr 6) is drawn nearly word for word from 1 Kgs 8, including the seven prayer occasions.

Narrowing the focus, parallels with David's bringing the ark to Jerusalem and the Davidic Covenant (2 Sam 6–7) also appear in this narrative of Solomon's prayer. These parallels include installing the ark (linking the old with the new), many sacrifices, and the king's leadership with a focus on Jerusalem.[8] One significant difference, however, is the glory cloud filling the temple—symbolizing the LORD's entrance—as the ark was installed (1 Kgs 8:10–13). This is not found in the Davidic installation ceremony in 2 Sam 6. Repeated citations of the Davidic Covenant (2 Sam 7) punctuate Solomon's prayer and its context (1 Kgs 8:17–19, 25; 9:5). Marc Brettler notes that 2 Sam 7 is blended with Deut 12:11 ("the place which the LORD your God will choose as a dwelling for his Name").[9] This "chosen place" (see also 1 Kgs 8:44, 48, "chosen

---

7. Hundley, *Gods in Dwellings*, 79.

8. Long, *1 Kings*, 97; see also Kang, *Persuasive Portrayal*, 241. Throntveit, *When Kings Speak*, gives an analysis of Solomon's prayer in 2 Chr 6 that parallels 1 Kgs 8.

9. All translations are from the NIV.

city") is subordinated to the choosing of David (1 Kgs 8:16) and totally absent from the original Davidic Covenant.[10] The theme of the incomparability of God is found in David's prayer (2 Sam 7:22) and echoed by Solomon in the opening (1 Kgs 8:23) and closing (8:60) of his prayer.

Brettler highlights the influence of Deut 4:29, "if from there you seek the LORD your God, you will find him if you look for him with all your heart and with all your soul," as reflected in a similar clause in 1 Kgs 8:48. The theme of repentance prominent in Deut 4:25–31 also fits with the prayer occasion of exile (1 Kgs 8:47–48; see also Deut 28:36, 64; Ps 106:6).[11] In addition to exile, a number of the crises evident in the prayer occasions are linked with the covenant curses as articulated in Deut 28: defeat (Deut 28:25); drought (Deut 28:23–24); disaster (Deut 28:22, 42).

Other intertextual connections are apparent. The phrase "ark of the covenant of the LORD" (1 Kgs 8:1, 6) is found in Deut 10:8; 31:9, 25, 26. But it occurs nowhere in the prophets or psalms, except in Jer 3:16. The rhetorical question of disdain (1 Kgs 9:8) is echoed from Deut 29:24, "All the nations will ask: 'Why has the LORD done this to this land? Why this fierce, burning anger?'" One of the most interesting intertextual references comes from the words "iron–smelting furnace" as a descriptor of Egypt (1 Kgs 8:51). It is found elsewhere only in Deut 4:20 and Jer 11:4.

There are also echoes from this prayer into the rhetoric and themes of Jeremiah, not surprising given that Judah and Jerusalem were on the cusp of disaster because of their disobedience. The title, "LORD, the God of Israel" is found in 1 Kgs 8:15, 17, 20, 23, 25 and often in Jeremiah (e.g., 11:3; 13:12; 21:4). The final ominous declaration of God's response to Solomon's Temple Prayer (9:9) reverberates in Jer 32:23, "So you brought all this disaster upon them."

---

10. Brettler, "Interpretation and Prayer," 20–21.

11. Brettler, "Interpretation and Prayer," 30. Levenson provides further details aligning the texts of Deut 4 and 1 Kgs 8 (Deut 4:39//1 Kgs 8:23; Deut 4:20//1 Kgs 8:51 and Deut 4:7//1 Kgs 8:52). Levenson concludes that 1 Kgs 8:23–53 "most closely resembles Deut 4:1–40" (*Sinai and Zion*, 161–62).

Section 2: Prayers of Kings

WHO WAS SOLOMON THE SUPPLIANT?

After reading 1 Kgs 1–11, one is struck by Solomon's absence from the narrative (in contrast to David in 1–2 Sam). In the succession narrative in 1 Kgs 1–2, Walsh correctly points out that it was Nathan and Bathsheba, not Solomon, who were concerned over Adonijah's succession plot at En Rogel. The narrative proceeds with dialogues between Nathan, Bathsheba, and David, while Solomon the "central figure remains off stage."[12] In contrast, Walsh observes that in this same narrative are many details about Adonijah, including his mother's name, a physical description of his being handsome, his primacy due to birth order after Absalom, and even David's permissive manner of rearing him (1 Kgs 1:6).[13] Yet there is no such detailed communication about Solomon.

The person of Solomon is discovered from others. Under divine direction, Nathan nick-named Solomon "Jedidiah" ("Loved by the Lord," 2 Sam 12:25). We learn more about Solomon from the hyperbolic accolades of the Queen of Sheba (1 Kgs 10) and Hiram's response (2 Chr 2:12–13) than from his own self-reporting. When his persona is revealed, it is often in the context of his official capacities: determining a just response to the two women with one baby (1 Kgs 3:16–28), the narrator's listing of his wisdom accomplishments (1 Kgs 4:29–34), or his organizational and bureaucratic achievements (1 Kgs 5). These brief officialese-type insights into Solomon's identity stand dwarfed by the long chapters extensively detailing the preparations and building of the temple and the royal palace (1 Kgs 5:1—9:10). Balentine suggests another entry point into understanding Solomon: "Biblical prayer is but one of the means afforded in Hebrew narrative for building character portraits."[14]

So who was Solomon? First and foremost, Solomon in this prayer narrative self-identified as the son of David (8:15, 17, 19, 20, 24–26; 9:4). In the opening of the prayer, the text portrays Solomon as a witness to the fulfillment of what God had promised to his father (8:24–26). The entire prayer narrative not only repeatedly recalls the Davidic covenant and Solomon's role in its fulfillment that had already occurred (8:15,

---

12. Walsh, "Characterization of Solomon," 472.
13. Walsh, "Characterization of Solomon," 473.
14. Balentine, *Prayer in the Hebrew Bible*, 49.

19, 20, 24–26; 9:5) but also Solomon's role as the one determining its future direction, if he kept the conditions of the covenant (8:25–26; 9:6). Reminiscent of the prayer of his father David, Solomon opened his prayer with "there is no God like you" (8:23, 60; 2 Sam 7:22). Ironically, when the celebration was finally completed and the huge assembly was dismissed, the chapter ends not with a reference to Solomon by name, but rather to David: "They blessed the king and then went home, joyful and glad in heart for all the good things the LORD had done for his servant David and his people Israel" (8:66). After all the building and dedicatory celebration Solomon still seemed to stand in his father's shadow, even in the divine response (1 Kgs 9:4–5).

Secondly, it was as David's son that Solomon built the temple that his father was not allowed to build (8:19; 1 Chr 22:8–9). In the "Protocol of Legitimation" (8:15–21),[15] Solomon established his right to build the temple. With a series of first-person references, Solomon re-cast himself as the temple-builder and moved out from under his father's shadow (8:20–21). In Solomon's brief "Prayer of the Presence" (8:12–13; recall Hundley's "metonymy of presence"), he celebrated the cloud of God's glory descending and filling the temple and said with apparent satisfaction, "I have indeed built a magnificent temple for you, a place for you to dwell forever" (v. 13). He called it a place for "you" to dwell (i.e., presence).[16] Thus, the narrative casts Solomon as the temple-building son of David.

In each of the seven prayer occasions, Solomon featured the centrality of the temple he had built as the conduit linking heaven and earth. He repeatedly emphasized the geo-spatial aspect of prayer. It was toward this earthly temple that the people were directed to pray to God who would hear in heaven (8:29, 31, 33, 35, 38, 42, 44, 48). When God responded, he acknowledged Solomon's role in building the temple: "I have consecrated this temple which you have built" (9:3). Solomon

---

15. DeVries, *1 Kings*, 125.

16. "The Name," a multivalent metonymic expression for God, is frequently found elsewhere in this prayer narrative and should not be restricted to distant transcendence (8:16–18, 29, 41, 43–44, 48; 9:3); see Richter, *The Deuteronomistic History*, 29; and contra Mettinger, *The Dethronement of Sabaoth*, 48.

surpassed his father in that he was the one who built the temple which his father could not (8:19).

In the final "blessing/praise" section (8:56–61), Solomon explicitly connected this completed work with the promises given to Moses, and also made a veiled allusion to Joshua who led the people to rest (8:56). This fit within the broader scope of redemptive history, moving from the Exodus event to God's presence in a presumably permanent dwelling. Solomon described that fulfillment in the words and phrases typical of the text of Joshua (1 Kgs 8:56–61; cf. Josh 21:44–45; 22:4–5; 23:1, 14). References to the Exodus also regularly punctuate this narrative's cultic opening (8:9) and the initial and final blessing/praise sections (8:16, 21, 51, 53). There is a movement from Moses (8:9) to David (8:15–26) and then a returning to Moses in the conclusion (8:53) followed by a Moses/Solomon nexus in the final "blessing/praise" section (8:56–61). The divine response, like the steady beat of a drum, revisits the promise already fulfilled to David (9:4–5) and the conditional aspect dependent on the obedience of David's son, Solomon, and his descendants (9:6–9).

The seven prayer occasions (8:31–51) at the heart of this lengthy prayer point to the intercessory role of Solomon as well as those who would follow. He knew the contents of the covenant sufficiently to detail the circumstances when the people would need divine assistance. The prayer occasions of defeat, siege, war, and exile all involved military conflict, certainly sources of anxiety, especially since these generally arose from more powerful nations round about. Prayer occasions of drought, blight, locusts, and other natural calamities, were all situations beyond his control as king and yet of great concern to his people.

Solomon humbly identified himself as a servant of the Lord (8:28–30, 52), in good company with David (8:24–26) and Moses (8:53, 56). In his self-description to the Lord at Gibeon, Solomon already declared he was but a small young man (*na'ar qaton* 1 Kgs 3:7). In the context of this prayer, he exclaimed, "But will God really dwell on earth? The heavens, even the highest heaven, cannot contain you. How much less this temple I have built!" (8:27). The metonymic presence represented in the presence-cloud filling the temple was a mere partial manifestation of God's full presence. Solomon humbly recognized that God's actual presence breaks the bonds of God's temple on earth to a vision of the fullness of God's presence burgeoning beyond the boundaries of heaven itself. He seems to have been keenly aware that the "magnificent temple I have built" (8:13) was totally incapable of rising to the grandeur of its divine Resident. Such humility provides a baseline for his prayers and ours.

THE SUPPLIANTS' EXPECTATIONS (1 KINGS 8:31-51)

Need coupled with a sense of helplessness, Solomon recognized, is often the spark that triggers prayer. The seven prayer occasions that Solomon delineated would have placed the suppliants squarely in that position: need for justice, condemning the guilty and establishing the innocent (vv. 31-32); experience of deserved defeat by enemies (vv. 33-34); drought (vv. 35-36); disasters of all kinds (vv. 37-40); the pious foreigner (vv. 41-43); call to war (vv. 44-45); exile (vv. 46-51).

The goals of prayer articulated by Solomon recognized the deserved covenant curses (Deut 28), but repeatedly implored God for forgiveness and for deliverance from the present or impending crises (8:30-59). In a remarkable petition, Solomon requested that whatever foreigners—who had heard of God's Name and power—were seeking would be granted even to them (8:43).

As Solomon prayed, he anticipated that those suppliants who came after him would engage God in the same manner. They would pray to God because they expected God to act. They would call on God who, with his "mighty hand and outstretched arm," had acted in the past to deliver Israel from Egypt (8:16, 21, 51; cf. Deut 4:34; 26:8; Jer 21:5; 32:21; Ezek 20:33-34). Solomon celebrated the fulfillment of the covenants with David (8:15, 20, 25-26; 9:5) and Moses (8:9, 21, 53, 56), expecting that pattern would continue. Solomon invoked God to protect the chosen city and the "temple I have built for your Name" (8:44, 48). The suppliants would continue to pray because they believed God would "hear from heaven"; it was a steady refrain (8:30, 32, 34, 36, 39, 43, 45, 49). Their prayer would be full of the hope and expectation that God would act on their behalf. Our prayers are also energized by that same hope and expectation.

Section 2: Prayers of Kings

THE SUPPLIANTS WHO WOULD FOLLOW SOLOMON

Solomon took the lead role as a suppliant in the prayer, summoning the people into his presence (8:1), turning and blessing them (8:14), and then standing, with hands spread to heaven, to pray (8:22). At the conclusion of his prayer, he rose before the altar, blessed the people (8:54–55), and later dismissed them (8:66). Solomon cast himself as a model suppliant with both his movements and his words.

These people were God's own special inheritance (8:51, 53). They were also God's servants (8:36) and his people (8:30, 43, 44, 50, 52, 59). Solomon encouraged the people to pray and make supplication or seek God's favor, directing the people to think of the temple not just as a place of sacrifice but primarily as a place of prayer (cf. Matt 21:13; Isa 56:7).[17] The suppliants would be keenly aware of the symbiosis between the temple and God's dwelling in heaven to which they were calling for forgiveness and divine engagement.

God's praying people had sinned (8:33, 35, 46, 50) and needed to confess his Name (loyalty/allegiance) after they had turned back to the Lord (8:33, 35, 47–48). From that position of repentance, forgiveness was repeatedly requested (8:30, 34, 36, 50). They turned back to God when they came face to face with God's covenantal chastisements. The seventh and most severe prayer occasion of exile prompted a three-fold confession: "We have sinned, we have done wrong, we have acted wickedly" (8:47; cf. Ps 106:6). Serious prayer is accompanied by repentance and confession of sin.

Another aspect of the paradigmatic suppliant in this prayer is the recognition that divine omniscience penetrates into each petitioner's heart (8:39). The intended response of the suppliants to that divine, intimate knowing is fearing the Lord (8:40). Wheeler notes that the closest verbal parallel to God's response based on his unique ("you alone") and complete knowledge of the human heart is found in Jeremiah (Jer

---

17. Levenson observed, "The Hebrew words for these two acts of worship [prayer and supplication], or their verbal counterparts, recur unremittingly throughout the third address (8:28, 29, 30, 33, 35, 38, 42, 44, 45, 47–49, 52). It is as though the author does not want us to forget that this is the one true and enduring aspect of the Temple" (*Sinai and Zion*, 164).

17:10; 32:19; cf. Ps 139:23).[18] The foreign pilgrim also was destined to fear the LORD "as do your own people Israel" (8:43). Thus, Israel prayed to One who knew them intimately, a knowledge that prompted them to fear the LORD and attempt to walk in his ways (cf. the parallel in 2 Chr 6:31). We pray to the same God for the same reason.

HOW IS GOD PORTRAYED IN THIS PRAYER?

The scene opened with the installation of the ark and concluded with the theophany of the glory cloud filling the newly-constructed temple (8:10–11). Solomon's brief "Presence Prayer" (8:12–13) designated the temple as "a place for you to dwell forever." There was a heightened sense of God's presence there. The temple was understood as a synecdoche/metonymy of presence (8:28–29), as observed in the close of the narrative where it says Solomon's prayer, the sacrifices, and the festival happened "before the LORD" (8:59, 64, 65).[19] In Solomon's concluding blessing/praise, he pleaded that God be with them "as he was with our fathers; may he never leave us or forsake us" (8:57). This once again features the notion of close divine presence and deliverance.

In the initial blessing/praise section (8:15–21), God is portrayed as the One who had made a promise to David and who now was fulfilling that promise in Solomon, the builder of the "temple for my Name" (8:16–20, 29, 44, 48). The Name Theology is prominent in the "Protocol of Legitimation," where Solomon established his right to build the temple (8:15–21) and in the prayer itself. It disappears in the concluding blessing/praise section (8:56–61) and the dismissal of the assembly (8:62–66), but reappears one final time in the post-prayer theophany (9:3). In one aspect this multivalent metonymy, "the Name," suggests the idea of presence. Yet in the prayer occasion regarding the pious foreigner, "the Name" clearly stood in for the notion of fame/reputation (8:41–43)[20] and signaled ownership (8:43). In the prayer occasions of war and exile, "the Name" also represented the concepts of ownership, possession, and authority (8:44, 48). On the occasions of defeat and

---

18. Wheeler, *Prayer and the Temple*, 141.

19. Wilson, *Out of the Midst of the Fire*, 65, 133, 156. See also Lister, *The Presence of God*, 211–15.

20. Richter, *The Deuteronomistic History*, 129.

drought, they would humbly confess "the Name" as the One whom they had offended with their sin (8:33, 35). In the final theophanic response to Solomon's Temple Prayer, God gave an anthropomorphic elaboration on "the Name": " . . . by putting my Name there forever. My eyes and my heart will always be there" (9:3; cf. 8:29). God would virtually be present.

Solomon asked that his words, "which I have prayed before the LORD, be near to the LORD" (8:59). Locating his "words" in a spatial framework ("near") is an unusual mixing of semantic domains as words are usually heard and remembered, not "near." Spatially, this may be developed as the "here but also there" concept; the modern notion of virtual presence or virtual reality may be helpful for our understanding of this aspect of divine presence evoked in prayer (e.g., "on earth as it is in heaven").

This mixing of semantic divergent domains is evident also in the beginning of Solomon's prayer; he asked that "your eyes to be open toward this temple night and day . . . so that you will hear the prayer your servant prays" (8:29). This same anthropomorphic juxtaposition of eyes and hearing closes the prayer (8:52). God's awareness was expected in many of the occasions themselves where defeat (8:33), drought (8:35), and exile (8:46) would be results of God's judgment for sin.

The call for God to "hear" is ubiquitous in this prayer (8:30 [2x], 32, 34, 36, 39, 43, 45, 49, 52). Repeatedly this is expressed as "hear from heaven [your dwelling place]" (8:30, 39, 43, 49). The word for "hear" when used by God is often coupled with a call for obedience (e.g., Deut 4:1; 5:1), but when used by the people in prayer to God it was a call for an active response of deliverance.

Other anthropomorphic expressions surface. First Kings 8:15 introduces the One "who with his own hand has fulfilled what he promised with his own mouth" (8:15). This prayer is a call for God to see and hear, and to respond with forgiveness and deliverance. The anthropomorphic reference to God's "mighty hand" and "outstretched arm" in regard to the pious foreigner (8:42) evokes Exodus imagery (Exod 6:6; Deut 4:34).

In sum, the expectations of those who would pray in earnest merged with the characterization of God. He would act on their behalf in keeping with the covenant, ultimately and sovereignly turning "our hearts to walk in all his ways" (8:58).

WHAT IS LEARNED ABOUT PRAYER FROM SOLOMON'S TEMPLE PRAYER?

Gregory Beale and John Walton have done much to show the cosmic Edenic connections to the tabernacle and temple. The temple ultimately binds heaven and earth vertically and God with his people horizontally.[21] The "temple" goes through multiple transformations from Eden to the tabernacle, to the Solomonic and second temples, to Jesus who refers to his body as a temple (John 2:19–22),[22] to Paul who references the people of God, collectively and individually, as a temple (1 Cor 3:16–17; 6:19), and finally to the eschatological universal expansion in Rev 21:22 where "the Lord God Almighty and the Lamb are its [New Jerusalem's] temple."[23]

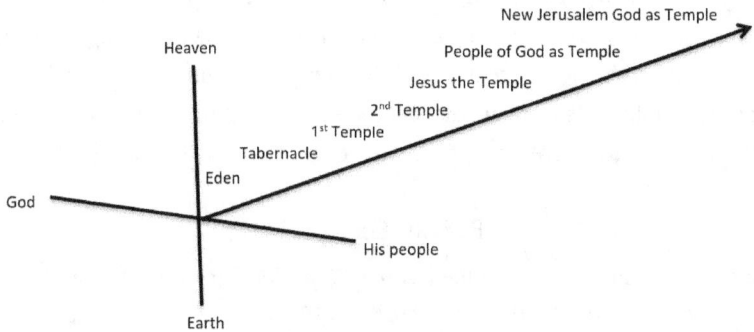

The narrative context into which Solomon's prayer is set is one small slice of that grand redemptive narrative with which God's people are privileged to join as active praying participants.

This magnificent Solomonic prayer reflects several significant parallels with the Lord's Prayer (Matt 6:9–13). Prayer addressed toward this temple is heard by God who is in heaven (cf. "Our Father who art in heaven"). The Solomonic prayer features the "Name" metonymy,

---

21. Beale, *The Temple and the Church's Mission*, 61, 66–71; Walton, *Genesis*, 147–51, 167.

22. See also Perrin, *Jesus The Temple*.

23. See Mathewson, *A New Heaven and a New Earth*.

and we are taught to pray "hallowed be your Name." Furthermore, as suppliants in Solomon's day were needy, we too pray from a position of need, "give us this day our daily bread." Repentance and prayer for forgiveness (8:30, 34, 35, 50) are echoed in our request to "forgive us our debts." Finally, as the Solomonic suppliant cries out for deliverance and rescue, so we cry out "deliver us from the evil one."

This prayer beautifully lit up the amber sky just before the dark nadir of night set in as this temple-building son of David went astray—using his gifts to build other temples as he descended into idolatry and abandoned his own admonitions (8:60; 9:9). Modern readers can learn much from the wisdom and piety of Solomon's Temple Prayer. It encourages us to humbly confess our sins, to cry out in prayer when faced with crises, and to make supplication to the One who will hear from heaven and forgive the sin of his servants and teach us the right way to live, delivering us as the people of his inheritance (8:35–36). We no longer pray toward the temple on Zion, but rather pray in the "Name" of Jesus. He is the temple who is transforming us as a believing community through the presence of his Holy Spirit into a temple made without hands. Finally, it is in New Jerusalem, where God himself is the eternal temple, that our prayers will give way to speaking with God face to face.

BIBLIOGRAPHY

Balentine, Samuel. *Prayer in the Hebrew Bible: The Drama of Divine-Human Dialogue.* OBT. Minneapolis: Fortress, 1993.

Beale, Gregory K. *The Temple and the Church's Mission: A Biblical Theology of the Dwelling Place of God.* NSBT 17. Downers Grove, IL: InterVarsity, 2004.

Brettler, Marc. "Interpretation and Prayer: Notes on the Composition of 1 Kings 8:15–23." In *Minhah le-Nahum: Biblical and other Studies Presented to Nahum M. Sarna in Honour of His 70th Birthday,* edited by Marc Brettler and Michael Fishbane, 17–35. JSOTSup 154. Sheffield: Sheffield University Press, 1993.

DeVries, Simon. *1 Kings.* WBC. Nashville: Thomas Nelson, 2003.

Hundley, Michael B. *Gods in Dwellings: Temples and Divine Presence in the Ancient Near East.* Atlanta: Society of Biblical Literature, 2013.

Hurowitz, Victor. *I Have Built You an Exalted House: Temple Building in the Bible in Light of Mesopotamian and North-West Semitic Writings.* JSOTSup 115. Sheffield: JSOT, 1992.

———. *Keeping Heaven on Earth: Safeguarding the Divine Presence in the Priestly Tabernacle.* Tübingen: Mohr Siebeck, 2011.

Kang, Jang. *The Persuasive Portrayal of Solomon in 1 Kings 1–11.* European University Studies, Series XXIII Theology. Berlin: Peter Lang, 2003.

Levenson, Jon D. *Sinai and Zion: An Entry into the Jewish Bible.* Minneapolis: Winston, 1985.

Lister, J. Ryan. *The Presence of God: Its Place in the Storyline of Scripture and the Story of Our Lives.* Wheaton, IL: Crossway, 2015.

Long, Burke O. *I Kings, with an Introduction to Historical Literature.* FOTL 9. Grand Rapids: Eerdmans, 1984.

Mathewson, David. *A New Heaven and a New Earth: The Meaning and Function of the Old Testament in Revelation 21:1—22:5.* New York: T. & T. Clark, 2003.

Mettinger, Tryggve. *The Dethronement of Sabaoth: Studies in the Shem and Kabod Theologies.* Lund: CWK Gleerup, 1982.

Parker, Ian. *Wisdom and Law in the Reign of Solomon.* Lewiston, NY: Edwin Mellen, 1992.

Perrin, Nicholas. *Jesus the Temple.* Grand Rapids: Baker, 2010.

Richter, Sandra L. *The Deuteronomistic History and the Name Theology: l^ešakkēn š^emô šām in the Bible and the Ancient Near East.* Berlin: de Gruyter, 2002.

Throntveit, Mark A. *When Kings Speak: Royal Speech and Royal Prayer in Chronicles.* Atlanta: Scholars Press, 1987.

Walsh, Jerome. "The Characterization of Solomon in 1 Kings 1–5." *CBQ* 57 (1995) 471–93.

Walton, John, *Genesis.* NIVAC. Grand Rapids: Zondervan, 2001.

Wheeler, Samuel B. "Prayer and the Temple in the Dedication Speech of Solomon 1 Kings 8:14–61." PhD diss., Columbia University, 1977.

Williams, D. S. "Once Again: The Structure of the Narrative of Solomon's Reign." *JSOT* 86 (1999) 49–66.

Wilson, Ian. *Out of the Midst of the Fire: Divine Presence in Deuteronomy.* SBLDS 151. Atlanta: Scholars, 1995.

4

Changing the Mind of God
The Prayer and Tears of King Hezekiah (2 Kings 20:1–6)

David T. Lamb

INTRODUCTION

WHEN KING HEZEKIAH OF Judah was sick and at the point of death, the prophet Isaiah informed the ruler that he would in fact die (2 Kgs 20:1). Hezekiah's short prayer (2 Kgs 20:2–3) curiously lacked a confession of sin or a request for healing, but included merely a solitary command for YHWH to "remember" (*zekhor-na*) his pious deeds and faithful lifestyle. YHWH heard his prayer, granted his unspoken request, and extended his life by fifteen years.

To understand the context of Hezekiah's prayer, I will first discuss royal prayers for longevity in both ancient Near Eastern (ANE) sources and the book of Kings. Then I will examine Hezekiah's point-of-death prayer in depth, and finally conclude by looking at the role piety and emotions play in a biblical theology of prayer.

David T. Lamb—*Changing the Mind of God*

ANE PARALLELS: LONG LIFE, A DIVINE GIFT FOR PRAYING, RIGHTEOUS RULERS

Numerous ANE inscriptions describe rulers who, like Hezekiah, prayed for, or received long lives because of their piety. In the ANE, the gods were often described as the source of long life for both Hittite (*ANET* 357b) and Egyptian rulers (Kamose, Thutmose III, and Ramesses II; *ANET* 199b, 232c; *COS* 2:8b).[1] Prayers were frequently made for royal longevity. A scribe prayed to Telipinus for "long years" for the Hittite ruler Murshili II (*ANET* 397c), Ashurnasirpal II of Assyria prayed that his days may be long and his years many,[2] and Sennacherib of Assyria, Hezekiah's adversary in 2 Kgs 18–19, prayed that his offspring would live forever.[3] (Instead of praying for the long lives of his sons, Sennacherib should have prayed that his sons would not commit patricidal regicide; see 2 Kgs 19:37.) Two West Semitic sources mention royal prayers for long life (for Kilamuwa: *ANET* 665c; for Azatiwada: *COS* 2:150b). Nebuchadnezzar II of Babylon prayed that Nabû would "decree the lengthening of my days" (*COS* 2:310). Just as Hezekiah appealed to YHWH for long life based on his righteousness, ANE rulers associated royal longevity with righteous behavior, including Yahdun-Lim of Mari (*ANET* 556b), Hammurabi of Babylon (in his code; *COS* 2:352b; *ANET* 178d), Hammurabi's son, Samsu-iluna (*COS* 2:258), and Sargon II of Assyria (*COS* 1:472d). Thus, in the ANE, long life for a ruler was perceived to be a gift of the gods. Kings and their officials would pray for it based on a ruler's piety. This pattern is found consistently throughout the ANE in Egyptian, Hittite, Babylonian, Assyrian, and West Semitic texts. What about Israelite sources?

ROYAL PRAYERS IN KINGS

While the Israelite monarchy was conceived as being "like all the nations" (Deut 17:14; 1 Sam 8:5), in terms of royal prayers things were a bit different. While ANE inscriptions record many rulers praying, only five rulers in the book of Kings prayed or asked prophets to pray for

---

1. On royal longevity in ANE sources, see Lamb, *Righteous Jehu*, 164–66.
2. Grayson, *Assyrian Rulers*, 231.
3. Luckenbill, *The Annals of Sennacherib*, 139.

Section 2: Prayers of Kings

them: Solomon, Jeroboam I, Jehoahaz, Hezekiah, and Josiah.[4] A brief summary of the results of their prayers will provide background for understanding the context of Hezekiah's prayer.

When YHWH appeared to Solomon in a dream and told him to ask for whatever he wanted, he asked for "a listening heart" (*lev shomeaʿ*) and YHWH granted his wish, although YHWH seemed surprised Solomon did not ask for a long life (1 Kgs 3:5–12) as ANE rulers did with their gods. In Solomon's temple dedication prayer, his request for YHWH's name to dwell in the temple for all time was responded to favorably (1 Kgs 8:29; 9:3); however, his request to have his heirs continue to reign over Israel was not, as his son Rehoboam lost the northern kingdom due to Solomon's apostasy (1 Kgs 8:25–26; 11:6, 11, 31–33).

Jeroboam, son of Nebat, told an anonymous man of God to pray for his leprous hand and it was instantly healed (1 Kgs 13:6).[5] Jehoahaz of Israel entreated the favor of YHWH when the nation was suffering under Syrian oppression, and YHWH therefore sent the nation a deliverer (2 Kgs 13:4).[6] Before his point-of-death prayer, Hezekiah prayed in response to Sennacherib's threat, laying the Assyrian letter before YHWH in the temple (2 Kgs 19:14–19), and he received a favorable response as YHWH promised to deliver the king and the city (2 Kgs 19:20–34). Josiah sent his officers to the prophetess Huldah to inquire of YHWH about the book that was found in the temple. Her response was that judgment was coming, but the king would be spared because he was repentant, humble, and wept before YHWH (2 Kgs 22:13, 19).

One other incident where prayer is not mentioned explicitly still needs to be discussed since it has several parallels to Hezekiah's point-of-death prayer. Ahab fasted, put on sackcloth, tore his clothes, and walked around despondently which prompted YHWH to tell Elijah

---

4. The prophets Elijah and Elisha also pray in the book of Kings (e.g., 1 Kgs 18:36; 19:4; 2 Kgs 4:33; 6:17, 18). See also Lamb, *Righteous Jehu*, 179–81.

5. Cohn compares Hezekiah's interaction with Isaiah to that of three other kings in 1 and 2 Kings (Jeroboam, Ahaziah, and Ben-Hadad), each of whom are ill and discuss with a prophet (Ahaziah, Elijah, and Elisha) whether or not they will recover ("Convention and Creativity," 603–16).

6. Many scholars think the anonymous deliverer was Adad-nirari III of Assyria. See Wiseman, *1 & 2 Kings*, 240.

that he would delay the judgment on Ahab's house to the next generation (1 Kgs 21:27–29). This incident is also included in this discussion because fasting and wearing sackcloth are consistently associated with prayer elsewhere in the Old Testament (Pss 35:13; 109:21–24; Jer 14:11–12; Joel 1:13–15; Dan 6:18; 9:3; 10:1–3). Comparable to a prayer, Ahab's behavior elicits a response from YHWH.

We can observe three similarities between these royal prayer narratives and Hezekiah's. First, four of the incidents involve prophetic mediators (Jeroboam and the man of God, Ahab and Elijah, Hezekiah and Isaiah, and Josiah and Huldah). Second, Jeroboam requests a healing just as Hezekiah did. Third, three of the rulers express intense emotions: Hezekiah and Josiah both weep and Ahab goes around dejectedly.

Among these six rulers, curiously, only two are evaluated as righteous (Hezekiah and Josiah). Prior to Hezekiah in the book of Kings, all rulers who pray (or fast) are evaluated as evil: Solomon, Jeroboam, Ahab, and Jehoahaz (1 Kgs 11:6; 14:9; 16:30; 2 Kgs 13:2). Surprisingly, YHWH generally responds positively to the prayers of these evil rulers. Thus, unlike the ANE conception of prayer, in Kings, favorable responses to prayer are not closely linked to royal righteousness. As we will see with Hezekiah, his righteousness does not appear to factor in YHWH's decision to heal him.

HEZEKIAH'S POINT-OF-DEATH PRAYER IN ISAIAH 38

Before looking at Hezekiah's point-of-death prayer (2 Kgs 20:1–6), we will make a few comments about the parallel account that appears in Isa 38:1–6.[7] The version in Isa 38 is substantially shorter than 2 Kgs 20 since it lacks four phrases present in 2 Kings (totaling eighteen words in Hebrew): (1) "Before Isaiah had gone out of the middle court" (*yesha'yahu lo' yatsa' khatser*[8] *hattikhonah*; from 2 Kgs 20:4a), (2) "The leader of my people" (*negid-'ammi*; from 2 Kgs 20:5a), (3) "I will heal

---

7. The Chronicles parallel (2 Chr 32:24) condenses the incident to one verse without offering anything unique so it will not be discussed here. For detailed discussions of the differences between 2 Kgs 20:1–6 and Isa 38:1–6, see Jones, *1 and 2 Kings*, 583–87 and Cogan and Tadmor, *II Kings*, 254–57.

8. Reading *khatser* with other Heb. mss, Q, and versions, instead of the MT's *ha'ir* (the city).

you. On the third day you shall go up to the house of YHWH" (*rofe' lak bayyom hashelishi ta'aleh bet yhwh*; from 2 Kgs 20:5), and (4) "For my own sake and for my servant David's sake" (*lema'ani ulema'an david 'avdi*; from 2 Kgs 20:6).

Other than these missing phrases, much of the language in 2 Kgs 20 and Isa 38 is identical, with two minor exceptions. Where the MT in 2 Kgs 20:2 merely has an implied pronoun ("he") as part of the primary verb, Isa 38:2 makes the identity of the subject explicit by including "Hezekiah" (*hizqiyyahu*). And the command at the beginning of Isaiah's second message is different; 2 Kgs 20:5 has the imperative of the verb *shuv* ("Turn") while Isa 38:5 has the infinitive absolute of the verb *halakh* ("Go"). The rest of this paper will focus on the account in 2 Kgs 20, since it is the longest and most comprehensive version of the incident.

HEZEKIAH'S POINT-OF-DEATH PRAYER IN 2 KINGS 20:1–6

Isaiah's Announcement: You Will Die

After looking at royal prayers in the ANE and in Kings, and the Isaianic parallel, we can now examine the narrative of Hezekiah's prayer in 2 Kgs 20. Hezekiah is so sick he is at the point of death (20:1). The only other time this form (*lamed* preposition with the infinitive of *mut*) is used in Kings for a ruler is when David gives his final charge to Solomon immediately before his death (1 Kgs 2:1). Like David, Hezekiah is literally at death's door. Isaiah appears, informing Hezekiah, "You will die" (*met 'attah*). In case that pronouncement was not clear enough, Isaiah adds, "And you shall not recover" (*velo' tikhyeh*). Isaiah's message may seem harsh, but it was the truth and it gave the king an opportunity to prepare for the inevitable.

Hezekiah's Prayer: Remember

In response to Isaiah's dire message, Hezekiah prays. We can observe four things about his prayer. First, Hezekiah appears to disobey YHWH's command to "put his house" in order. Perhaps God wanted him to set up his successor just as David did with Solomon (1 Kgs 2:1–12), or write his final will.⁹ We may not be sure what God wanted Hezekiah to do, but the text records him doing nothing to get his house in order.

Second, Hezekiah begins his prayer by giving God a command, "remember" (*zekhor-na*), which is ironic since he seems to be disobeying God's command to him.¹⁰ He reminds God by laying out his spiritual resume, walking in faithfulness and a whole heart, doing good in God's eyes, items which presumably would have been missing from the resumes of his evil predecessors.¹¹

Third, Hezekiah never asks God to heal him (like Jeroboam) or to extend his life (as do Ashurnasirpal II or Nebuchadnezzar II). While we cannot be certain that healing was what Hezekiah had in mind, Wray Beal's conclusion that his command to remember implies a "petition for healing" is reasonable.¹² Hezekiah has just been told he would die, so the subject of his health would have been on his mind.¹³ And, as we saw above, righteousness and long life were often linked in ANE prayers (see also Deut 17:19–20). YHWH also states that the healing was a direct result of hearing Hezekiah's prayer. Hezekiah seems to assume that if God remembers his piety, a supernatural healing will soon follow.

Fourth, like Josiah, the righteous king who followed him, Hezekiah weeps bitterly (2 Kgs 22:19). A literal translation here would be "Hezekiah wept a great weeping" (20:3) since both the verb (*bakhah*) and the related noun (*bekhi*) are used. Thus, the text emphasizes the ruler's emotional response. Earlier in his reign, when he heard about

---

9. See Cogan and Tadmor, *II Kings*, 254.

10. Wray Beal observes that Hezekiah prayed for the city before (2 Kgs 19), but now it is on his own behalf (*1 & 2 Kings*, 480). Leithart notes that Hezekiah is sometimes accused of praying in a self-righteous or self-interested manner, but "this kind of prayer is common in the Psalms" (*1 & 2 Kings*, 260).

11. Hezekiah's prayer is expressed in classic Deuteronomistic language: "whole heart," "walked before you in faithfulness," "done what is good in your sight." See Jones, *1 & 2 Kings*, 586; Cogan and Tadmor, *II Kings*, 254.

12. Wray Beal, *1 & 2 Kings*, 481. Barnes also notes that Hezekiah received fifteen more years because "he dared to pray for them." (*1–2 Kings*, 346).

13. Hezekiah's pre-occupation with his own welfare is evidenced as he does not appear to be bothered when Isaiah tells Hezekiah about the upcoming exile which will negatively affect his descendants since "there will be peace and security" in his days (2 Kgs 20:19).

the message from Sennacherib's official, Hezekiah tore his clothes, put on sackcloth, and went to the temple (2 Kgs 19:1).

YHWH's Response: Fifteen More Years

YHWH's response to Hezekiah's prayer was immediate. Before Isaiah had even left the palace complex, God told his prophet to go back and tell Hezekiah that his prayer had been heard, his tears had been seen, and his life would therefore be extended by fifteen years.[14] God did remember Hezekiah. Even though there is no record of Hezekiah obeying YHWH's command, the text states that YHWH listened to Hezekiah's.[15] It thus appears that Hezekiah's prayer changed the mind of YHWH.[16] I will next address three possible objections to this conclusion.

THREE OBJECTIONS

Objection #1: Isaiah changed his mind, not God. According to this objection, Isaiah's first oracle here was like Nathan's first message to David in 2 Sam 7 to build the temple, which was later corrected by YHWH (2 Sam 7:3–4).[17] Thus, the first messages of Nathan to David, and Isaiah to Hezekiah were not from God, but merely from the prophet. However, there is a significant difference between Nathan's two oracles and Isaiah's two oracles. The prophetic messenger formula ("Thus says YHWH," *koh 'amar yhwh*), used to give authority to Nathan's second message to David not to build, is absent from the first one to build (2 Sam 7:3–5). But the prophetic messenger formula is present in both Isaiah's message about Hezekiah's extended life span in 20:5 and in his initial message about Hezekiah's imminent death in 20:1, suggesting that, unlike Nathan's two messages to David, both of Isaiah's messages

---

14. Hezekiah's evil heir Manasseh appears to have been born during these additional fifteen years of his life (2 Kgs 20:21—21:1); see also Barnes, *1–2 Kings*, 344.

15. A similar phenomenon occurs after the incident of the golden calf (Exod 32:10–14) when YHWH tells Moses to leave him alone and he does not, and then Moses tells YHWH to relent and he does.

16. John Cassian says God "chose to break his own word . . . rather than show himself inexorable because of an inflexible decree" (ACCS V:223).

17. Barnes focuses not on YHWH's change, but that of the prophet Isaiah in both 2 Kgs 19 and 20 (*1–2 Kings*, 337, 338, 344).

to Hezekiah originated from God and had God's full endorsement. It was not Isaiah who changed his mind.

Objection #2: Hezekiah's healing was God's plan. According to this objection, God was already planning to heal Hezekiah, and the reason God told him beforehand was to invite Hezekiah to intercede in order for YHWH to then heal him. Wiseman states here that "prayer and God's answer are both part of his plan."[18]

However, there are at least three problems with this perspective. First, there are no hints in the text that Hezekiah's healing was part of God's plan all along. That is not what the text says. In fact, the text states the opposite quite clearly (see the next point). In order to argue it was part of God's plan, one has not just to read between the lines, but to add elements to the story.

Second, God said in the first message that Hezekiah was going to die, expressed both positively (you shall die) and negatively (you shall not recover).[19] If God were planning to heal him from the beginning, he should not have said Hezekiah will die. If we think God was planning on healing Hezekiah while he was saying Hezekiah will not recover, we essentially make God into a liar.[20] Thus, this solution to the problem of a mind-changing God results in a bigger problem of a deceptive or manipulative God.

Third, God states in the second message that he is going to add fifteen years to Hezekiah's life because God heard his prayer and saw his tears. The context therefore suggests that the additional fifteen years are a direct result of Hezekiah's prayer and not a result of a pre-ordained plan.

Objection #3: God does not change his mind. According to this objection, other Scriptures inform us that God does not change his mind,

---

18. Wiseman, *1 & 2 Kings*, 286. Zwingli states that Hezekiah's additional fifteen years were planned by God "*before* the establishment of the world" (Cooper and Lohrman, eds., *Reformation Commentary*, 489).

19. Fretheim describes God's initial word to Hezekiah as "not conditional, no ifs ands or buts" (Fretheim, *Kings*, 208).

20. Pellikan realizes that Hezekiah's fifteen-year extension could make God appear deceptive, but he denies this conclusion about God ("who does not lie") because "divine providence is not changed" (Cooper and Lohrman, eds., *Reformation Commentary*, 489).

so he cannot be doing that in 2 Kgs 20 with Hezekiah. However, the issue is more complicated than the advocates for divine immutability here might lead us to think. The witness of Scripture on this issue suggests that God both does not change and that he does, depending upon the context.[21] We will now turn to the relevant texts.

Divine Immutability Texts

There are four primary Old Testament texts that support the idea that God does not change and three of them use the verb *nakham* ("to repent" or "change one's mind").[22] I refer to these as the divine immutability texts. Balaam delivers an oracle to Balak declaring that God is not like a human who changes his mind (*nakham*), so he will not curse the people he has promised to bless (Num 23:19). Samuel tells Saul that YHWH is not like a human that he would change his mind (*nakham*) regarding the judgment that he would tear away the kingdom from Saul and give it to his neighbor David (1 Sam 15:29). YHWH himself declares that he does not change (*shanah*), and, therefore, Israel has not perished (Mal 3:6). The psalmist explains that YHWH will not change his mind (*nakham*) about his decision to make the addressee a priest forever, in the order of Melchizedek (Ps 110:4). Thus, we find at least one reference supporting the idea that God does not change in each of the three divisions of the Hebrew Bible: one in the Torah, two in the Prophets, and one in the Writings.

Divine Mutability Texts

However, offsetting these four divine immutability texts, are nineteen divine mutability texts in the Old Testament that support the idea that God does change. Most of these references (except Num 14:20, and the Hezekiah prayers in 2 Kgs 20 and Isa 38) use the same verb *nakham* that appears in three of the immutability texts.

---

21. See also my discussions of this topic in Lamb, *God Behaving Badly*, 135–52, and Lamb, "The Immutable Mutability," 25–38.

22. The verb *nakham* can mean "to comfort or console" (e.g., Gen 24:67; 2 Sam 13:39), or as it does in these divine (im)mutability contexts "to be sorry, repent, change one's mind" (Butterworth, "נחם," 82).

Both after the golden calf and the refusal to enter the land, Moses intercedes with YHWH who then twice relents from punishment (Exod 32:14; Num 14:20). After David's census, YHWH relents and stops the pestilence (2 Sam 24:16; 1 Chr 21:15). The psalmist narrates how, after his people cried, YHWH relented according to his steadfast love (Ps 106:45). The book of Jeremiah repeatedly describes God as changing his mind (Jer 18:8, 10; 26:3,13; 42:10). In one of Jeremiah's oracles, God says he has relented so often that he is tired of it (Jer 15:6). Jeremiah also records an incident where Hezekiah, after hearing from the prophet Micah, prayed and convinced YHWH to change his mind (Jer 26:19). Two texts from the Minor Prophets describe how relenting from judgment is a part of God's character (Joel 2:13–14; Jonah 4:2), and three other prophetic references narrate him relenting (Amos 7:3, 6; Jonah 3:9–10).

There are far more texts in the Old Testament supporting the idea that God does change his mind than those supporting the idea that he does not. Therefore, the argument that Hezekiah could not change God's mind based on other Scriptures is not compelling. In fact, Hezekiah's point-of-death prayer fits a consistent pattern of God relenting in response to prayer, which appears twice each in the Torah and the Writings, and fifteen times in the Prophets. While numerous Old Testament individuals experienced or described God as changing his mind, Hezekiah is among an elite group with Moses (Exod 32:14; Num 14:20) and Amos (Amos 7:3, 6), who change God's mind on two separate occasions.

Reconciling Immutability with Mutability

How do we reconcile the texts that describe God as changing with the ones that describe him as not changing? In contexts where there is doubt whether or not God will be faithful, the text declares that he does not waiver in his commitments. It is not simply that God does not ever change, but specifically that he does not change regarding his promises to his covenant people.

In contexts of imminent judgment from God, when people repent, he changes his mind and shows mercy. It is not that God always changes and is inconsistent, but specifically in situations where people deserve punishment, when they repent, he consistently changes from judgment to grace.

As we look at the contexts of these passages, we see not a divine contradiction but a consistent pattern. The Old Testament characters themselves understood both the changing and unchanging aspect of God's nature. According to the Old Testament, God is predictably flexible, constantly changeable, and immutably mutable, at least in regards to showing mercy toward repentant sinners.

WHY DID GOD CHANGE HIS MIND FOR HEZEKIAH?

YHWH showed mercy toward Hezekiah, but not because he repented for sinful behavior. Both the narrator and Hezekiah himself state that he was righteous (2 Kgs 18:3–6; 20:3). Why did God change his mind in Hezekiah's case? Assessing motive is always difficult, but YHWH gives clues in his message to the king. YHWH's response was immediate, before Isaiah even left the palace grounds, so he did not need a lot of time to deliberate. Before examining the two factors emphasized in the text, I want to briefly discuss two reasons that do not seem to contribute to God's decision to give the king fifteen more years.

Hezekiah's piety does not appear to be a major factor prompting God to change his mind. Hezekiah focused his prayer on his pious behavior, so he thought the prayers of a righteous man "availeth much" (see Jas 5:16), a perspective that is consistent with what was observed above in ANE royal prayers. But YHWH does not mention anything about Hezekiah's righteousness, which does not necessarily mean the king's piety made no difference, merely that it was not a factor YHWH chose to highlight. An additional reason we could conclude that piety did not play a role in Hezekiah's case is that, as we saw earlier in Kings, God responded positively to the prayers and fasts of three rulers who are described as unrighteous (Jeroboam, Ahab, and Jehoahaz).

If piety was not a major factor, what about Hezekiah's ancestry? At the beginning and end of YHWH's second message he mentions Hezekiah's ancestor David (20:5, 6), which could lead one to assume that Hezekiah's Davidic ancestry was a factor.[23] And YHWH specifi-

---

23. Hobbs thinks Hezekiah's prayer is self-centered and lacking in faith, and God acts in response because of David, not Hezekiah, who he characterizes as unbelieving

cally states that he is acting "for the sake of my servant David" (20:6). However, at the end of this message David is recalled in the context of explaining why Jerusalem will be defended. There is no explicit link between David and the extension of Hezekiah's life. If his relationship to his ancestor David were important, Hezekiah could have been healed earlier, prior to his prayer, because the prayer obviously had no impact on his ancestry. Neither Hezekiah's piety, nor his ancestry appear to have been major factors in his healing.

The two factors mentioned by YHWH to Hezekiah for the healing are merely that he prayed and that he wept. Between the preamble of the second message ("Thus says YHWH, the God of David your father;" 20:5) and the announcement of healing ("Behold, I will heal you;" 20:5), YHWH focuses not on Hezekiah's piety or his ancestry, but on his prayer and his tears.

YHWH highlights these factors two ways. First, mentioning Hezekiah's prayer and tears immediately before the healing announcement suggests there is causality—that the prayer and the tears have resulted in the healing. The "Behold I" (*hinni*) serves not only to get Hezekiah's attention, but to link what has just been noted with what is about to happen, like an implicit "Therefore."

Second, YHWH's observation of Hezekiah's behavior is expressed in poetic parallelism, in contrast to the prosaic nature of the surrounding narrative. Most English translations capture the poetic cadence well, but the parallelism comes through more clearly in the Hebrew (20:5).

"I have heard your prayer" (*shama'ti 'eth-tefillathekha*)

"I have seen your tears" (*ra'ithi 'eth-dim'athekha*)

YHWH's language here in his second message to Hezekiah is reminiscent of the beginning of the Exodus story as the narrator informs the reader why God was about to begin a process of deliverance.

"And God heard their groaning" (*vayyishma' 'elohim 'eth-na'aqatham*) (Exod 2:24).

(2 *Kings*, 296).

Section 2: Prayers of Kings

"And God saw the people of Israel" (*vayyar' 'elohim 'eth-bene yisra'el*) (Exod 2:25).

The same two sensory verbs used in 2 Kgs 20:5, "heard" (*shama'*) and "saw" (*ra'ah*) are used in Exod 2 to describe what motivated God to intercede and call Moses at the burning bush to deliver his people.[24] Curiously, the verb "remember" (*zakhar*) used by the narrator in Exodus, "And God remembered his covenant" (*vayyizkor 'elohim 'eth-beritho*; Exod 2:24) and used by Hezekiah in his prayer (20:3), is absent where we might expect it in YHWH's second message to Hezekiah. We assume YHWH remembered Hezekiah's righteousness since it was a major part of the ruler's prayer, which YHWH states that he heard. But the fact that "remember" is not mentioned by YHWH here is striking, particularly in light of the fact that he mentions these two other verbs from Exod 2. God wanted to highlight not Hezekiah's remembered righteousness, but his prayer and his tears.

RIGHTEOUSNESS, EMOTIONS, AND CHANGE

As I draw theological conclusions about royal prayers in Kings generally and about Hezekiah's point-of-death prayer specifically, I will focus on three words: righteousness, emotions, and change. First, righteousness is not as important as we may think in prayer. I believe the prayers of righteous men and righteous women "availeth much," but in the book of Kings, piety does not seem to be a major factor for God as he answers prayers for both evil and righteous rulers. God is so eager to be compassionate in these contexts that he listens to the prayers of everyone who turns to him and asks for help. When King Hezekiah highlights his righteousness, God does not mention it, but is merely pleased that he prayed. This conclusion may be considered bad news for all the righteous people out there, that there is not necessarily an inside track toward a favorable response from God, but for those of us who do not perceive ourselves to be particularly righteous, this message is great news.

Second, emotions are more important than we may think in prayer. The text emphasizes Hezekiah's tears. Hezekiah "wept a great

---

24. The same two verbs are repeated in Exod 3:7 as YHWH speaks to Moses.

weeping" (20:3) and God responded favorably when he saw the king's tears (20:5). The tears of both Hezekiah and Josiah are mentioned specifically by YHWH himself as a positive factor when he responds to their prayers. God is moved by emotional prayers. While God sees Hezekiah's tears, the vast majority of commentators do not. Alter, Barnes, Cogan and Tadmor, Fretheim, Fritz, Jones, Leithart, Sweeney, and Wiseman completely ignore Hezekiah's tears, making no mention of them.[25] One commentator, Wray Beal, mentions Hezekiah's tears briefly.[26] God viewed Hezekiah's expressions of emotions highly positively, but another commentator, Hobbs, viewed them highly negatively: "the news . . . sent Hezekiah into a sulk! . . . Hezekiah's weeping [was] presumably for himself!"[27] Apparently biblical scholars are either uncomfortable talking about emotions or they do not think they are significant to warrant a comment. YHWH not only talks about them, but they have a profound impact on him, significant enough to get him to change his mind. The narrative of Hezekiah's point-of-death prayer clearly suggests that the God of the Bible is swayed by emotional outbursts associated with prayer.

Third, change is something God does in response to prayer. Most commentators on this passage ignore the issue of God changing his mind, or somehow explain that it was part of God's sovereign plan (with little textual evidence to support this view). Fretheim, however, states it boldly, "God changes his mind," and then he proceeds to discuss "the power of prayer to effect changes in God's word."[28] If Hezekiah's God-changing prayer were unique in Scripture, then perhaps we should be reticent to make applications for today, but as we have seen, numerous other biblical characters prompted God, through prayer, to change his mind. Many of you may not need additional motivation to pray. You wake up, eager to pray; you go through your day in a constant state of

---

25. Alter, *The Former Prophets*; Barnes, *1–2 Kings*; Cogan and Tadmor, *II Kings*; Fretheim, *Kings*; Fritz, *1 & 2 Kings*; Jones, *1 & 2 Kings*; Leithart, *1 & 2 Kings*; Sweeney, *I & II Kings*; Wiseman, *1 & 2 Kings*.

26. Wray Beal, *1 & 2 Kings*, 480.

27. Hobbs, *2 Kings*, 290.

28. Fretheim, *Kings*, 205, 208. Fretheim understandably wonders why Hezekiah does not pray for divine change about Isaiah's pronouncement about his descendants and concludes he did not because it does not affect him personally.

Section 2: Prayers of Kings

prayerful meditation. But for those of us who find it difficult to make time to pray, or who wonder what difference it makes, an image of a God who listens, responds, and even changes in response to prayer is a powerful motivator. It makes one want to pray, which ultimately should be our goal as we reflect on our theology of prayer.

BIBLIOGRAPHY

Alter, Robert. *Ancient Israel: The Former Prophets: Joshua, Judges, Samuel, and Kings*. New York: Norton, 2013.

Barnes, William H. *1–2 Kings*. Carol Stream, IL: Tyndale, 2012.

Butterworth, Mike. "נחם." In *NIDOTTE* 3:81–83.

Cogan, Mordecai, and Hayim Tadmor. *II Kings*. AB 11. New York: Doubleday, 1988.

Cohn, Robert L. "Convention and Creativity in the Book of Kings: The Case of the Dying Monarch." *CBQ* 47 (1985) 603–16.

Cooper, D., and J. Lohrman, eds. *Reformation Commentary on Scripture*. OT Vol. V. Downers Grove, IL: InterVarsity, 2016.

Fretheim, Terence E. *First and Second Kings*. Westminster Bible Companion. Louisville: Westminster John Knox, 1999.

Fritz, Volkmar. *1 & 2 Kings*. Minneapolis: Fortress, 2003.

Grayson, A. K. *Assyrian Rulers of the Early First Millennium BC I (1114–859 BC)*. Toronto: University of Toronto, 1991.

Hobbs, T. R. *2 Kings*. WBC. Waco, TX: Word, 1985.

Jones, G. H. *1 and 2 Kings*. Vol. 2. NCBC. Grand Rapids: Eerdmans, 1984.

Lamb, David T. *God Behaving Badly: Is the God of the Old Testament Angry, Sexist and Racist?* Downers Grove, IL: InterVarsity, 2011.

———. "The Immutable Mutability of YHWH" in *STR* 2.1 (2011) 25–38.

———. *Righteous Jehu and his Evil Heirs: The Deuteronomist's Negative Perspective on Dynastic Succession*. Oxford: Oxford University Press, 2007.

Leithart, Peter. *1 & 2 Kings*. Brazos Theological Commentary. Grand Rapids: Brazos, 2006.

Luckenbill, D. D. *The Annals of Sennacherib*. Chicago: University of Chicago Press, 1921.

Sweeney, Marvin. *I & II Kings*. OTL. Louisville: Westminster John Knox, 2007.

Wiseman, Donald J. *1 & 2 Kings*. TCOT. Downers Grove, IL: InterVarsity, 1993.

Wray Beal, Lissa M. *1 & 2 Kings*. AOTC. Downers Grove, IL: InterVarsity, 2014.

5

"We Do Not Know What We Should Do, but Our Eyes Are on You"
The Prayer of King Jehoshaphat in 2 Chronicles 20:6–12

Brittany Kim

INTRODUCTION

Second Chronicles 17–20 greatly expands on the portrait of Jehoshaphat, the ninth century king of Judah, found in 1 Kgs 22. The additional materials include an account of a Moabite-Ammonite-Meunite campaign against Judah, in which the Chronicler narrates Jehoshaphat's prayer of lament as well as YHWH's favorable response and miraculous deliverance of his people (2 Chr 20:1–30). Jehoshaphat's prayer (vv. 6–12) demonstrates significant dependence on Israelite traditions and prior biblical texts concerning the promises to Abraham, the conquest and other military victories, and the building and dedication of the temple.[1] It is unclear to what extent the Chronicler used

---

1. YHWH's response through Jahaziel in vv. 14–17 also exhibits dependence on previous traditions, in particular the Exodus (Exod 14:13–14; on this parallel, see further Amzallag, "Subversive Dimension," 181–82), conquest (Josh 10:14), and David's commissioning of Solomon (1 Chr 28:20). However, this essay will focus on Jehoshaphat's prayer itself.

Section 2: Prayers of Kings

oral or written sources in constructing this account and Jehoshaphat's prayer in particular.[2] However, given the significant connections between Jehoshaphat's prayer and other material in Chronicles, the specific wording of the prayer seems to derive primarily from the Chronicler rather than Jehoshaphat himself.[3] In this essay I will analyze the prayer offered by the Chronicler's Jehoshaphat, giving particular attention to both its structure and intertextual allusions, in order to see how it serves the Chronicler's aim of presenting a foundation for hope for the postexilic Jews seeking restoration. I will then conclude with some theological reflections and consider how Jehoshaphat's prayer may inform the prayers of Christians today.

THE STRUCTURE OF JEHOSHAPHAT'S PRAYER

Jehoshaphat's prayer in 2 Chr 20:6–12 is prompted by messengers coming to inform him that a Moabite–Ammonite–Meunite coalition is marching against Judah.[4] Jehoshaphat's response is to immediately "set his face to seek (*darash*) YHWH and proclaim a fast over all Judah" (v. 3), leading the people of Judah to gather together so that they too may "seek (*baqash*) YHWH" and solicit his intervention (v. 4).[5] He

---

2. See the discussion by McKenzie, "Trouble with King Jehoshaphat," 310–12; Rainey, "Mesha's Attempt," 174; Sugimoto, "Chronicles as Independent Literature," 73.

3. See also McKenzie, "Trouble with King Jehoshaphat," 311; Klein, *2 Chronicles*, 282; Kalimi, *Reshaping of Ancient Israelite History*, 27–28. Therefore, references to Jehoshaphat throughout the essay should be understood as designating "the Chronicler's Jehoshaphat."

4. In 2 Chr 20:1, the MT identifies both the second and third groups as Ammonites. Along with most translations, I follow the LXX in taking the third group as Meunites (cf. 1 Chr 4:41; 2 Chr 26:7), assuming a metathesis in the consonantal text from an original *hm'vnym* to *h'mvnym*. See Knoppers, "Reform and Regression," 516n45; cf. Thompson, *1, 2 Chronicles*, 292–93. Later in the passage, the third party is described as "(the inhabitants of) Mount Seir" (vv. 10, 22–23), a location that is elsewhere connected to Edom (e.g., Gen 36:8; Deut 2:5). For further discussion, see Japhet, *I & II Chronicles*, 785–86; Dillard, *2 Chronicles*, 155–56.

5. All translations are mine unless otherwise noted. Beentjes contends that "the motif of 'seeking YHWH' will appear to be the criterion with which the Chronicler is screening and evaluating the kings theologically" ("Aspects of Innerbiblical Interpretation," 63).

then offers a prayer of lament, which—together with its frame in vv. 5 and 13—exhibits a chiastic pattern:[6]

- A: "And Jehoshaphat *stood ('amad)* in the assembly of Judah and Jerusalem in *the house (bayit) of YHWH before (lifne)* the new court" (v. 5)

  - B: "and said, 'YHWH, God of our fathers, *are you not (halo')* God in the heavens? And [do you not] rule over all the kingdoms of the nations?[7] And in your hand are *strength (koakh)* and might, and no one can withstand you.'" (v. 6)

    - C: "Did not you, our God, *dispossess (yarash)* the inhabitants of this land from before your people Israel and *give (natan)* it to the offspring of Abraham, your friend, forever?" (v. 7).

      - D: "And they dwelt in it and built for you in it a sanctuary for your name, saying, 'If disaster comes upon us, sword, judgment,[8] or pestilence or famine, we *will stand ('amad) before (lifne)* this *house (bayit)* and *before (lifne)* you, for your name is in this *house (bayit)*, and we will cry out to you from our distress, and you will hear and save'" (vv. 8–9).

    - C': "And now look, the children of Ammon and Moab and Mount Seir—which you did not *give (natan)* to Israel to enter when they came from the land of Egypt, for they turned aside from them and did not destroy them—look, they are repaying us by entering to drive us out from your

---

6. For an analysis of the prayer in the form of a lament, see Endres, "Theology of Worship," 178.

7. There is debate over how far the question extends. Here I assume that the initial "are not" also governs the second clause, introducing two rhetorical questions (see the NRSV and NASB; also Klein, 2 *Chronicles*, 279; Beentjes, "Aspects of Innerbiblical Interpretation," 65–66), but some translations take only the first clause as a question (see the NIV and ESV).

8. Alternatively, the verse could read "sword *of* judgment" (see Japhet, *I & II Chronicles*, 791; Williamson, *1 and 2 Chronicles*, 296). Others suggest emending *shefot* ("judgment") to *shetef* ("flood") (Klein, 2 *Chronicles*, 279; Dillard, 2 *Chronicles*, 151–53).

> *possession (yerushah)*, which you *gave (natan)* to us *to possess (yarash)*" (vv. 10–11).
>
> B': "Our God, *will you not (halo')* execute judgment against them? For there is no *strength (koakh)* in us before this great multitude that is coming against us, and we do not know what we should do, but our eyes are on you" (v. 12).
>
> A': "And all Judah *was standing ('amad) before (lifne)* YHWH, even their little ones, their wives, and their children" (v. 13).

In a chiastic structure, the emphasis falls on the central point, and here that point (D) is further highlighted by its correspondence with the frame (A/A'). Following this chiastic pattern, I will analyze Jehoshaphat's prayer from the outside in, though I will delay discussion of the framing verses in order to consider them along with the center.

B/B': YHWH's "Strength" vs. the People's Lack of "Strength"

Jehoshaphat begins and ends his prayer by contrasting YHWH's "strength" with the people's lack of "strength." His initial rhetorical questions in *B* (introduced by *halo'*) may contain a hint of complaint: If YHWH is truly ruler over all, then why is he allowing the attacking nations to threaten Judah?[9] His prayer concludes in *B'* with a matching rhetorical question (also introduced by *halo'*), which serves to solicit this mighty God's help on behalf of his powerless people.[10]

YHWH's Sovereign Rule in David's Prayer
(2 Chr 20:6 // 1 Chr 29:11–12, 18)

The *B* section first notes YHWH's particular relationship with Judah's ancestors. Troy Cudworth argues that in Chronicles, the epithet "God of the fathers" consistently "evokes YHWH's promise to the patriarchs

---

9. See also Endres, "Theology of Worship," 178; Kuntzmann, "La définition d'un type," 38.

10. Commenting on these verses, Balentine says that "often in Kings and Chronicles, *hălō'* functions not to introduce a question but to stress a positive assertion" (*Prayer in the Hebrew Bible*, 99). Therefore, he sees Jehoshaphat's "language serv[ing] as a declaration of doxology, not complaint" (p. 100). However, in my view, the rhetorical questions serve to exert pressure on YHWH to act in accordance with the implied affirmative responses.

that he would provide their descendants (i.e., Israel) with a secure place in the land as long as they remain faithful to him,"[11] a theme to which Jehoshaphat returns in v. 7. Here, however, he turns his attention toward YHWH's sovereignty over the whole earth, deliberately echoing David's prayer in 1 Chr 29:10–19:[12]

2 Chr 20:6	1 Chr 29:11–12, 18
YHWH, God of our fathers (ʾelohe ʾavotenu), are you not God *in the heavens* (*bashamayim*)? *And [do you not] rule over all* (*veʾattah moshel bekhol*) the kingdoms of the nations. *And in your hand are strength and might* (*uveyadekha koakh ugevurah*), and no one can withstand you.	All that is *in the heavens* (*bashamayim*) and on the earth belongs to you ... *And you rule over all* (*veʾattah moshel bakkol*). *And in your hand are strength and might* (*uveyadekha koakh ugevurah*)[13] ... *YHWH, God of* (*ʾelohe*) *Abraham, Isaac, and Israel, our fathers* (*ʾavotenu*)

Jehoshaphat, however, makes two additions that apply David's statements to his current situation. First, he specifies that YHWH's universal rule is over the "kingdoms of the nations," thus noting its relevance for the attacking peoples.[14] Second, he draws out one implication of YHWH's sovereign rule that should give hope to Judah, declaring, "and no one can withstand you." Jehoshaphat implies that if YHWH is who David said he was, then he should have both the power to deliver Judah from the impending threat and the relational motivation to do so. And that message applies also to the Chronicler's postexilic audience in their struggles with the people of the land.[15]

---

11. Cudworth, "God of the Fathers," 484.

12. On the allusion, see Beentjes, "Aspects of Innerbiblical Interpretation," 65–66; also Lynch, *Monotheism and Institutions in the Book of Chronicles*, 246–47, who observes that "the Chronicler consistently portrays [Jehoshaphat] in Davidic terms."

13. Japhet observes that the phrase *koakh ugevurah* ("strength and might") occurs only in these two verses in the OT (*Ideology of the Book of Chronicles*, 44n143).

14. Beentjes, "Aspects of Innerbiblical Interpretation," 66.

15. Although I do not assume a specific date for Chronicles, I read it against the general background suggested by Ezra-Nehemiah, with which it shares many affinities.

Section 2: Prayers of Kings

No Strength against the Multitude in the Time of Asa
(2 Chr 20:12 // 2 Chr 14:11 [10])

The address shifts in B' from "God of our fathers" (v. 6) to "our God" (v. 12; also v. 7), connecting the present generation with their ancestors and highlighting YHWH's continued relationship with his people as a basis for Jehoshaphat's plea.[16] The particular form of intervention Jehoshaphat calls for—that YHWH would "execute judgment (*tishpat*) against" Judah's enemies—is probably, in part, designed to form a play on his own name, which means "YHWH has judged."[17] The king's name serves as a witness to YHWH's character and a ground for hope that YHWH will act to vindicate his people.

The prayer concludes with an acknowledgement of the people's utter helplessness, which echoes King Asa's prayer when facing an attack by the vast army of Zerah the Ethiopian in 2 Chr 14:11 [10]:[18]

2 Chr 20:12	2 Chr 14:11 [10]
Our God (*'elohenu*), will you not execute judgment against them? For there is *no strength* (*'en . . . koakh*) in us before this great multitude (*hehamon . . . hazzeh*) that *is coming against* us (*habba' 'alenu*), and we do not know what we should do, but our eyes are on you.	YHWH, there is no [difference] for you between helping the mighty or the one who has *no strength* (*'en koakh*).[19] Help us, YHWH *our God* (*'elohenu*), for we lean upon you and in your name we *have come against* (*va'nu 'al*) this multitude (*hehamon hazzeh*).

Asa's prayer implies that "the one who has no strength" applies first and foremost to himself (or to Judah more generally). Jehoshaphat then follows in Asa's footsteps, also preparing for the onslaught of a

---

16. Similarly, Beentjes, "Aspects of Innerbiblical Interpretation," 67, concerning v. 7.

17. See Beentjes, "Aspects of Innerbiblical Interpretation," 70.

18. On the allusion, see Rösel, ". . . dann will ich vom Himmel her hören," 357n12. Although Dillard does not note these verbal links, he contends that the Chronicler modeled his account of Jehoshaphat on that of Asa ("Chronicler's Jehoshaphat," 17–22; cf. Hill, *1 & 2 Chronicles*, 485; Amar, "Form and Content," 1–24).

19. The syntax of this sentence is difficult. Literally, the Hebrew reads, "YHWH, there is no one/thing with you to help between the great and the one who has no strength." For similar translations, see the NRSV; Klein, *2 Chronicles*, 208. Alternatively, it could mean, "there is none like you to help, between the mighty and the weak" (ESV; cf. Japhet, *1 & II Chronicles*, 711).

"multitude" by acknowledging his lack of strength.[20] However, unlike Asa, Jehoshaphat seeks YHWH's help *before* organizing his army for battle, suggesting a greater reliance on YHWH.[21] With no clear path forward, Jehoshaphat casts himself on YHWH, hoping YHWH will rescue him as he did Asa. For the audience of Chronicles, the connections between these narratives establish a pattern of how YHWH works among his people when they are utterly dependent on him.

C/C': The Conquest and Its Limits

The C and C' sections of Jehoshaphat's prayer focus on both the conquest and its limits, noting that YHWH gave Israel their land but that he also gave surrounding lands to the Ammonites, Moabites, and Edomites.

Land Promise Rooted in YHWH's Relationship with Abraham (2 Chr 20:7 // Isa 41:8)

In C Jehoshaphat draws on standard language to describe the conquest of Canaan, though he accentuates YHWH's action without noting the role that the Israelites played in "dispossessing" (*hiphil* of *yarash*) the Canaanites (see, e.g., Deut 9:3).[22] Moreover, he once again uses a rhetorical question marked by *halo'* ("did you not"), suggesting that

---

20. This may seem odd in light of the apparent claim of 2 Chr 17:14–19 that Jehoshaphat had over one million armed men at his disposal. The Hebrew word *'elef*, translated here as "thousand," can also mean "clan," and a related word (*'alluf*) means "chief." Therefore, some scholars have suggested that Chronicles is counting not "thousands" of soldiers but either "units" of a much smaller size (Mendenhall, "Census Lists," 60–62) or "specially trained leaders" (Payne, "Validity of the Numbers," 218). Others argue that the numbers are exaggerated, perhaps "serv[ing] only to indicate Jehoshaphat's high standing before God" (Klein, "Reflections on Historiography," 646; for a different perspective, see Amzallag, "Subversive Dimension," 184–85). Another possible explanation for Jehoshaphat's desperation, despite his apparently vast army, is that it reflects the Chronicler's postexilic situation when the weakness of the Judahite community necessitates complete reliance on YHWH (see Beentjes, "War Narratives," 594–95).

21. Rösel, ". . . dann will ich vom Himmel her hören," 357n12. Knoppers suggests that Jehoshaphat's final words serve not merely to acknowledge his helplessness and dependence on YHWH but also as a form of "leading the people in typical sacral war fashion by consulting the deity" for instructions ("Jerusalem at War," 69).

22. See Kuntzmann, "La definition d'un type," 39.

Section 2: Prayers of Kings

YHWH needs to be reminded of his gift of the land. And by noting the eternality of the promise, the prayer emphasizes its continuing relevance both to Jehoshaphat's time and to the Chronicler's postexilic situation.[23]

Jehoshaphat also connects Israel's inheritance of the land all the way back to YHWH's relationship with Abraham, describing the patriarch as YHWH's "friend." This expression, denoting the intimacy of YHWH's relationship with Abraham, is found elsewhere only in Isa 41:8, and the Chronicler may be intentionally alluding to that text:[24]

2 Chr 20:7	Isa 41:8
Did you not, our God, ... give [this land] to the *offspring of Abraham*, your *friend* (*zera' 'avraham 'ohavekha*),[25] forever?	But you, Israel, my servant, Jacob, my chosen one, *offspring of Abraham*, my *friend* (*zera' 'avraham 'ohavi*)

Addressing the situation of Judean exile, Isa 41 reaffirms YHWH's choice of Israel and promises that he will deliver them from their exilic overlords (see vv. 10–12). YHWH's words of reassurance on that occasion are also appropriate to those in the Chronicler's audience who still face threats from foreign peoples. They can rest in the knowledge that YHWH's commitment to Abraham, his friend, bridges the gulf of separation experienced during the exile and provides the basis for the reestablishment of YHWH's earlier promises to those who have returned to the land.

YHWH's Gifts of Land to Edom, Moab, and Ammon (2 Chr 20:10–11 // Deut 2:4–5, 9, 19)

In *C'* Jehoshaphat addresses the current situation, drawing YHWH's attention to the unwelcome presence of their enemies with a double exclamatory, "look!" (*hinneh*, vv. 10, 11). But before he describes the immediate crisis, he adds an important parenthetical note about the

---

23. See Beentjes, "Aspects of Innerbiblical Interpretation," 67–68.

24. See also Kuntzmann, "La définition d'un type," 39; Knoppers, "Jerusalem at War," 66–67. On the nature of Abraham's friendship with YHWH, see Dietrich, "Friendship with God," 166–69.

25. In place of the (*qal*) active participle in the MT (*'ohavekha*), the LXX has a passive participle (*ēgapēmenō*).

history of Israel's relationship with these people groups (or in the case of the Meunites, with their geographical region), alluding to Deut 2:[26]

2 Chr 20:10–11	Deut 2:4–5[28]
And now look, the children of Ammon and Moab and *Mount Seir*—which you did *not give (loʾ-nathattah)* to Israel to enter . . . , for they turned aside from them and did not destroy them—look, they are repaying us by entering to drive us out from your *possession*[27] (*yerushatekha*), which you gave to us to possess.	You are about to pass into the border of your brothers, the children of Esau, who dwell in Seir, . . . be very careful. Do not provoke them, for I will *not give (loʾ-ʾetten)* you any of their land . . . because I have given Esau *Mount Seir* as a *possession (yerushah)*.

Whereas 2 Chr 20:11 uses *yerushah* to speak of YHWH's "possession," Deut 2 applies it to Edom, Moab, and Ammon.[29] So YHWH's favor and generosity in ensuring the "possession" of these nations (Deut 2:5, 9, 19) has created a situation in which Moab, Ammon, and Edom's neighbors—the Meunites—now have the ability to threaten both YHWH's own "possession" and his covenant people, whom he has chosen to "possess" (*yarash*) it. The function of Jehoshaphat's statement is to place the blame for the current crisis on YHWH.[30] Because YHWH did not allow Israel "to enter" (*lavoʾ*) their lands, these nations are now "entering" (*lavoʾ*) Israel with the intent of removing YHWH's people from their land in a reverse conquest, offering poor repayment for Israel's prior restraint and threatening to undo YHWH's work in planting Israel in the land.

However, in contrast to Jehoshaphat's claim, Deut 2 actually indicates that YHWH does permit Israel to enter the territories of Edom, Moab, and Ammon, though he gives the people orders not to "provoke them" (vv. 5, 9, 19). According to Num 20:14–21, it was the Edomites

---

26. On this allusion, see Beentjes, "Aspects of Innerbiblical Interpretation," 69–70.

27. The LXX and Tg. have "our possession" in place of the MT's "your possession," but most English translations follow the MT (see the ESV, NRSV, NASB, NLT).

28. See also similar statements about the Moabites and Ammonites in vv. 9 and 19.

29. Beentjes also observes that six out of the fourteen occurrences of *yerushah* appear in Deut 2 ("Aspects of Innerbiblical Interpretation," 69–70).

30. See Kuntzmann, "La définition d'un type," 40.

who would not allow the Israelites to pass through their land.³¹ By omitting the role played by the nations themselves in refusing entrance to the Israelites, Jehoshaphat emphasizes YHWH's culpability.³² Moreover, he also highlights the Israelites' submission to YHWH's command, noting that they "turned aside from [these nations] and did not destroy them" (2 Chr 20:10). This indicates that their current suffering is a direct consequence of their earlier obedience to YHWH, and it underscores the contrast between their behavior and that of their enemies.³³ Given the threat to both Israel and YHWH's own plans, Jehoshaphat implies that YHWH must act.³⁴ And the reminder that the land is YHWH's possession, which he gave to Israel, should comfort the postexilic Jews who are unable to establish complete control over the land.

A/D/A': Standing Before YHWH('s House): The Hope of Deliverance in Solomon's Temple Dedication Prayer (2 Chr 20:9 // 2 Chr 6:28–30)

In the center of his chiastic prayer (*D*) Jehoshaphat alludes to Solomon's temple dedication prayer found in 2 Chr 6:14–42, following its repeated three-part structure:³⁵

	2 Chr 20:9	2 Chr 6:28–30³⁶
1	If disaster comes upon us, sword, judgment, or *pestilence* (*dever*) or *famine* (*ra'av*),	If there is *famine* (*ra'av*) in the land, if there is *pestilence* (*dever*), . . . if their enemies besiege them in the land at their gates . . .
2	we will stand before *this house* (*habbayit hazzeh*) and before you, for your name is in *this house* (*babbayit hazzeh*), and we will cry out to you from our distress,	any prayer, any supplication that is made by any man or by all your people Israel, who . . . spread out their palms toward *this house* (*habbayit hazzeh*),

---

31. Cf. Judg 11:17 concerning Moab, as well as Deut 23:3–6 [4–7], which condemns Moab and Ammon for not greeting Israel with food on their journey to Canaan.

32. Beentjes, "Aspects of Innerbiblical Interpretation," 69.

33. See Japhet, *I & II Chronicles*, 791.

34. Rösel, ". . . dann will ich vom Himmel her hören," 356.

35. See further Beentjes, "Aspects of Innerbiblical Interpretation," 68–69; Knoppers, "Jerusalem at War," 67–68.

36. See also the parallel sequence in vv. 34–35.

| 3 | and *you will hear* (*tishma'*) and save. | then *may you hear* (*tishma'*) from heaven, your dwelling place, and forgive and give to each whose heart you know according to his ways. |

First, Jehoshaphat describes the problems Solomon addresses, including the current crisis of danger by "sword." Second, he notes the response of the people to their situation of distress, following Solomon in emphasizing the central importance of "this house" as the site toward which the people direct their pleas for help. Jehoshaphat's further statement that YHWH's "name is in this house" suggests that YHWH has "a personal stake in this particular national crisis."[37] Although Jehoshaphat's description of people "stand[ing]" before the temple as they seek YHWH's help (20:9b) has no counterpart in Solomon's prayer, it reflects the posture of Solomon and the people prior to the temple dedication prayer (6:3, 12–13), which is replicated by Jehoshaphat and the Judeans in the passage's frame (A and A').

Moreover, while Solomon speaks of the people's "prayer" and "supplication," Jehoshaphat describes them as "cry[ing] out (*za'aq*)" to YHWH. The Chronicler may use this verb because it appears earlier in the narrative of Jehoshaphat's ill-advised alliance with King Ahab in the latter's attack on Ramoth-gilead, which states that "Jehoshaphat cried out (*yiz'aq*), and YHWH helped him" (18:31). Although King Ahab dies in the battle, Jehoshaphat escapes unharmed. Therefore, his life is a testament to how YHWH responds with deliverance when his people "cry out" to him (cf. 1 Chr 5:20).

Finally, following the third part of Solomon's prayer, Jehoshaphat anticipates YHWH's response. Like Solomon, he stresses how YHWH will "hear" his people's pleas for help, but he uses different terminology to convey the result. Since Judah has done nothing to provoke this war, Jehoshaphat ignores Solomon's repeated emphasis on YHWH's forgiveness (see 6:21, 25, 27, 30, 39), declaring merely that YHWH will "save" his people.

While the focus on the temple comes to the fore here, it is woven in more or less subtle ways throughout Jehoshaphat's prayer. Verse 8

---

37. Knoppers, "Jerusalem at War," 68. See also the mention of YHWH's "name" in 6:34.

connects the emphasis on conquest in C and C' with the temple, saying that those who lived in the land built "a sanctuary for [YHWH's] name." As Beentjes observes, it seems that for the Chronicler, "the purpose of the conquest is the Temple."[38] Moreover, the Davidic prayer that Jehoshaphat echoes in *B* is a prayer David offers after collecting materials for the building of the temple (1 Chr 29:10–19). And when Jehoshaphat says in B' "our eyes (*'enayim*) are on you," he mirrors YHWH's gaze, whose "eyes (*'enayim*)" are fixed on those who gather at the temple to pray (2 Chr 7:15). Finally, when Jehoshaphat and the people gather at the temple to "seek" (*darash*, *baqash*) YHWH in *A* and *A'*, their actions are grounded in YHWH's response to Solomon's temple dedication prayer. There YHWH promises that if his people "seek" (*baqash*) him, he will indeed "hear" the humble and contrite prayers of his people and "heal their land" (7:14).[39] However, Jehoshaphat's call for a fast in v. 3 goes beyond the guidelines for soliciting YHWH's help found in the temple dedication account, demonstrating the urgency of the Judeans' entreaty.[40]

Clearly, the temple is of central importance to Jehoshaphat's prayer, with the summary of Solomon's prayer of dedication for the temple forming the focal point. It is interesting to note, however, that despite the Chronicler's emphasis on Solomon elsewhere (2 Chr 1–9), he is not named here as either the builder of the temple or the one who offers the dedication prayer. Instead, Jehoshaphat's prayer democratizes these roles—it is the offspring of Abraham who constructed YHWH's sanctuary and prayed that YHWH would hear their cries offered before it. This allows for an easy identification with the people of Jehoshaphat's

---

38. Beentjes, "Aspects of Innerbiblical Interpretation," 68; see also Japhet, *I & II Chronicles*, 790; Kuntzmann, "La définition d'un type," 40.

39. See also Klein, *2 Chronicles*, 286.

40. Elsewhere in Chronicles, fasting is found only in conjunction with mourning for Saul and his sons (1 Chr 10:12), but in other OT texts fasting is used to solicit YHWH's help in times of trouble (e.g., 2 Sam 12:16, 21–23; Joel 2:15–17; see Way, "צוּם," 781–82). While fasting could also be a sign of repentance (e.g., Neh 9:1–2), there is no indication of repentance (or a need to repent) in 2 Chr 20. See Strübind, *Tradition als Interpretation*, 182; contra Williamson, *1 and 2 Chronicles*, 295.

generation and particularly the postexilic audience of the Chronicler, which lacks a Davidic king and must put their hope in the temple.[41]

THE THEOLOGICAL SIGNIFICANCE OF JEHOSHAPHAT'S PRAYER

As we have seen, the Chronicler's account of Jehoshaphat's prayer is carefully structured and highly dependent on earlier biblical texts. The intentional allusions function theologically to convey three primary messages. First, the allusion to Israel's dealings with Moab, Ammon, and Edom at the time of the conquest vindicates Israel of any wrongdoing and places the culpability for the current situation on YHWH himself. Combining these traditions with Solomon's temple dedication prayer gives further weight to Jehoshaphat's plea for help. If YHWH promised that he would restore his people when they suffer for their sins and repent, how much more should he be willing to protect them now when they are suffering for their obedience! This mixing of traditions also offers assurance to the Chronicler's postexilic audience that YHWH will respond to the unjust persecution they face from the people in the land.

Second, the allusions evoke memories of past instances of YHWH's mighty deliverance—the conquest (2 Chr 20:7), Asa's victory over Zerah the Ethiopian (2 Chr 20:12 // 14:11 [10]), and the return from exile (2 Chr 20:7 // Isa 41:8). For the Chronicler's audience, these recollections function as a montage highlighting how YHWH has repeatedly and consistently redeemed his people whenever they have turned to him, thus instilling hope that he will continue to do so in the present.

Finally, these allusions seek to remind YHWH of his promises to Israel and demonstrate how those promises are still relevant both to Jehoshaphat's situation and to that of the Chronicler's postexilic audience. Jehoshaphat recalls YHWH's eternal gift of the land to Israel, and the allusion to Isa 41:8 shows that YHWH's commitment to Abraham transcends even the exile, providing a basis for the Chronicler's

---

41. See further Beentjes, "Aspects of Innerbiblical Interpretation," 68. On the significance of the Chronicler's historical context, see Davies, "Defending the Boundaries," 54.

postexilic audience to hope in YHWH's continued protection. Also, by summarizing Solomon's prayer of dedication, Jehoshaphat calls on YHWH to remember his promise to respond to the cries of his people when they "seek" him at his temple (2 Chr 7:14). That promise is firmly rooted in YHWH's covenant relationship with his people (see Deut 4:7), which, in turn, is built on the foundation of YHWH's response to his people's cries at the exodus (Exod 2:23–25). And the Chronicler's account conveys the idea that "the same God who answered the prayers of Jehoshaphat, spoken in the first temple, is available to the Chronicler's audience at the second temple."[42] The rebuilt temple offers the postexilic Jews access to the God of the ancestral promises, who rules over the whole cosmos.

JEHOSHAPHAT'S PRAYER AS A MODEL FOR CHRISTIANS TODAY

But how can Jehoshaphat's prayer serve as a model for Christians today, who are living in a different redemptive-historical moment—without the land or the temple or the blessings of God's covenant with Israel, which promise peace and prosperity in this life? When devoted Christ-followers face pandemics, cancer diagnoses, violence, poverty, hunger, racism, oppression, or other threats to their life and well-being, they do not have any assurance that God will soon intervene to relieve their suffering as he did for Jehoshaphat. However, as Christoph Rösel points out, the tension between God's immediate response to prayer and his hiddenness is found even within the OT itself, as is clear from a comparison of 2 Chr 20 with the lament psalms.[43] Sometimes as Christians, our experience is more like that of the psalmists who bemoan God's silence or of the postexilic Jews awaiting the complete fulfillment of the prophetic promises than that of Jehoshaphat.

Nevertheless, I think Jehoshaphat's prayer can inform our prayers in a few ways. First, it is remarkably YHWH-centered.[44] Jehoshaphat begins by piling up descriptions of YHWH's might and ends with the people's gaze fixed on YHWH. Moreover, the prayer is peppered

---

42. Knoppers, "Jerusalem at War," 76.
43. Rösel, ". . . dann will ich vom Himmel her hören," 365–66.
44. See Balentine, *Prayer in the Hebrew Bible*, 100, 102.

throughout with verbal forms describing YHWH's actions—past, present, and future: YHWH "dispossessed" and "gave" (vv. 7, 11), he "rules" (v. 6), and he will "hear" and "save" (v. 9). Thus, Jehoshaphat encourages us to ground our own petitions in YHWH's nature and characteristic deeds.

Second, although we cannot simply coopt the blessings of YHWH's covenant with Israel, as if they directly apply to us today, we can still imitate Jehoshaphat's reliance on God's promises. In contrast to Jehoshaphat, we cannot expect that God will necessarily deliver us when we face hardship on account of our obedience. After all, 1 Pet 4:12–19 declares that we should "not be surprised" when we suffer for following Christ (cf. 2 Tim 3:12). However, as Christians, we can trust in God's promise that he will one day destroy all forms of suffering and even death itself so that we can experience the fullness of life he intended in the new heavens and new earth (Rev 21–22). And we can persistently ask that God's kingdom would come in our lives now as it is in heaven.

Third, we can follow Jehoshaphat in calling to mind past acts of God's deliverance as a basis for hope that he can also bring about deliverance in the present situation. Indeed, Jehoshaphat's own story provides further testimony to YHWH's salvific deeds. As the narrative in 2 Chron 20 plays out, not only does YHWH give Judah victory over their enemies, but he fights the battle for them so that they do not have to do anything (vv. 15–30). Remembrance is central to OT faith, and the Israelites' struggle to trust is often linked to their tendency to forget what YHWH has done for them.[45] Recounting the testimony of Israel and the church—and recalling our own personal stories of how God has been faithful to us in the past—strengthens our faith in his power and goodness and gives us hope that he will ultimately make all things right.

Finally, we can adopt Jehoshaphat's posture of absolute dependence on God. In modern American culture, which valorizes self-sufficiency, it can be difficult to admit weakness. But when we fail to acknowledge our limitations, we can wear ourselves down trying to resolve our troubles or spiral out of control if our efforts fail. When,

---

45. See further Jebasingh, "Theological Appraisal," 75–88.

like Jehoshaphat, "we do not know what we should do" (2 Chr 20:12), confessing that only God has the power to help us and fixing our eyes on him can bring rest and relief from our futile striving.[46] Rösel cites a sermon that Dietrich Bonhoeffer preached on 2 Chr 20:12 in 1932 in the midst of the uncertainty of life in Germany between the world wars, which declares:[47]

> We look to you . . . as those who do not know at all what they should do but who know that you forgive sins and are merciful, as those who have no firm ground under their feet anymore but are grasped and held over the abyss of the bottomless void from above by you, who know that your paths and your commandment are hidden in this world under the cross, but that they shall be revealed in your kingdom.[48]

Like Bonhoeffer, we may sometimes feel like we are hanging "over the abyss of the bottomless void," but we can trust that we are "grasped and held" there by God and that ultimately the fullness of God's kingdom will come. Reading Jehoshaphat's prayer within the context of the larger biblical witness encourages us to wait with our gaze fixed on God until he responds with salvation, even if we must wait until this mortal life has passed away and the splendor of the new creation has come.

BIBLIOGRAPHY

Amar, Itzhak. "Form and Content in the Story of Asa in 2 Chr 13:23b–16:14: A Diachronic-Synchronic Reading." *VT* 69 (2019) 1–24.

Amzallag, Nissim. "The Subversive Dimension of the Story of Jehoshaphat's War against the Nations (2 Chron. 20:1–30)." *BibInt* 24 (2016) 178–202.

Balentine, Samuel E. *Prayer in the Hebrew Bible: The Drama of Divine-Human Dialogue*. OTB. Minneapolis: Fortress, 1993.

---

46. I do not mean to suggest that we should not use whatever means are at our disposal to try to overcome the problems we face. But sometimes there is no human solution to our struggles, or our solutions prove woefully inadequate.

47. Rösel, ". . . dann will ich vom Himmel her hören," 367. For examples of how Jehoshaphat's prayer was used by sixteenth-century Lutherans, see Haemig, "Jehoshaphat and His Prayer," 522–35.

48. Bonhoeffer, "Staying Grounded in Turbulent Times," 77.

Beentjes, Pancratius C. "Aspects of Innerbiblical Interpretation in 2 Chronicles 20." In *Tradition and Transformation in the Book of Chronicles*, 61–77. SSN 52. Leiden: Brill, 2008.

———. "War Narratives in the Book of Chronicles: A New Proposal in Respect of Their Function." *HvTSt* 59 (2003) 587–96.

Bonhoeffer, Dietrich. "Staying Grounded in Turbulent Times." In *The Collected Sermons of Dietrich Bonhoeffer*, Vol. 2, edited by Victoria J. Barnett, 71–78. Translated by Claudia D. Bergmann et al. Minneapolis: Fortress, 2017.

Cudworth, Troy D. "The 'God of the Fathers' in Chronicles." *JBL* 135 (2016) 438–91.

Davies, Philip R. "Defending the Boundaries of Israel in the Second Temple Period: 2 Chronicles 20 and the 'Salvation Army.'" In *Priests, Prophets and Scribes: Essays on the Formation and Heritage of Second Temple Judaism in Honour of Joseph Blenkinsopp*, edited by Eugene Ulrich et al., 43–54. JSOTSup 149. Sheffield: Sheffield Academic, 1992.

Dietrich, Jan. "Friendship with God: Old Testament and Ancient Near Eastern Perspectives." *SJOT* 28 (2014) 157–71.

Dillard, Raymond B. *2 Chronicles*. WBC 15. Waco: TX: Word, 1987.

———. "The Chronicler's Jehoshaphat." *TJ* 7 (1986) 17–22.

Endres, John C. "Theology of Worship in Chronicles." In *The Chronicler as Theologian: Essays in Honor of Ralph W. Klein*, edited by M. Patrick Graham et al., 165–88. London: T. & T. Clark, 2003.

Haemig, Mary Jane. "Jehoshaphat and His Prayer among Sixteenth-Century Lutherans." *Church History* 73 (2004) 522–35.

Hill, Andrew E. *1 & 2 Chronicles*. NIVAC. Grand Rapids: Zondervan, 2003.

Japhet, Sara. *1 & II Chronicles*. OTL. Louisville: Westminster John Knox, 1993.

———. *The Ideology of the Book of Chronicles and Its Place in Biblical Thought*. Winona Lake, IN: Eisenbrauns, 2009.

Jebasingh, Jebamony, "A Theological Appraisal of זכר (Remembrance)." *Bangalore Theological Forum* 45 (2014) 75–88.

Kalimi, Isaac. *The Reshaping of Ancient Israelite History in Chronicles*. Winona Lake, IN: Eisenbrauns, 2005.

Klein, Ralph W. *2 Chronicles*. Hermeneia. Minneapolis: Fortress, 2012.

———. "Reflections on Historiography in the Account of Jehoshaphat." In *Pomegranates and Golden Bells: Studies in Biblical, Jewish, and Near Eastern Ritual, Law, and Literature in Honor of Jacob Milgrom*, edited by David P. Wright et al., 643–57. Winona Lake, IN: Eisenbrauns, 1995.

Knoppers, Gary N. "Jerusalem at War in Chronicles." In *Zion, City of Our God*, edited by Richard S. Hess and Gordon J. Wenham, 57–76. Grand Rapids: Eerdmans, 1999.

Section 2: Prayers of Kings

———. "Reform and Regression: The Chronicler's Presentation of Jehoshaphat." *Bib* 72 (1991) 500–24.

Kuntzmann, Raymond. "La définition d'un type au fil d'une lecture intertextuelle (2 Ch 20,5–13)." In *Typologie biblique: De quelques figures vives*, Lectio divina, edited by Raymond Kuntzmann, 35–47. Paris: Editions du Cerf, 2002.

Lynch, Matthew. *Monothesim and Institutions in the Book of Chronicles: Temple, Priesthood, and Kingship in Post-Exilic Perspective*. FAT 2.64. Tübingen: Mohr Siebeck, 2014.

McKenzie, Steven L. "The Trouble with King Jehoshaphat." In *Reflection and Refraction: Studies in Biblical Historiography in Honour of A. Graeme Auld*, edited by Robert Rezetko et al., 35–47. VTSup 113. Brill: Leiden, 2007.

Mendenhall, George E. "The Census Lists of Numbers 1 and 26." *JBL* 77 (1958) 52–66.

Payne, J. Barton. "The Validity of the Numbers in Chronicles: Part 2." *BSac* 136 (1979) 206–20.

Rainey, A. F. "Mesha's Attempt to Invade Judah (2 Chron 20)." In *Studies in Historical Geography and Biblical Historiography: Presented to Zecharia Kallai*, edited by Gershon Galil and Moshe Weinfeld, 174–76. VTSup 81. Leiden: Brill, 2000.

Rösel, Christoph. "'. . . dann will ich vom Himmel her hören.': 2. Chronik 20 und die Theologie des Gebets in den Chronikbüchern." *Theologische Beiträge* 43 (2012) 353–68.

Strübind, Kim. *Tradition als Interpretation in der Chronik: König Josaphat als Paradigma chronistischer Hermeneutik und Theologie*. BZAW 201. Berlin: de Gruyter, 1991.

Sugimoto, Tomotoshi. "Chronicles as Independent Literature." *JSOT* 55 (1992) 61–74.

Thompson, J. A. *1, 2 Chronicles*. NAC 9. Nashville: Broadman & Holman, 1994.

Way, Robert J. "צום." In *NIDOTTE* 3:780–83.

Williamson, H. G. M. *1 and 2 Chronicles*. NCBC. Eugene, OR: Wipf & Stock, 1982.

Section 3

Prayers of Prophets

6

A Prophet like Fire, Burned Out, and Rekindled

Exploring the Significance of Elijah's Prayers (1 Kgs 17–19)

MICHAEL WIDMER

INTRODUCTION

ELIJAH IS REMEMBERED AS a man of prayer (Jas 5:16–18), a "prophet like fire, whose words burned like a torch" (Sir 48:1),[1] and one who possessed tremendous courage and faith. Not unlike Moses, Elijah single-handedly confronted idolatrous monarchs in the name of God. Through the power of intercessory prayer Elijah revived the son of a widow (1 Kgs 17:21–22) and achieved an amazing victory for YHWH over the prophets of Baal (1 Kgs 18). In persistent prayer Elijah claimed God's promise to send rain (1 Kgs 17:1, 14; 18:41–46). The Bible, however, also reveals another side of Elijah. After his public triumph on Mount Carmel, Elijah fled from Jezebel, seemed confused, and even asked God to take his life (1 Kgs 19:3–4). Scripture paints a rich and complex portrayal of one of the great prophetic intercessors.

---

1. Unless otherwise indicated, biblical quotes are taken from the NRSV.

Section 3: Prayers of Prophets

The enduring value of Elijah's prayers is not undisputed. Werline, for example, questions to what degree Elijah's prayers are models of faith for the church. He reckons that when God answered the prophet's prayer with fire from heaven, the author used prayer to sanction Elijah's killing of the Baal prophets.

> Frankly, I do not see how one can ever redeem the act of prayer in this particular text. It is dark and disturbing . . . A faith intimately connected to these stories is dangerous, as is prayer modeled on the Mount Carmel text.[2]

Werline does acknowledge that not all of Elijah's prayers sanction violence. He points to Elijah's prayer for the widow's son, but notes that Elijah's prayer for the revival of the boy testifies to a potency often ascribed to shaman-like figures, who are associated with an uncontrollable and dangerous power.[3] I do not deny for a moment the hermeneutical complexities that Elijah and his prayers raise. However, I doubt whether the category of shaman does justice to the biblical portrayal of Elijah. James refers to Elijah as "a human being like us" (Jas 5:17) and upholds the prophet as a model of a righteous person, full of faith and earnest prayer. Following the conviction of the writer of 2 Timothy, I intend to explore in what ways Elijah's prayers are "useful for teaching, for reproof, for correction, and for training in righteousness" (2 Tim 3:16).

READING ELIJAH'S PRAYERS AGAINST THE CENTRAL ISSUES OF 1 KINGS 17–19

The underlying concern that pervades the entire Elijah narrative is the battle between YHWH and Baal (16:31–33, 17:24, 18:39, 19:19–21).[4] Leading up to the final confrontation on Mount Carmel, ch. 17 raises the issues of who controlled the rain, provided the food, and had power over life and death. Was it YHWH or Baal? The prophet of YHWH or the prophets of Baal? God's sovereign kingship was challenged and Israel's exclusive covenant relationship with YHWH was once again

---

2. Werline, *Pray*, 39.
3. Werline, *Pray*, 37.
4. von Rad, *Theologie*, 33.

fundamentally endangered by the specter of idolatry (cf. Exod 20:1–2, 32–34). No more serious matter could be faced by a prophet of YHWH. Against this background, Elijah the Tishbite appeared abruptly on the scene and declared to the idolatrous monarch a drought in the name of YHWH (17:1).

"STANDING BEFORE GOD"

Elijah introduced himself as one who stands before YHWH, the living God (17:1, 18:15). Standing before YHWH (*'md lifne yhwh*), is one of the characteristic terms to describe the role of the prophetic intercessor.[5] In the presence of God, the prophet received divine instructions regarding what to say to the people. At the same time, standing before God presented an opportunity to engage with the divine decision-making process and to advocate on behalf of a third party (cf. Gen 18:22–23; Jer 15:1). Although v. 1 does not explicitly state that the drought was brought about by YHWH's word, 17:14 confirms that Elijah spoke on God's behalf (see also 18:1). Taken out of context, the declaration that there would be no rain except by Elijah's word might create the impression that Elijah claimed to have the power to bring about miracles, suggesting an exaggerated sense of self-importance. The prophetic assertion, "except by *my* word," however, has to be read in relation to the role of the one who stood before God. This could either mean, as James seems to understand, that there would be no rain except by Elijah's word of prayer (Jas 5:17–18), or that Elijah faithfully proclaimed what he was commissioned to say. Chapters 17 and 18 consistently present Elijah as an exemplary model of an obedient servant of YHWH, who listened, spoke, and acted according to divine instruction (17:3–5, 8–10; 18:1–2, 15, 36).

The contest between Elijah and the prophets of Baal in ch. 18 forms a first climax within the larger narrative. The accounts of God's provision for Elijah and later for the widow of Zarephath (1 Kgs 17) illustrate how God was preparing his prophet for the great public showdown on Carmel by teaching him lessons of prayer and trust.

---

5. Widmer, *Standing in the Breach*, 381–84.

Section 3: Prayers of Prophets

ELIJAH, THE WIDOW OF ZAREPHATH AND HER SON

After many days, the son of Elijah's hostess became severely ill and died ("there was no breath left in him"). The grief-stricken mother lashed out at Elijah:

> What have you against me, O man of God? You have come to me to bring my sin to remembrance, and to cause the death of my son! (17:18)

In the presence of Elijah, the widow felt her unworthiness exposed (cf. Luke 5:8). The mother perceived the death of her son as a divine punishment. Since YHWH usually informs his prophets in advance about forthcoming judgments, in order to give them a chance to warn and advocate on behalf of the sinful party, Elijah's lack of forewarning suggests that the sudden death of the boy was not a divine punishment (cf. Amos 3:7; Gen 18:17; Exod 32:7–14). This is confirmed by the fact that Elijah had no answer to the women's accusation, only a question for God. In the OT, praying for the restoration of someone's life was an extremely daring undertaking. Only Elijah and his successor Elisha sought to invoke YHWH's lordship over death (2 Kgs 4:32–36).

Elijah's Prayer for the Revival of the Son

> He cried out to the LORD, "O LORD my God, have you brought calamity even upon the widow with whom I am staying, by killing her son?" Then he stretched himself upon the child three times, and cried out to the LORD, "O LORD my God, let this child's life come into him again." (17:20–21)

Elijah's prayer was provoked by the widow's accusation. Elijah, in turn, accused YHWH of killing the boy (17:18–20), mediating and representing the mother's concern. Earlier, Elijah had spoken God's word to the widow (17:13–14); now Elijah spoke the widow's words to YHWH. Elijah's double cry expressed urgency and disagreement and made it evident that he would not allow the death of the boy go unchallenged.

Elijah's intercession was an accusatory cry of compassion on behalf of his generous host. This is confirmed by Elijah referring to his hostess as a "widow." Widows belonged to the most vulnerable people in society and thus stood under YHWH's special protection (Deut 24:19–21). This, as Kiuchi rightly discerns, suggests that Elijah maximized his prayer appeal for divine mercy and compassion (cf. Luke 7:13).[6] Following his accusatory cry, Elijah stretched himself three times upon the body of the child and continued his prayer.

"Elijah Stretched Himself upon the Child": An Intercessory Prayer Act?

The meaning of Elijah's gesture is not entirely clear. Some argue that Elijah followed an existing ritual, where he hoped to transfer the illness from the boy into his own body.[7] Verses 18 and 20, however, indicate that the boy was already dead. Did Elijah seek to transfer some of his own life to the boy? Elisha engaged in a similar ritual (2 Kgs 4:34).[8] Perhaps the prayer was considered insufficient for the resuscitation process (cf. 2 Kgs 20:1–7).

Kiuchi explores the meaning of Elijah's gesture against the theme of uncleanness and the law (Lev 21:1–3; Num 9:6–7). His investigations lead him to conclude that by stretching himself on the dead child, Elijah made himself deliberately unclean and, thus, would not be in a condition to be heard by God. This seeming paradox of Elijah violating the cultic law and yet praying to a holy God for healing leads Kiuchi to conclude that Elijah deliberately took the role of a sacrificial victim by anathematizing himself on behalf of the dead boy (cf. Rom 9:3). He argues that:

> Within the framework of sacrificial thinking, Elijah is not viewed as violating the uncleanness laws . . . To put it another way, the principle of giving life over to death, which constitutes the essence of atonement in animal sacrifice (Lev 17,11), can also be seen in a spiritual dimension such as intercession.[9]

---

6. Kiuchi, "Elijah," 77.

7. Sweeney, *I & II Kings*, 215. Some commentators see here parallels with healing magic known from Mesopotamia and Canaan. See Montgomery, *Kings*, 296.

8. Montgomery, *Kings*, 296.

9. Kiuchi, "Elijah," 78.

Section 3: Prayers of Prophets

At first reading, one might question whether "self-sacrificial intercession" is contained in Elijah's prayer-gesture. However, Kiuchi has provided a coherent and creative argument that potentially sheds light on sacrificial theology (cf. Gal. 3:13). Nevertheless, we cannot be absolutely certain about the meaning of Elijah's gesture. Whatever the exact meaning, v. 22 clearly states that "the LORD listened" to Elijah's cry. Any magical element can be ruled out, as the revival is clearly ascribed to God's intervention in answer to Elijah's intercession. YHWH, the LORD of life, who gives and takes the breath of life (Deut 32:39; Ps 104:29), allowed himself to be moved by the prayer of his prophet.

Chapter 17 as a whole portrays how the prophet's faith was being trained to trust God in difficult circumstances.[10] Elijah was ready to face his overwhelming opposition on Carmel.

THE CONFRONTATION

YHWH, Baal, and their Prophets

Following YHWH's instructions, Elijah summoned Ahab to assemble the entire people along with Jezebel's prophets to Mount Carmel (18:24). Elijah's challenge to Israel brought the central issue to the fore:

> "How long will you go limping with two different opinions?
> If the LORD is God, follow him; but if Baal, then follow him."
> (18:21)

Ever since Mount Sinai, YHWH demanded exclusive covenant commitment (Exod 20:3). Elijah's name ("my El is Yah") underlines where the prophet's loyalty lay. From Israel, however, Elijah did not receive any answer (18:21). The northern kingdom, prompted by Jezebel's zeal, promoted Baalism over Yahwism (18:13). As a result, the people found themselves in a difficult and dangerous situation. For Elijah, however, it was clear that this was not a time for compromise (Deut 5:7–9).

Against the overwhelming majority of Baal and Asherah prophets, Elijah referred to himself as the only prophet of YHWH left (18:22) and set the rules for the contest:

---

10. Dharamraj, *A Prophet*, 19, adds that 1 Kgs 17 establishes "Elijah's authenticity to the reader."

> "Let two bulls be given to us . . . Then you call on the name of your god and I will call on the name of the LORD; the god who answers by fire is indeed God." (1 Kgs 18:23–24)

This time the people expressed their approval, indicating possible discomfort with their syncretism. The prophets of Baal went first. DeVries rightly identifies the verb "to answer" (*'anah*) as a keyword in the contest. The people did not answer Elijah (18:21). "The god who *answers* by fire is indeed God" (cf. 18:24).[11] The prophets of Baal called out, "O Baal, answer us!" (*'anenu*), and Elijah said, "Answer me, O LORD, answer me"! (*'aneni*, 18:26, 37). When, at midday, there was still "no voice, and no answer" (*ve'en 'oneh*, 18:26; see also v. 29), Elijah mocked his opponents and Baal (18:27). There was "no answer" because Baal was a "sheer delusion" (cf. Isa 41:29).[12]

When it was Elijah's turn to prepare for his offering, the movement of the narrative shifts from the frantic rituals of the Baal prophets to the deliberate and symbolic preparations of Elijah. He rebuilt the broken altar of YHWH on behalf of all Israel, reminding them of their identity as YHWH's chosen and redeemed covenant people (18:30–32; Exod 19–24). The narrative further emphasizes Elijah's instructions to pour out twelve buckets of water over the burnt offering. This excessive amount would demonstrate that only a miracle could ignite the drenched sacrifice. It might also emphasize the costliness of the libation sacrifice and Elijah's confidence that YHWH would send rain soon (1 Kgs 18:36).[13]

For our purpose, it is particularly interesting to note the contrast of prayer styles and objectives between the prophets of Baal and Elijah. The former were characterized by ritual dancing, endless shouting, and manipulative rituals, whereas Elijah's prayer was concise and

---

11. DeVries, *1 Kings*, 226.

12. Childs, "On Reading the Elijah Narratives," 132.

13. It might also echo Samuel's covenant renewal ceremony at Mizpah. At that time, Israel turned away from the Baals and Astartes, poured out water before the YHWH, and repented of their apostasy. Subsequently Samuel offered up a prayer and sacrifice on behalf of Israel (1 Sam 7:3–12). See Widmer, *Standing in the Breach*, 177–90, for a detailed reading.

intentional (cf. Matt 6:7). It had mainly a twofold objective: YHWH's glory and Israel's return to the God of their fathers.

Elijah's Intercession for the Glory of YHWH and Israel's Recommitment

> At the time of the offering of the oblation, the prophet Elijah came near and said, "O Lord, God of Abraham, Isaac, and Israel, let it be known this day that you are God in Israel, that I am your servant, and that I have done all these things at your bidding. Answer me, O Lord, answer me, so that this people may know that you, O Lord, are God, and that you have turned their hearts back." (18:36–37)

After preparing the sacrifice, Elijah approached the altar at the established time. He replaced the name Jacob with Israel, reminding the people that it was YHWH who gave them their name and identity (cf. Gen 32:28). Elijah prayed that YHWH would establish beyond doubt that he, and not Baal, was God in Israel. Coupled with the petition for an unmistakable revelation from YHWH was Elijah's prayer that the people would recognize him as YHWH's rightful prophet, who was following divine instructions. The prophet's final petition focused on Israel: "Answer me, O Lord, answer me, so that this people many know that you, O Lord, are God" (18:37). Elijah pleaded twice, "answer me." He acknowledged that it would be by YHWH's sovereign power alone that the people would turn back to their God. The contest was not designed "to determine who is effective in the art of summoning the deity,"[14] as if Elijah has to prove himself as some kind of shaman. God's sovereignty is underlined by Elijah's final plea in v. 37, which is both intriguing and ambiguous.[15]

> "... answer me, so these people will know that you, Lord, are God, and that you *are turning* their hearts back again" (*ha-sibota et-libbam achoranit*, 18:37, NIV 2011).

---

14. As Balentine, *Prayer in the Hebrew Bible*, 54.
15. DeVries, *1 Kings*, 230, described the wording as "enigmatic unless emended."

This rendering suggests that Elijah prayed that YHWH would turn Israel's wavering hearts back to covenant fidelity. An "evangelistic" plea that God would win back Israel's allegiance[16] fits the context and would be in line with the prayers of other prophets (e.g. Deut 30:6; Jer 31:18).[17] The verb "turning," however, is in the past tense (e.g., "have turned," *hifʿil* perfect), even though Israel had not yet turned back to YHWH (18:39).

> ". . . answer me, so that this people may know . . . that you *have turned* their hearts back." (18:37 NRSV)

This translation itself could be interpreted in two different ways. Perhaps Elijah was praying that the people would come to know that it was YHWH who had turned their hearts back to him[18] Or v. 37b could also be taken as Elijah's assertion that YHWH himself had caused Israel's turning away; now, the people would come to realize that turning to Baal was in fact YHWH's judgment.[19] The implication would be that if YHWH himself caused the people to turn away from him, only God could bring them back to the covenant relationship. Either of these interpretations underlines God's sovereignty over Israel's heart condition.

Elijah's intercession was immediately answered. YHWH consumed the burnt offering in a dramatic and unmistakable way by sending fire from heaven (18:38; cf. 2 Kgs 1:10, 12; Lev 9:24). As the divine fire fell (*nfl*), the people fell (*nfl*) on their faces and confessed: "YHWH, he is God, YHWH, he is God! (*yhvh huʾ haʾelohim*)"[20] (18:39). Immediately after their confession, Elijah tested the people's commitment by commanding them to seize the prophets of Baal.[21] At the Kishon, river Elijah himself killed the prophets with a sword (18:40, 19:1).

---

16. NJB: ". . . so that this people may know that you . . . are winning back their hearts."

17. Hawkins, *While I Was Praying*, 90.

18. Keil argued that the perfect tense here denotes "not only what has already occurred, but what will still take place and is as certain as if it had taken place already" (Keil and Delitzsch, *Commentary*, para. 6340).

19. See also DeVries, *1 Kings*, 230, and Nelson, *Kings*, 118.

20. Author's translation.

21. Wray Beal, *1 & 2 Kings*, 245.

SECTION 3: PRAYERS OF PROPHETS

Killing the Prophets of Baal

When modern interpreters come to a disturbing passage such as this one, it is essential to understand it within the wider Old Testament context in order to evaluate its abiding significance. YHWH's great anger over the worship of Baal during Ahab's reign (1 Kgs 16:33–17:1) was his covenant response as the people flaunted the command not to have any other gods. As God's prophet, Elijah was following the Torah, which stipulates that: "Whoever sacrifices to any god, other than the LORD alone, shall be devoted to destruction" (Exod 22:20). By purging Israel of false prophets and idolatry, Elijah, in contrast to Ahab, was a faithful observer of the covenant stipulations (Deut 13:5, 13–18, 17:2–7; 1 Kgs 18:18).

God's Promise of Rain Claimed in Prayer

Following the eventful contest on Carmel, Elijah withdrew to the top of the mountain and assumed a posture of prayer, bowing with his head between his knees (18:42). Initially "there was nothing" apart from God's promise and the prophet's faith (18:43). What God had promised (18:1) still needed to be claimed in ongoing prayer. Seven times Elijah instructed his servant to check whether his prayer was being answered. While YHWH had previously answered Elijah instantly, this time the prophet needed to persist patiently in prayer. At the appearance of only a small cloud, Elijah commissioned his servant in faith to announce that God would bring about heavy rain (18:44). With the arrival of the storm, YHWH demonstrated once again that he, not Baal, was Master over the elements and that Elijah was his prophet. This episode demonstrates well how the divine will is interrelated with prophetic proclamation and intercession.

ELIJAH'S FLIGHT, LAMENT, AND JOURNEY TO THE MOUNTAIN OF GOD

When the Phoenician Queen Jezebel, conspicuously absent from Mount Carmel, learned of the fate of her prophets, she vowed to kill Elijah (19:4). In fear Elijah "fled for his life." After a day's flight into the wilderness, Elijah was exhausted, lamenting: "It is enough; now, O

LORD, take away my life (*nafshi*), for I am no better than my ancestors (*'avoth*)" (19:4). Although Elijah was not the only prophet who wished to die (Num 11:15; Jonah 4:3, 8), only Elijah dared to address God in such a curt and abrupt way.[22] Earlier Elijah pleaded with YHWH to return "life" (*nefesh*) to the dead boy (17:21), now the prophet asked God to take his "life" (*nefesh*).

The events on Mount Carmel had been a tremendous emotional roller-coaster, followed by great physical exertion that would have left the fittest totally exhausted. Moreover, it looks as if, in spite of the victory on Carmel, Elijah feared that he had not achieved anything that was of more lasting value in the fight against Baalism than his ancestors. Elijah might be referring particularly to his spiritual fathers (*'av*), the prophets (cf. 2 Kgs 2:12).[23] Von Rad suggested that Elijah's depression was caused by what the prophet perceived to be the end of the Yahwistic faith (19:10).[24]

God did not respond in words to Elijah's lament. Instead YHWH sent his messenger to look after the physical needs of the weary man (19:7). In the strength of the received meal, Elijah embarked on a forty-day journey to Horeb, the mountain of God (19:8). Moses twice spent forty days on the mountain of God (Exod 24:18, 34:28; Deut 10:10); echoes of Moses abound in these verses.

ELIJAH ON HOREB: FOLLOWING IN THE FOOTSTEPS OF MOSES

On arrival at Horeb, Elijah came to *the* cave (Hebrew: *hamme'arah*, 19:9). If this is a deliberate reference to the same cave where Moses experienced the fullest revelation of YHWH after his intercessory prayer (Exod 33:19—34:7), then perhaps Elijah also was seeking a revelation from God. Judging from God's question, however, YHWH did not fully approve of Elijah's presence: "What are you doing here?" (19:9). Elijah replied:

---

22. Thiel, *Könige*, 249.
23. See Thiel, *Könige*, 253.
24. von Rad, *Theologie*, 30.

Section 3: Prayers of Prophets

> "I have been very zealous for the LORD . . . for the Israelites have forsaken your covenant, thrown down your altars, and killed your prophets with the sword. I alone am left, and they are seeking my life . . ." (19:10)

YHWH did not directly respond to Elijah's lament; instead he instructed him as he had Moses: "Go out and *stand* on the mountain *before the* LORD, for the LORD is about to pass by" (19:11; cf. Exod 34:5–6). It looks as if God was calling his prophet to get ready for intercession. After all, Elijah had introduced himself as one who *stands before the* LORD (17:1; 18:15). YHWH's summons was followed by three mighty manifestations that are reminiscent of God's theophany on Sinai (Exod 19:16–25), with the significant difference that this time YHWH was not in any of these awesome phenomena. After the fiery showdown on Carmel, God chose to reveal himself in the "sound of sheer silence" (19:11–12).[25]

Not unlike Moses, Elijah needed protection from the divine glory when he went out of the cave (19:13; cf. Exod 33:20). YHWH repeated the question: "What are you doing here, Elijah?" This time, it sounds as if the LORD expected his prophet not just to "stand at the entrance of the cave," but to take his place before YHWH (19:11–13). After the golden calf apostasy, when YHWH descended in a cloud and passed before Moses, he quickly bowed his head and pleaded for the pardon of the idolatrous people (Exod 34:5–9).[26] Elijah, however, failed to respond in intercession in God's presence.[27] Instead of praying for the idolatrous Israelites, Elijah seemed preoccupied with himself. He repeated the same lamenting words as before (19:10, 14). From this peculiar repetitive dialogue, one gets the impression that "Elijah is in exactly the same place after the theophany as before . . . still feeling just as sorry for himself as ever."[28]

The prophet's response is not only characterized by self-pity, but also by a distortion of reality. Did Elijah not just succeed in rebuilding

---

25. See Dharamraj, *A Prophet*, 70–94, for helpful discussions of the ambiguous Hebrew expression (*qol demamah daqqah*).

26. For a detailed reading of Exod 32–34, see my *Moses, God, and the Dynamics*.

27. Middleton, "God's Loyal Opposition," 61–62.

28. Nelson, *Kings*, 125.

the broken altar of YHWH (18:30–32)? As a result of YHWH's revelation, did not Israel just confess YHWH as God (18:39)? Moreover, why does Elijah blame Israel for killing YHWH's prophets, when Obadiah told him that it was Jezebel (18:4, 13)? In fact, Israel helped Elijah to kill the prophets of Baal. As for Elijah lamenting that he alone is left, was he not told that there were at least a hundred hidden prophets of YHWH who remain (18:13)? Does Elijah regard them as mere royal cult prophets (cf. 1 Kgs 22:6)? What about Elijah's delusion that Israel seeks to kill him, when in fact it was Jezebel (19:2)?[29] In other words, Elijah's lament reveals a man in despair, lacking clear judgment.

YHWH did not reprimand Elijah nor attempt to comfort or correct him at this stage. Instead, God recommissioned his prophet for a new task. We notice the same divine strategy in the case of Jeremiah. Several times God replied to the "weeping prophet" by giving him a new mission (Jer 15:19–21; 18:19—19:3).[30] Not unlike in Jeremiah's case, the divine command to Elijah might well have the additional figurative meaning of: "Go, return (*shuv*) on *your way* (*derekh*) . . ." (19:15), in the sense of get back to your prophetic duties.

Elijah Recommissioned

God sent Elijah back with a mission to anoint Hazael, Jehu, and Elisha. Through a complex web of geo-political and religious circumstances, YHWH would use each of these individuals to bring divine judgment on the idolatrous generation and purify Israel of Baal idolatry (1 Kgs 19:17; 2 Kgs 9–10). The battle against Baalism was won on Carmel, but the war was not over yet.[31]

According to von Rad, the climax and key to the account are found in YHWH's answer (19:18) to Elijah's lament; Elijah was not alone. Seven thousand faithful worshippers of YHWH were left.[32] It is as if YHWH was assuring Elijah not to worry about the future of God's people. Strengthened by the divine word, Elijah responded to YHWH's command, returned from Horeb, and called Elisha into his services

29. Jones, *Sharing*, 101.
30. Widmer, *Standing in the Breach*, 396–406.
31. Waltke, *Old Testament Theology*, 718.
32. von Rad, *Theologie*, 28–30.

(19:19). That led, in turn, to the subsequent anointing of the other two as kings of Syria and the northern kingdom, Israel.

Although several intertextual indicators suggest that Elijah did not live up to the Mosaic intercessory ideal on Horeb, YHWH patiently listened to the lament of his prophet and recommissioned him. The accounts of Naboth's vineyard and King Ahaziah's Baal idolatry confirm that Elijah was fully restored to his prophetic ministry (1 Kgs 21; 2 Kgs 1). Elijah had his weaknesses and was admonished by God for these. It is important to note, however, that God vindicated his servant in a unique way in the end (2 Kgs 2:1–18). Little wonder that later biblical authors judged Elijah's life and ministry as overwhelmingly positive (Mal 4:5–6; Luke 1:16–17; Jas 5:17–18).

FURTHER THEOLOGICAL REFLECTIONS

Elijah's Prayers and Jesus' Authority

In his Nazareth synagogue sermon, Jesus referenced Elijah's revival of the widow's son (Luke 4:14–30). Several chapters later, Luke includes the narrative of Jesus raising from the dead the son of the widow from Nain (7:11–17). Luke underlines parallels, but also important differences. Although Elijah was the first person in the Bible who challenged the finality of death and prevailed, Jesus did not have to pray and engage in a ritual, but simply commanded the dead person to rise.

Another Lukan passage with echoes of Elijah is where James and John asked whether they should pray down fire in Elijah fashion upon inhospitable Samaritans (Luke 9:52–54). James and John's intention might be described as an imprecatory prayer. In Elijah's case the fire came—two times—as a demonstration of YHWH's power over Baal and as a confirmation that Elijah was truly a man of God (1 Kgs 18:36–38; 2 Kgs 1:10–14). Jesus, however, rebuked James and John, and that was the end of the matter. Instead, Jesus prayed for the forgiveness of his adversaries from the cross (Luke 23:34).

Pray like Elijah: A Model of Faith and Perseverance

James encourages his readers to pray for each other when sick and refers to Elijah as a model (Jas 5:16–18). By the first century BCE, Elijah was depicted in heroic terms (Sir 48:1–14). "In Judaism Elijah's reputation for prayer was frequently mentioned and enhanced over time and became a prototype for intercessory prayer (2 Esdr 7:109; Josephus, *Ant.* 14.22; m Taanith 2.4; 3.8)."[33] By saying that Elijah was "a human being like us," James appears not only to counter popular legends of the time, but also to attribute to Elijah weaknesses that are common to any believer.

At first sight, Elijah's prayer for the revival of the widow's son (1 Kgs 17:17–24) would seem the more suitable illustration for James' purposes. The answer to Elijah's prayer for "healing" of the dead boy happened instantly. James, however, highlights the perseverance of Elijah when he was praying for rain. Although 1 Kgs 18:1 does not explicitly say that the prophet prayed for the drought (Jas 5:17), based on God's word, Elijah prevailed in praying for the rain (18:42). McKnight helpfully draws out some implications by saying that James encourages: "those who do God's will . . . to pray as Elijah did, with fervency, and they too can bring healing, both physical and spiritual, to the community."[34]

The Elijah narrative contains several miraculous elements that might feel foreign to modern readers. Nevertheless, the underlying conviction that YHWH is a living God who hears and is both able and willing to act in response to prayer is as foundational to faith now as it was then.

A Prayer for God's Glory, Liberation from Idolatry, and Human Action

Elijah's intercession on Mount Carmel provides an abiding model precisely because it is essentially a prayer for YHWH's glory (18:37–38). The King of the universe battles all forms of idolatry because they seek to diminish the glory that belongs rightfully to him alone (Deut 6:14–15).

The power of idolatry has been a constant danger to believers throughout the ages. The summons to undivided loyalty to and love for God, as expressed in the *Shema* (Deut 6:4–5), resurfaces in Jesus'

33. McKnight, *James*, 450.
34. McKnight, *James*, 452.

teaching that "No one can serve two masters" (Matt 6:24). Elijah's prayer can be read as a prayer that seeks to liberate people from idolatry and expose it for what it is: a destructive illusion that imprisons people. Israel was imprisoned by the tyranny of Ahab and Jezebel as they compelled the worship of Baal, who was believed to hold power over rain and death. YHWH demonstrated through his prophet that both rain and death are in his power alone (cf. Deut 10:12; Matt 6:31–32).

According to Elijah's prayer, a show of divine power would not suffice in enabling the people to recommit to YHWH. Israel's liberation depended on another ingredient, namely, on God's turning their hearts (18:37). The Carmel duel illustrates that both God's revelation and the people's faith are divine gifts that need to be claimed through intercession. This recognition ought to be balanced with the fact that prophetic prayer usually goes hand in hand with human action. Confronting a monarch with his sin and then mocking 850 hostile prophets (18:10–40) are the marks of somebody who is prepared to lay down his life for the glory of God and the redemption of the people (18:13). The bold acting faith of people like Elijah creates space for YHWH to demonstrate that he is the living God.[35] Fretheim goes so far as to say, "God's work in the world is always mediated."[36]

The Abiding Spirituality of the Lament

Elijah's prayers give voice to different shades of the lament. The prophet's prayer for the widow's boy is characterized by a critical and accusatory tone. Lamenting and complaining to God on behalf of a third party is an audacious form of advocacy for those who do not have a voice before the heavenly Judge (Exod 5:22–23). Just as other intercessors questioned the fundamental assumption about YHWH being a righteous Judge (Gen 18:22–33; Jer 12:1–2), so also Elijah gave voice to the apparent injustice and refused to settle for the way things seemed to be (17:20–21).

There is, however, another aspect to the laments of Elijah. On his escape to Horeb, Elijah's prayer displays despair and depression. This is in line with most prophets' experience: confronting covenant

---

35. Jones, *Sharing*, 102–3.
36. Fretheim, *Kings*, 99.

trespassers in the name of God leads inevitably to tensions, persecution, and suffering (Jer. 26:1–11; Matt 5:10–12). After Elijah's great victory on Carmel, he had no strength left for complaint and petition. Suffering from burnout, Elijah could only see the dark side of past, present, and future (19:4, 10, 13–14). Nevertheless, God did not directly engage with the content of the prophet's lament. After providing for the physical needs of his servant, YHWH did not allow the lamenting prophet to get lost in his misguided worries, but re-commissioned Elijah with new responsibilities. Nelson offers the following comment: "Depressed persons cannot usually be talked out of their gloom. What does sometimes help is a sense of purpose, and that is exactly what God provides with a new commission."[37]

In sum, Elijah's prayers encompass dynamics that are fundamental to biblical faith—obedient submission, loyal opposition, faithful perseverance, unrestrained expression of pain in lament, as well as recommitment to God and his mission.

BIBLIOGRAPHY

Balentine, Samuel E. *Prayer in the Hebrew Bible: The Drama of Divine-Human Dialogue*. OBT. Minneapolis: Fortress, 1993.
Childs, Brevard S. "On Reading the Elijah Narratives." *Int* 34 (1980) 128–37.
DeVries, Simon J. *1 Kings*. WBC 12. Waco, TX: Word, 1985.
Dharamraj, Havilah. *A Prophet Like Moses? A Narrative-Theological Reading of the Elijah Stories*. PBM. Milton Keynes: Paternoster, 2011.
Fretheim, Terence E. *First and Second Kings*. Westminster Bible Companion. Louisville: Westminster John Knox, 1999.
Hawkins, Ralph K. *While I Was Praying: Finding Insights about God in Old Testament Prayers*. Macon, GA: Smyth & Helwys, 2006.
Jones, Paul Hedley. *Sharing God's Passion: Prophetic Spirituality*. Milton Keynes: Paternoster, 2012.
Keil, C. F., and F. Delitzsch, *Commentary on the Old Testament*. 10 volumes. Peabody, MA: Hendrickson, 1996.
Kiuchi, Nobuyoshi. "Elijah's Self-Offering: 1 Kings 17,21." *Bib* 75 (1994) 74–79.
McKnight, Scot. *The Letter of James*. NICNT. Grand Rapids: Eerdmans, 2011.

---

37. Nelson, *Kings*, 127.

Section 3: Prayers of Prophets

Middleton, Richard J. "God's Loyal Opposition: Psalmic and Prophetic Protest as a Paradigm for Faithfulness in the Hebrew Bible." *CATR* 5 (2016) 51–65.

Montgomery, James A. *A Critical and Exegetical Commentary on the Book of Kings*. ICC. Edinburgh: T. & T. Clark, 1951.

Nelson, Richard D. *First and Second Kings*. IBC. Louisville: John Knox, 1987.

Rad, Gerhard von. *Theologie des Alten Testaments Band 2: Die Theologie der prophetischen Überlieferungen Israels*. 10th ed. Munich: Kaiser, 1993.

Sweeney, Marvin A. *I & II Kings*. OTL. Louisville: John Knox, 2007.

Thiel, Winfried. *1. Könige 17–22*. BKAT. Göttingen: Vandenhoeck & Ruprecht, 2019.

Waltke, Bruce K., and Charles Yu, *An Old Testament Theology: An Exegetical, Canonical, and Thematic Approach*. Grand Rapids: Zondervan, 2007.

Werline, Rodney. *Pray Like This: Understanding Prayer in the Bible*. Edinburgh: T. & T. Clark, 2007.

Widmer, Michael. *Moses, God, and the Dynamics of Intercessory Prayer*. FAT 2.8. Tübingen: Mohr Siebeck, 2004.

———. *Standing in the Breach: An Old Testament Theology and Spirituality of Intercessory Prayer*. Siphrut 13. Winona Lake, IN: Eisenbrauns, 2015.

Wray Beal, Lissa M. *1 & 2 Kings*, AOTC 9. Nottingham: Apollos, 2014.

7

Joyously Drawing Water from the Springs of Salvation
Praise as Structure and Goal of the Book of Isaiah

Mark J. Boda

THE STUDY OF PRAYER within the Hebrew Bible has undergone significant shifts over the past quarter century. Earlier studies employed diachronic methodologies, especially form and tradition criticism, which often extracted prayers from their literary contexts to identify their function within the religion of ancient Israel (*Sitz im Leben*). More recent analysis has focused on synchronic strategies to discern the function of prayers within their literary settings (*Sitz in der Literature* or *Sitz im Buch*).[1]

My initial treatment of prayer forms in Isaiah focused on the role of lament or songs of disorientation at key points in the macrostructure of Isaiah (esp. Isa 6, 40, and 49).[2] This present investigation shifts the focus to the role played by depictions of, calls to, or expressions of

---

1. Compare my earlier Boda, *Praying the Tradition* with Boda, "Prayer as Rhetoric." For the general trend in analysis of forms in the Old Testament, see Sweeney and Ben Zvi, eds., *Changing Face*; Ben Zvi and Floyd, eds., *Writings and Speech*; Buss and Stipe, *Changing Shape*; cf. Toffelmire, "Form Criticism."

2. Boda, "Uttering Precious."

Section 3: Prayers of Prophets

praise and thanksgiving in the structure of the book.³ It will show that while lament is acknowledged as a key expression for this community experiencing the discipline of Yahweh prophesied in Isa 6, it is praise that comprises the ultimate goal of the Isaiah tradition, which explains the importance of praise in the structure of the book as a whole.

ISAIAH 40-55: PRAISE BEYOND LAMENT

Isaiah 49:13 and 54:1

In my earlier work on lament in Isaiah, I noted the appearance of praise at the seam between the two major sections in Isa 40–55. Isaiah 40–55 is divided into two major sub-sections by the description of a lament by two different speakers who are then addressed directly in the prophetic material that follows.⁴ Isaiah 40:27 gives voice to the lament of Jacob/Israel ("My way is hidden from Yahweh, and the justice due me escapes the notice of my God"), while 49:14 gives voice to the lament of Zion/Jerusalem ("Yahweh has forsaken me, and Yahweh has forgotten me").⁵ Isaiah 49:1–12 represents the climax of the section addressing the lament of Jacob/Israel, identified as "My Servant Israel" (49:3). Just before introducing the lament of Zion/Jerusalem in 49:14, however, the one(s) responsible for Isa 40–55 provide(s) a call for praise in 49:13:

> Shout for joy (*rnn*), O heavens! And rejoice (*gyl*) O earth!
> Break forth into joyful shouting (*ptskh rinnah*), O mountains!
> For the LORD has comforted (*nkhm*) his people
> And will have compassion on his afflicted.⁶

Here, entities of creation (heavens, earth, mountains) are called to praise Yahweh for granting the comfort (*nkhm*) first mentioned in Isa 40:1. But while Servant Israel (49:3) has received comfort, there is yet another entity that awaits salvation: Zion/Jerusalem, and her lament

---

3. As will soon be evident, the vocabulary of joy is inextricably linked with praise and thanksgiving throughout Isaiah as is the vocabulary of mourning with lament.

4. For the data on this division see Boda, "Walking in the Light," 68; cf. Goldingay, *Isaiah*, 280.

5. On the rhetorical role of the laments in Isa 40–55 see esp. Westermann, *Isaiah 40–66*, 218–19; Oswalt, *Isaiah 40–66*, 303.

6. Translations here will be drawn from NASB, revised at times for author's preference.

cuts off any premature response of praise that might arise from creation. It is this second lament that is addressed throughout Isa 49:14—54:17, as the saved Servant now plays a role in transforming the situation of Zion/Jerusalem. By the end of this second part of Isa 40-55 the same vocabulary that was used to call creation to praise in 49:13 (*rnn, ptskh rinnah*) is now directed in 54:1 towards Zion/Jerusalem, whose lament has been answered by Yahweh through the victory of his mighty arm through the Servant.

> "Shout for joy (*rnn*), O barren one, you who have borne no *child*;
> Break forth into joyful shouting (*ptskh rinnah*) and cry aloud,
> you who have not travailed;
> For the sons of the desolate one *will be* more numerous
> Than the sons of the married woman," says the LORD.

The call to praise in Isa 49:13 thus concludes the literary section that precedes it (40:27—49:12), but also foreshadows the goal of the following literary section, which reaches its climax in the repetition of praise vocabulary in 54:1 directed towards Zion/Jerusalem.

Praise Pericopae in Isaiah 40-55

Isaiah 49:13 and 54:1 show the key role played by praise in the superstructure of Isa 40-55. They are not alone, however, within this section of Isaiah, but are joined by a series of calls to or depictions of joyful praise, which punctuate Isa 40-55:

42:10-12

[10] Sing to the LORD a new song,
Sing His praise (*tehillah*) from the end of the earth!
You who go down to the sea, and all that is in it.
You islands, and those who dwell on them.
[11] Let the wilderness and its cities lift up *their voices*,
The settlements where Kedar inhabits.
Let the inhabitants of Sela shout for joy (*rnn*),
Let them shout from the tops of the mountains.
[12] Let them give glory (*kavod*) to the LORD
And declare His praise (*tehillah*) in the coastlands.

Section 3: Prayers of Prophets

44:23

Shout for joy (*rnn*), O heavens, for the Lord has done *it*!
Shout joyfully (*rw'*), you lower parts of the earth;
Break forth into a shout of joy (*ptskh rinnah*), you mountains,
O forest, and every tree in it;
For the Lord has redeemed Jacob
And in Israel He shows forth His glory (*p'r*).

48:20

Go forth from Babylon! Flee from the Chaldeans!
Declare with the sound of joyful shouting (*rinnah*), proclaim this,
Send it out to the end of the earth;
Say, "The Lord has redeemed His servant Jacob."

49:13

Shout for joy (*rnn*), O heavens! And rejoice (*gyl*), O earth!
Break forth into joyful shouting (*ptskh rinnah*), O mountains!
For the Lord has comforted His people
And will have compassion on His afflicted.

51:3

Indeed, the Lord will comfort Zion;
He will comfort all her waste places.
And her wilderness He will make like Eden,
And her desert like the garden of the Lord;
Joy (*sason*) and gladness (*simkhah*) will be found in her,
Thanksgiving and sound of a melody.

52:7–10

⁷How lovely on the mountains
Are the feet of him who brings good news,
Who announces peace
And brings good news of happiness,
Who announces salvation,
And says to Zion, "Your God reigns!"

⁸Listen! Your watchmen lift up *their* voices,
They shout joyfully (*rnn*) together;
For they will see with their own eyes
When the LORD restores Zion.
⁹Break forth (*ptskh*), shout joyfully (*rnn*) together,
You waste places of Jerusalem;
For the LORD has comforted His people,
He has redeemed Jerusalem.
¹⁰The LORD has bared His holy arm
In the sight of all the nations,
That all the ends of the earth may see
The salvation of our God.

54:1

"Shout for joy (*rnn*), O barren one,
you who have borne no *child*;
Break forth into joyful shouting (*ptskh rinnah*) and cry aloud,
you who have not travailed;
For the sons of the desolate one *will be* more numerous
Than the sons of the married woman," says the LORD.

55:12

For you will go out with joy (*simkhah*)
And be led forth with peace;
The mountains and the hills will break forth into shouts of joy
(*ptskh rinnah*) before you,
And all the trees of the field will clap *their* hands.

Some have noted how these praise pericopae appear at the end or beginning of subsections within Isa 40–55,[7] but, besides their role within

---

7. The importance of the praise pericopae for the structure of Isa 40–55 was identified long ago by Greßmann, "Die Literarische Analyse Deuterojesajas," but more recently Westermann, *Sprache und Struktur*; Mettinger, *Farewell to the Servant Songs*, and Beaucamp, *Le Livre de la Consolation*, in particular have shown the importance of the various praise pericopae (esp. 42:10–12; 44:23; 45:8; 48:20–21; 49:13; 51:3; 52:9–10; 54:1–3); cf. Beaucamp, "Chant Nouveau du Retour"; "Le IIe Isaïe." Blenkinsopp (*Isaiah 40–55*, 61) is more hopeful about this approach, while Goldingay and Payne (*Isaiah 40–55*, 21) are more skeptical. Childs (*Isaiah*, 387) identifies the hymn of praise as a "literary device" which "seems to be characteristic

Section 3: Prayers of Prophets

their respective literary contexts, there appears to be a progression within these praise pericopae throughout Isa 40–55, based on our earlier observation of the linchpin praise pericope in Isa 49:13. Prior to this point in Isa 40–55, the praise pericopae have a cosmic or international emphasis, calling for praise in the context of either creation or the nations. It is this broader form of praise that is in view in Isa 49:13 and that is cut short by the lament of Zion/Jerusalem in 49:14, which introduces the second major section of Isa 40–55. After this point, calls for and depictions of praise are focused on Zion and her people, reaching a climax in the previously mentioned 54:1, in which the vocabulary of 49:13 reappears but is now directed towards Zion herself. After this point, the depiction of praise in 55:12 extends joyful praise once again to creation.

This pattern of praise pericopae reinforces the structural importance of Isa 49:13–14 as linchpin within Isa 40–55 and emphasizes how forms related to lament and praise are key to interpreting this section of Isaiah.

Isaiah 43 and 51: From Lament to Praise

Praise, however, appears in several other places in Isa 40–55. Isaiah 43:18–21 speaks of God's creation of a roadway in the wilderness and notes how the beasts of the field will glorify and the people of God will praise Yahweh.

> [18] Do not call to mind the former things,
> Or ponder things of the past.
> [19] Behold, I will do something new,
> Now it will spring forth;
> Will you not be aware of it?
> I will even make a roadway in the wilderness,
> Rivers in the desert.
> [20] The beasts of the field will glorify (*kvd*) Me,
> The jackals and the ostriches,
> Because I have given waters in the wilderness
> And rivers in the desert,
> To give drink to My chosen people.
> [21] The people whom I formed for Myself

---

of the entire book."

Will declare My praise (*tehillah*).

This connection between the wilderness roadway and praise is reminiscent of 51:3, mentioned above, but also of 51:11:[8]

> And the ransomed of the LORD will return
> And come with joyful shouting (*rinnah*) to Zion,
> With everlasting joy (*simkhah*) upon their heads.
> They will find gladness (*sason*) and joy (*simkhah*),
> And sorrow (*yagon*) and sighing (*'anakhah*) will flee away.

Here, we see the key contrast between the former state of lament (sorrow, sighing) and the new state of praise (joy, gladness). This then is an important reminder of the superstructure of Isa 40–55. Lament is answered by prophetic oracles after the laments of Israel/Jacob in 40:27 and 49:14, but scattered throughout the oracular response are praise pericopae designed to shape a shift from lament to praise.[9] This evidence explains why the opening commission of Isa 40–55 is *nakhamu nakhamu* ("comfort, comfort"), consolation directed towards the lamenting community and city. The sign that the community is comforted is the joyful praise described throughout.

BEYOND ISAIAH 40–55: FROM LAMENT TO PRAISE IN ISAIAH 1–39 AND 56–66

Isaiah 35

Isaiah 51:11 and its contrast motif (lament to praise) prompt us to move beyond the literary boundaries of Isa 40–55 and see the impact of praise on the remainder of the book. Isaiah 51:11 is drawn from the final, climactic verse of Isa 35 (v. 10), a chapter that begins in similar fashion in 35:1–2:

> [1]The wilderness and the desert will be glad (*sys*),
> And the Arabah will rejoice (*gyl*) and blossom;
> Like the crocus

---

8. See the wilderness imagery used in 41:18, 19; 49:10–12.

9. See the superb review of the various forms and passages of praise in Isa 40–55 in Whybray, *The Second Isaiah*, 30–34. He reminds us that these "are to be thought of as simply part of Deutero-Isaiah's message" (32).

Section 3: Prayers of Prophets

> ²It will blossom profusely
> And rejoice (*gyl*) with rejoicing (*gilah*) and shout of joy (*rnn*).
> The glory of Lebanon will be given to it,
> The majesty of Carmel and Sharon.
> They will see the glory (*kavod*) of the Lord,
> The majesty (*hadar*) of our God.

Thus, Isa 35 emphasizes at its end the contrast motif of lament to praise, foreshadowing the major rhetorical goal of Isa 40–55.[10]

Isaiah 56–66

This same rhetorical goal is evident in the final section of Isaiah, chs. 56–66. It is first encountered in 57:18–19 where mourning is met with comfort from God:

> ¹⁸"I have seen his ways, but I will heal him;
> I will lead him and restore comfort (*nikhumim*) to him and to his mourners (*'avel*),
> ¹⁹Creating the fruit/utterance of the lips.
> Peace, peace to him who is far and to him who is near,"
> Says the Lord, "and I will heal him."

Similar are two praise pericopae found near the end of Isa 56–66, both of which contrast past or present lament with a call to joy.

65:18–19

> ¹⁸But be glad (*sys*) and rejoice (*gyl*) forever in what I create;
> For behold, I create Jerusalem *for* rejoicing (*gilah*)
> And her people *for* gladness (*masos*).
> ¹⁹I will also rejoice (*gyl*) in Jerusalem and be glad (*sys*) in My people;
> And there will no longer be heard in her
> The voice of weeping (*bekhi*) and the sound of crying (*ze'aqah*).

---

10. On the key role played by Isa 35 in the book of Isaiah see Steck, *Bereitete Heimkehr*, especially in light of the connections with Isa 40 and Isa 32–34. Steck also notes close connections to Isa 60–62 with parallels between 35:8–10 and 62:10–12.

66:10

> Be joyful (*smkh*) with Jerusalem
> and rejoice (*gyl*) for her, all you who love her;
> Be exceedingly glad (*masos*) with her,
> all you who mourn (*'avel*) over her.

But key to the development of this motif in Isa 56–66 is the declaration of the Servant figure at the very center of the collection in ch. 61:[11]

> ¹The Spirit of the Lord GOD is upon me,
> Because the LORD has anointed me
> To bring good news to the afflicted;
> He has sent me to bind up the brokenhearted,
> To proclaim liberty to captives
> And freedom to prisoners;
> ²To proclaim the favorable year of the LORD
> And the day of vengeance of our God;
> To comfort (*nkhm*) all who mourn (*'avel*),
> ³To grant those who mourn (*'avel*) *in* Zion,
> Giving them a garland instead of ashes,
> The oil of gladness (*sason*) instead of mourning (*'evel*),
> The mantle of praise (*tehillah*) instead of a spirit of fainting.
> So they will be called oaks of righteousness,
> The planting of the LORD, that He may be glorified (*p'r*).[12]

Here we see once again the shift from mournful lament to joyful praise as evidence of the comforting agenda set out in Isa 40:1.

Isaiah 24–27

Within Isa 1–39 praise also appears in what is often called "The Isaiah Apocalypse" in Isa 24–27. While there is significant interpretive debate over the meaning of this section, there is no question that praise is essential to its message. The opening, ch. 24, begins with a depiction of

---

11. On the structural role of Isa 61 as well as Isa 60, 62, which surround it, see Westermann, *Isaiah 40–66*, 296; Blenkinsopp, "Second Isaiah," 198. Notice how the servant articulates his mission in ch. 61 while Zion's salvation is highlighted in chs. 60, 62, expressing in chiastic fashion the linear flow of Isa 40–55.

12. Notice the use of (*p'r*) throughout Isa 40–66 to indicate the glorification of Yahweh through his salvation of Israel (44:23; 49:3; 60:21; 61:3).

Section 3: Prayers of Prophets

the judgment of Yahweh on the land/earth and this judgment brings an end to joyful activity (v. 7: *smkh*; v. 8: *mesos* 2x; v. 11: *simkhah, mesos*) replacing it with lament (v. 4: *'avel*; v. 7: *'avel, 'nkh*). However, a description of joyful praise breaks in at 24:14–16a:

> [14]They raise their voices, they shout for joy (*rnn*);
> They cry out from the west concerning the majesty of the Lord.
> [15]Therefore glorify (*kvd*) the Lord in the east,
> The name of the Lord, the God of Israel,
> In the coastlands of the sea.
> [16a]From the ends of the earth we hear songs, "Glory (*tsevi*) to the Righteous One."

The referent of those who raise their voices here is highly debated, but the previous verse appears to provide it in the reference to the gleanings, that is, the remnant that will emerge from the destruction of the city.[13] Whoever they are they, whether Gentile or Jew, they declare praise in an international global context. This praise, however, is cut short by the cry of lament in 24:16b:

> But I say, "I waste away! I waste away![14] Alas for me!
> The treacherous deal treacherously,
> And the treacherous deal very treacherously."

For the autobiographical voice of 24:16b, the praise of 24:14–16a is premature and inappropriate.[15] Only after the judgment of 24:17–23,

---

13. See Motyer, *Isaiah*, 166–67. Oswalt (*Isaiah 1–39*, 450) identifies them as the oppressed emerging from the city of chaos. Loete ("Premature Hymn," 232–33) argues that it is the "inhabitants of the earth," especially because of the address to them in v. 17b. He goes on to note the contrast between the desolation in "the middle of the earth" in 24:13 and the praise arising from "the ends of the earth" in 24:16, suggesting that while "the few people that remain in the 'the middle of the earth' have no reason for joy, those living on the edges of the earth praise YHWH in joyful hymns, because they believe they have escaped his judgement" (234). It is uncertain why Beuken ("Prophet Leads the Readers," 124) thinks that "the imagery of the gleanings (24:12–13) excludes the very possibility that anything has survived."

14. The translation here is controversial. The present translation is based on the cognate *rzh* (be lean); see *DCH* 7:459, which also suggests a connection to *raz* (secret).

15. With Loete, "Premature Hymn," contra Beuken ("Prophet Leads the Readers," 133–34), who treats the waw-relative prefix conjugation "I said" in 24:16d as the background for rather than contrast to the preceding joyous praise. See the use

which climaxes with Yahweh reigning on Mount Zion, do we then hear the autobiographical voice express praise to Yahweh in 25:1–5. After a prophetic vision of Yahweh's future redemptive actions related to Zion, Isa 25:9 provides a future depiction of praise by the community *bayom hahu'* (in that day):

> And it will be said in that day,
> "Behold, this is our God for whom we have waited that He might save (*ysh'*) us.
> This is the LORD for whom we have waited;
> Let us rejoice (*gyl*) and be glad (*smkh*) in His salvation (*yeshu'ah*)."

Some have explained the response of the autobiographical voice in 24:16b by reference to Isa 21:1–4, where the prophet does not gloat over divine judgment in sympathy for those affected.[16] However, the first description of judgment in 24:1–13 only mentions the destruction of the city, while the restoration of the reign of Yahweh on Mount Zion is reserved until the second description of judgment in 24:17–23. It is only after this restoration at Zion that we hear the autobiographical voice join in the praise.

Praise is also present in the prayer comprising Isa 26, although here praise plays a subsidiary role to the calls to trust and requests for divine aid in this chapter. This prayer begins with a celebration of the restoration of Jerusalem, a fitting response in light of the restoration of the reign of Yahweh on Mount Zion.

Isaiah 24–27 thus echoes some of what we have seen in Isa 40–55, an initial praise of Yahweh that is identified as premature praise and silenced by a cry of lament until Yahweh's rule is restored in Zion, a restoration that prompts praise.[17] The praise expressed here is clearly related to the divine judgment on the earth-city in ch. 24, which many have linked to the overthrow of Babylon.[18] It is only when the reign

---

of the waw-relative prefix conjugation in Joel 2:18–19; cf. Wolff, *Joel and Amos*, 54.

16. See e.g., Seitz, *Isaiah 1–39*, 183, 185; Goldingay, *Isaiah*, 140; Motyer, *Isaiah*, 167.

17. It is the rejection of the praise of 24:14–16a that leads Williamson (*Book Called Isaiah*, 177), to dismiss any connection between Isa 24–27 and Isa 40–55, and yet it is rejection of such praise that forges the closest connection to 49:13–14.

18. See Seitz (*Isaiah 1–39*, 175, 178–9), for connections between chs. 24–27 and

of Yahweh is restored in Zion that we find approval for praise. This pattern is similar to Isa 40–55. Here the phrase "in that day" indicates that this praise is intended for the remnant that will emerge from exile, shaping the agenda for restoration and preparing readers of Isaiah for the second half of the book.

Isaiah 12

We began this review of praise in Isaiah at the center of Isa 40–55 (49:13) and have progressively moved out from that center to show the impact of praise forms on material within the surrounding sections of Isaiah. We first addressed chs. 40–55, then chs. 56–66, followed by chs. 1–39. We now come to our final key praise pericope in Isa 12, which represents the first major pericope dominated by praise forms that a reader encounters in the book of Isaiah.

Isaiah 12 has often been divided into two basic form units, separated by nearly identical phrases (*ve'amareta/ve'amaretem bayom hahu'*, then you will say in that day) in 12:1 and 12:4. However, this structural division does not take into account the voicing shifts throughout the chapter,[19] since 12:1a speaks to a masculine singular audience, who are given words expressed to God in the first common singular (12:1b–2), and 12:3–4a speaks to a masculine plural audience, who are given words calling a masculine plural audience to thanksgiving and praise (12:4b–5) and then calling a feminine singular audience identified as "the inhabitant of Zion" (12:6).[20] This suggests then that 12:3 lays the foundation for the second command to speak in 12:4a. This shifting between voices involving common singular, masculine singular, masculine plural, and feminine singular audiences is strikingly similar to what we find in Isa 40:1–11. The use of the second masculine singular address in 12:1a followed by the first common singular thanksgiving in

---

chs. 13–14. Johnson (*Chaos to Restoration*) links this to Jerusalem as judged in 597. Goldingay (*Isaiah*, 138) also notes lexical connections to Jerusalem, which suggests that it may remind Judeans that this depiction relates to their own culpability.

19. On voicing see Mandolfo, *God in the Dock*; Jacobson, *Many Are Saying*; Dobbs-Allsopp, *On Biblical Poetry*. For its use in Isaiah see Heffelfinger, *I Am Large*, in Psalms see Boda, "Varied and Resplendid Riches."

20. See Sweeney, *Isaiah 1–39*, 198; also the domain analysis in Wieringen, "Isaiah 12:1–6."

12:1b–2 suggests the only first common singular referent that we find in Isaiah: the prophetic intermediary, as seen in the autobiographical accounts in chs. 6, 8, as well as in the prophetic commissioning of ch. 40 and servant declarations in chs. 40–66. The shift from a second masculine singular audience using first common singular words in 12:1–2 to a second masculine plural audience calling for thanksgiving/praise from masculine plural and feminine singular audiences in 12:3–6 suggests that instructions are being given for both an individual, who will express thanksgiving for personal salvation, and for a group, which will call a community to thanksgiving/praise. The address to the female inhabitant of Zion is strikingly similar to what we find in Isa 40, while the focus on God's comfort in 12:1 is reminiscent of the initial call to comfort at the outset of Isa 40. Williamson has identified other significant connections between Isa 12 and Isa 40–55, including the similar form of eschatological hymns of praise at the conclusion to sections and similar themes with at times identical vocabulary.[21]

While sensitive to the broader context of Isaiah (esp. ch. 40), we should not miss the close connection between Isa 12 and its immediate literary context.[22] The employment of the phrase *bayom hahu'* (in that day) in 12:1 and 4 connects these pericopae to the series of identical phrases throughout Isa 7–11, revealing that the praise and thanksgiving provided here are designed for those who will emerge as the remnant after the judgement of Yahweh. Furthermore, Isa 8:18 identifies Isaiah's children as well as Isaiah himself as "signs and wonders in Israel from Yahweh of hosts, who dwells on Mount Zion." We can see how the names of the children presented in Isa 7–12 are employed in the vocabulary of the various prophetic announcements, but we should not miss the plays on Isaiah's name (*yeshaʿyahu*) in Isa 12, at the seam between the two constituent sections:[23]

---

21. Williamson, *Book Called Isaiah*, 120–23. Of course, one must be wary of limiting oneself to connections between Isa 12 and 40ff in light of the caution of Childs, *Isaiah*, 108–9.

22. Williamson (*Book Called Isaiah*, 118) notes that Isa 12 has a "number of connections with the previous chapters, which suggest that it has been shaped to function as a conscious conclusion."

23. See Seitz, *Isaiah 1–39*, 112–13; Williamson, *Book Called Isaiah*, 123; cf. Boda, "Signs and Wonders."

Section 3: Prayers of Prophets

²Indeed, God is my salvation (*yeshuʻah*),
I will trust and not be afraid;

For Yah Yahweh is my strength and song,
And He has become my salvation (*yeshuʻah*).
³You will joyously (*sason*) draw water
From the springs of salvation (*yeshuʻah*).

Not only are there connections to that which precedes Isa 12, but we can also see connections to that which follows. While 12:1–2 focuses on the future comfort afforded to the people of God once Yahweh's anger expressed throughout chs. 7–11 subsides, 12:3–6 adds to this a more global dimension, calling those who give thanks to express their praise in the hearing of the peoples (*ʻammim*) and all the earth (*kol haʾarets*). This global dimension foreshadows the international and cosmic context of Isa 13–27.[24] The reference to praise "in that day" also brings to mind the provision of praise expressions in Isa 24–27, especially 25:1–9, which has a similar structure: beginning with the first common singular voice of the prophet praising (12:1–2//25:1–5), followed by a prophetic declaration of redemption (12:3//25:6–8) which prompts communal praise (12:4–5//25:9–10a).[25] This evidence highlights the function of Isa 12 within its immediate canonical literary context, but the earlier evidence also shows how Isa 12 is foreshadowing what is to come in Isa 40–66, which provides insight into the remnant that will emerge in that day (*bayom hahuʾ*).[26] The structure of a masculine plural audience among the nations in 12:4b–5 followed by a feminine singular audience in 12:6 matches the structure of Isa 40–55 with its focus on the community in exile in 40:27–49:13 and then Zion/Jerusalem in 49:14–54:17.

Once again, we see the important role played by praise/thanksgiving forms employed in Isa 12 for the structure of the book of Isaiah,

---

24. As also Smith, *Isaiah 1–39*, 280. This would be another example of what Goldingay and Payne (*Isaiah 40–55*, I:21), drawing on Mettinger's (*Farewell to the Servant Songs*) earlier work, call "gemstone passages . . . that relate to what precedes as well as to what follows."

25. Beuken, "Prophet Leads the Readers," 144–55; cf. Oswalt (*Isaiah 1–39*, 459) for connections between 25:1–5 and ch. 12.

26. As Williamson (*Book Called Isaiah*, 112) noted: "the chapter functions just like the eschatological hymns of praise in 40–55."

both in terms of this immediate section of 1–39 but also in terms of developments in the entire book.

CONCLUSION

Isaiah's commission in Isa 6 reveals that praise is foundational to Isaiah's calling. Before he utters his lament in 6:11 ("How long?") and even prior to his fearful cry of ruin in 6:5 ("Woe to me"), we are presented with a worshipful scene of praise in the divine council: "Holy, holy, holy is Yahweh Almighty; the whole earth is full of his glory" (6:3). We see from the outset that Isaiah's calling as prophet emerges out of a praise environment focused on the holiness of Yahweh. It is not surprising that the theme of this initial praise would dominate the text of the book of Isaiah from beginning to end, and also would be identified by the people as the dominant message of Isaiah's oral proclamations (30:9–11). This thrice holy God will produce a "holy seed," and the sign of this remnant will be praise of Yahweh as first encountered around his heavenly throne.[27] The emergence of this worshipping remnant is developed throughout Isaiah, beginning in Isa 12,[28] then Isa 24–27, Isa 35, and reaching its climax in Isa 40–66.[29] While lament is acknowledged as a key expression for this community experiencing the discipline of Yahweh prophesied in Isa 6, it is praise that comprises the ultimate goal of the Isaiah tradition, which explains its importance to the structure of the book as a whole.[30]

---

27. The remnant leitmotif consistently appears throughout all of these pericopae in Isaiah. This was apparent in the praise pericopae in Isa 40–55, where we find calls to or descriptions of joyful praise intertwined with commands to depart from Babylon (48:20; 52:7–12; 55:12) or descriptions of the wilderness roadway from exile (43:18–21; 51:11). Isaiah 35 continues this interconnection between joyous praise and the returning remnant, as does Isa 61:1–3. The praise in Isa 24:14–16a arises from "the gleanings" of 24:13, suggesting the remnant community. So also the people of God who will praise "in that day" in Isa 12 is clearly identified in Isa 11:11–16 as "the remnant of his people who will remain" (11:11, 16). On remnant, see the classic work of Hasel, *The Remnant*.

28. Notice how Isa 12 ends with a focus on the "Holy One of Israel," echoing the beginning of Isa 6 and bringing closure to the section Isa 6–12; cf. Wieringen, "Isaiah 12,1–6," 171.

29. This would explain why Nurmela (*Mouth of the Lord*) identifies the Psalter as the dominant source of inner-biblical allusion in Isa 40–66.

30. See my analysis of the Book of the Twelve in Boda, "Deafening Call," where I identify a rhetorical strategy of three calls to silence interlaced with three calls to joy.

Section 3: Prayers of Prophets

This is an important reminder for communities of faith shaped by the book of Isaiah. While lament is clearly heard by God in the throne room of heaven and there is space for its expression on earth, praise is the ultimate goal of the human journey. In this way Isaiah echoes the inner voice of the Psalmist expressed in the refrains of Pss 42–43:

> Why are you in despair, O my soul?
> And why have you become disturbed within me?
> Hope in God, for I shall again praise Him

BIBLIOGRAPHY

Beaucamp, Paul-Évode. "'Chant Nouveau Du Retour' (Isa 42:10–17): Un Monstre de l'Exégèse Moderne." *Revue des sciences religieuses* 56 (1982) 145–58.

———. "Le IIe Isaïe (Is XL, 1–XLIX, 13)—Problème de l'Unité du Livre." *Revue des sciences religieuses* 62 (1988) 218–26.

———. *Le Livre de la Consolation d'Israël: Isaïe 40–55*. Lire la Bible. Paris: Cerf, 1991.

Ben Zvi, Ehud, and Michael H. Floyd, eds. *Writings and Speech in Israelite Prophecy and Ancient Near Eastern Prophecy*. SymS 10. Atlanta: Society of Biblical Literature, 2000.

Beuken, Wim. "The Prophet Leads the Readers into Praise: Isaiah 25:1–10 in Connection with Isaiah 24:14–23 Seen against the Background of Isaiah 12." In *Studies in Isaiah 24–27: The Isaiah Workshop—De Jesaja Werkplaats*, edited by Hendrik Jan Bosman and Harm W. M. van Grol, 121–156. Oudtestamentische Studiën 43. Leiden: Brill, 2000.

Blenkinsopp, Joseph. *Isaiah 40–55: A New Translation with Introduction and Commentary*. AB 19A. New York: Doubleday, 2002.

———. "Second Isaiah—Prophet of Universalism." In *The Prophets*, edited by Philip R. Davies, 186–206. The Biblical Seminar 42. Sheffield: Sheffield Academic, 1993.

Boda, Mark J. "A Deafening Call to Silence: The Rhetorical 'End' of Human Address to the Deity in the Book of the Twelve." In *The New Form Criticism and the Book of the Twelve*, edited by Mark J. Boda et al., 164–85. ANEM 10. Atlanta: Society of Biblical Literature, 2015.

The three calls to silence appear as direct protest prayers disappear and the calls to joy are given the final word. The calls to joy are directed towards Zion and thus are similar to the pattern we have discovered in Isaiah in which Zion's joy is key to the rhetorical goal. In contrast, there is no equivalent call to silence in Isaiah, although protest does disappear.

———. "Prayer as Rhetoric in the Book of Nehemiah." In *New Perspectives on Ezra-Nehemiah: History and Historiography, Text, Literature, and Interpretation*, edited by Isaac Kalimi, 279–96. Winona Lake, IN: Eisenbrauns, 2012.

———. *Praying the Tradition: The Origin and Use of Tradition in Nehemiah 9*. BZAW 277. Berlin: de Gruyter, 1999.

———. "The Signs and Wonders of Salvation: Beholding Isaiah and His Children." In *Is the Gospel Good News?*, edited by Stanley E. Porter, 25–40. McMaster New Testament Series 16. Eugene, OR: Pickwick, 2019.

———. "'Uttering Precious Rather Than Worthless Words': Divine Patience and Impatience with Lament in Isaiah and Jeremiah." In *Why?—How Long?: Studies on Voice(s) of Lamentation Rooted in Biblical Hebrew Poetry*, edited by Mark J. Boda et al., 83–99. T. & T. Clark Library of Biblical Studies. New York: Bloomsbury, 2014.

———. "'Varied and Resplendid Riches': Exploring the Breadth and Depth of Worship in the Psalter." In *Rediscovering Worship: Past, Present, Future*, edited by Wendy Porter, 61–82. McMaster New Testament Series 13. Eugene, OR: Pickwick, 2015.

———. "Walking in the Light of Yahweh: Zion and the Empires in the Book of Isaiah." In *Empire in the New Testament*, edited by Stanley E. Porter and Cynthia Long Westfall, 54–89. McMaster New Testament Studies 10. Eugene, OR: Pickwick, 2011.

Buss, Martin J., and Nickie M. Stipe. *The Changing Shape of Form Criticism: A Relational Approach*. HBM 18. Sheffield: Sheffield Phoenix, 2010.

Childs, Brevard S. *Isaiah*. OTL. Louisville: Westminster/John Knox, 2001.

Dobbs-Allsopp, F. W. *On Biblical Poetry*. Oxford: Oxford University Press, 2015.

Goldingay, John. *Isaiah*. NIBC. Peabody, MA: Hendrickson, 2001.

Goldingay, John, and David Payne. *Isaiah 40–55*. 2 vols. ICC. London: T. & T. Clark, 2005.

Greßmann, Hugo. "Die Literarische Analyse Deuterojesajas." *ZAW* 34 (1914) 254–97.

Hasel, Gerhard F. *The Remnant: The History and Theology of the Remnant Idea from Genesis to Isaiah*. Berrien Springs, MI: Andrews University Press, 1972.

Heffelfinger, Katie M. *I Am Large, I Contain Multitudes: Lyric Cohesion and Conflict in Second Isaiah*. BibInt 105. Leiden: Brill, 2011.

Jacobson, Rolf A. *Many Are Saying: The Function of Direct Discourse in the Hebrew Psalter*. JSOTSup 397. London: T. & T. Clark International, 2004.

Johnson, Dan G. *From Chaos to Restoration: An Integrative Reading of Isaiah 24–27*. JSOTSup 61. Sheffield: JSOT, 1988.

Section 3: Prayers of Prophets

Loete, Joseph. "A Premature Hymn of Praise: The Meaning and Function of Isaiah 24:14–16c in Its Present Context." In *Studies in Isaiah 24–27: The Isaiah Workshop—De Jesaja Werkplaats*, edited by Hendrik Jan Bosman and Harm W. M. van Grol, 226–38. Leiden: Brill, 2000.

Mandolfo, Carleen. *God in the Dock: Dialogic Tension in the Psalms of Lament*. JSOTSup 357. London: Sheffield Academic, 2002.

Mettinger, Tryggve N. D. *A Farewell to the Servant Songs: A Critical Examination of an Exegetical Axiom*. Scripta Minora Regiae Societatis Humaniorum Litterarum Lundensis. Lund: CWK Gleerup, 1983.

Motyer, J. A. *Isaiah: An Introduction and Commentary*. TOTC 18. Downers Grove, IL: InterVarsity, 1999.

Nurmela, Risto. *The Mouth of the Lord Has Spoken: Inner-Biblical Allusions in Second and Third Isaiah*. Studies in Judaism. Lanham, MD: University Press of America, 2006.

Oswalt, John N. *The Book of Isaiah, Chapters 1–39*. NICOT. Grand Rapids: Eerdmans, 1986.

———. *The Book of Isaiah, Chapters 40–66*. NICOT. Grand Rapids: Eerdmans, 1997.

Seitz, Christopher R. *Isaiah 1–39*. IBC. Louisville: John Knox, 1993.

Smith, Gary V. *Isaiah 1–39*. NAC. Nashville: Broadman & Holman, 2007.

Steck, Odil Hannes. *Bereitete Heimkehr: Jesaja 35 als Redaktionelle Brücke zwischen dem Ersten und dem Zweiten Jesaja*. SBS 121. Stuttgart: Verlag Katholisches Bibelwerk, 1985.

Sweeney, Marvin A. *Isaiah 1–39 with an Introduction to Prophetic Literature*. FOTL 16. Grand Rapids: Eerdmans, 1996.

Sweeney, Marvin A. and Ehud Ben Zvi, eds. *The Changing Face of Form Criticism for the Twenty-First Century*. Grand Rapids: Eerdmans, 2003.

Toffelmire, Colin. "Form Criticism." In *Dictionary of the Old Testament: Prophets*, edited by Mark J. Boda et al., 257–71. Downers Grove, IL: IVP Academic, 2012.

Westermann, Claus. *Isaiah 40–66: A Commentary*. OTL. London: S. C. M., 1969.

———. *Sprache und Struktur der Prophetie Deuterojesajas*. Stuttgart: Calwer, 1981.

Whybray, R. Norman. *The Second Isaiah*. OTG. Sheffield: JSOT, 1983.

Wieringen, A. L. H. M. van. "Isaiah 12,1–6: A Domain and Communication Analysis." In *Studies in the Book of Isaiah: Festschrift Willem A. M. Beuken*, edited by J. T. A. G. M. Van Ruiten and M. Vervenne, 257–71. BETL 132. Louvain: Leuven University Press/Peeters, 1997.

Williamson, H. G. M. *The Book Called Isaiah: Deutero-Isaiah's Role in Composition and Redaction*. Oxford: Oxford University Press, 1994.

Wolff, Hans Walter. *Joel and Amos: A Commentary on the Books of the Prophets Joel and Amos*. Translated by Samuel Dean McBride. Hermeneia. Philadelphia: Fortress, 1977.

8

"Do Not Pray, Plead, or Pester Me Because No One is Listening" (Jeremiah 7:16)

ELAINE A. PHILLIPS

INTRODUCTION

WHAT DO WE DO with this command (Jer 7:16) from God to Jeremiah *not* to pray for the people of Judah, especially since Jeremiah heard it in one form or another four times (see also 11:14; 14:11–12; 15:1–4)? This admonition has garnered a number of interpretations, some of them questioning the character of God.

In preparation for our investigation, we must review the importance of promise, obedience, and communication in the covenant relationship between God and God's people. That relationship unfolded in the context of Israel's checkered history, a descending spiral of disobedience, only infrequently interrupted by a reformation. It will be important to view through Jeremiah's eyes the strained covenant bond between God and God's people at the end of the Judean monarchy.

As we address Jeremiah's role at the cusp of heading into exile, we will attempt to reconstruct the historical backdrop against which we might position these commands from the LORD not to pray for the people.[1] No matter how we weave these admonitions into the historical context(s), at stake are God's faithfulness to the covenant and what kind of person Jeremiah proved to be in his most impossible position.

COVENANT AS RELATIONSHIP

God's covenant with Israel at Sinai had established a relationship that was brimming with promises—blessings, land, freedom from bondage, and God's unfailing covenant love (*khesed*). These people were God's kingdom of priests, a holy nation (Exod 19:6), and were called to hear and obey God's Torah (Exod 24:3–4; Deut 4:1–2). Everything—geopolitics, social structures, worship—was to happen within this covenant context. Unswerving devotion and communication were foundational.

Ministers of the Covenant: Prophets and Priests

Prophets were in a unique mediating position not even experienced by the priesthood, significant as that role was. The priests offered sacrifices and burned incense as they made atonement for God's people and symbolically bore them into God's presence. They functioned as mediators in the Tabernacle/temple, a most dangerous place because of the searing holy Presence of God. Along with the Levites and elders, priests were also charged with mediating God's word to the people through their role as Torah teachers (Deut 31:9–13).

Prophets, on the other hand, *spoke for* God into the immediate circumstances, often in very explicit, forceful, and unusual terms. God commissioned his "servants, the prophets" to tend to the covenant, generally at times when Israel's side of the relationship was fracturing badly. "Thus saith the Lord. . ." introduced their pronouncements as

---

1. There are multiple gnarly issues with which to contend in conjunction with the words of Jeremiah, e.g., dating and composition of oracles, relationship to Josiah's reforms, Deuteronomistic influence, and the final shaping of the Jeremiah tradition. The complexities of these issues are ably presented in the introductions to most commentaries. I shall mention the most salient as they arise but do not intend a comprehensive summary of any of them. For good treatments, see Bright, *Jeremiah*; Thompson, *Jeremiah*; and the introductory observations of Seitz, "The Prophet Moses."

they both rebuked the people for flagrant disregard for God's authority, and offered encouragement to the faithful.[2]

The Nature of Prophetic Intercession[3]

In significant instances, prophets also spoke *to* God—questioning, challenging, pleading, and interceding. In Abraham Joshua Heschel's words:

> The prophet is not only a censurer and accuser, but also a defender and consoler. Indeed, the attitude he takes to the tension that obtains between God and the people is characterized by a dichotomy. In the presence of God, he takes the part of the people. In the presence of the people, he takes the part of God.[4]

These servants of the LORD followed the pattern initiated by Moses, the consummate prophet (Deut 5:28–31;18:15–22). On the heels of the golden calf incident, Moses pleaded with God not to destroy the apostate people and not to desert them, but to continue to go with them to the Land God had promised to the patriarchs (Exod 32–34). That signature encounter with the LORD gave Moses and all the prophets who followed him the theological foundation for appealing to the Name and character of God (Exod 34:6–7). The balance between compassion, forgiveness, and boundless patience, on the one hand, and "visiting the iniquity," on the other, was heavily tilted toward unfailing covenant love. Nevertheless, underlying that declaration we see the persistent need for intercession on behalf of transgressors. Prayer and covenant were intertwined.

The prophetic intercessors appealed to the character of God on behalf of those whose moral frailty brought their relationship with God

---

2. Some of the prophets—Moses, Samuel, Ezekiel, and Jeremiah—whose prayers are recorded in the Hebrew Bible also served as priests.

3. Seitz ("The Prophet Moses," 5–8) uses the term "bi-directional" to draw attention to the intercessory aspect of the prophetic office. With Jeremiah, something went terribly amiss.

4. Heschel, *The Prophets*, 24. Heschel reiterates the point with specific reference to Jeremiah (p. 121).

into jeopardy.[5] God expected the prophet to stand in the gap (Ezek 22:30–31) because once the prophet moved out of that breach, God's wrath would come upon the people.[6]

Sadly, both prophets and priests also easily went astray. This was no more evident than in those last dark days of Judah when politics and religion were inextricably enmeshed, and both powerful offices were aligned against Jeremiah (Jer 5:31; 6:13; 8:10; 13:13; 23:11, 33–34; 26:7–16). Even the prophets and priests already in exile had adopted deceit and lies as the foundation of their messages (29:1–10).

COVENANT RELATIONSHIP STRAINED TO THE BREAKING POINT

Israel's track record in the Land had been set early on during the period of the Judges. In a nutshell, the pattern consisted of apostasy, oppression from enemies, repentance on the part of the people, deliverance by one of God's chosen individuals, and a repetition of the cycle that was usually worse than the previous episode. Kings, once the Davidic dynasty was inaugurated, were remembered in terms of whether they had been faithful to lead the people in accordance with Torah or not. Most of them were not. There were several notable exceptions, particularly Hezekiah and Josiah, who led the people to nation-wide reformations. Even these, however, were painfully short-lived, especially the latter.

The Reformation Attempt Under Josiah

It does not take much reading between the lines of Jeremiah to get the picture that Josiah's celebrated "reform," as dramatic as it was, did not have a lasting impact. To be sure, the temple was cleansed, the Torah found, idols were smashed throughout the Land, and they celebrated the Passover, all in Josiah's eighteenth year (2 Kgs 22–23; 2 Chr 34). Josiah, however, reigned a total of thirty-one years. We have to ask what happened in the following decade. It seems that the idolatrous ideologies, promulgated for the preceding fifty-five years by Manasseh,

---

5. Widmer, *Standing in the Breach*, 6.
6. Widmer, *Standing in the Breach*, 402–3.

were just too ingrained.[7] However we parse the nature and extent of the reform, immediately following the accolades for Josiah at the end of his reign (2 Kgs 23:25), God declared it was time to respond in accordance with the covenant (2 Kgs 23:26–27; Jer 15:4) because of all the evil that *Manasseh* had done.[8]

Jeremiah's Covenant-Based Indictment

Jeremiah accused God's people of refusing correction (5:3) and abandoning Torah (9:13 [12]), indulging their own selfish natures and tearing apart the bonds of the covenant relationship. The "stubbornness of their evil hearts" characterized Israel from the day they left Egypt, and it got steadily worse (7:22–26; 11:7–8).

The first place they turned were "other gods" that seduced the people away from the Lord. The list is familiar—carved images and foreign idols (8:19), Baal (9:14 [13]; 11:13, 17), and the "queen of heaven" (7:18). They burned their sons and daughters in fire (7:31). In tones that echo Ps 115 and Isa 44–45, Jeremiah contrasted God's absolute majestic power with the impotence of objects constructed by humans (10:1–16).

There are repeated accusations of falsehood woven into the fabric of judgment. Their "houses are full of deceit," like cages of birds (5:27). The prophets and priests were false and the people loved it that way (5:30–31; 6:13–15, echoed in 8:10–12). The invective against false prophets grew ever stronger (14:14–16; 23:9–40). There were geo-political interests underlying the radical differences between Jeremiah and his false contemporaries.[9] Most damning were the presumptuous declarations of allegiance to the temple all the while engaging in "abominations"—the Lord's indelicate word for their behavior (7:4–10). In his world awash with despair and dashed expectations, Jeremiah even

---

7. Thompson, *Jeremiah*, xxxii–xxxiii. No doubt Manasseh's wholesale pro-Assyrian stance had repudiated everything Hezekiah had accomplished, and the people turned again to the Assyrian gods.

8. Second Chronicles 33:10–17 attests to Manasseh's humble return to the God of his fathers when he was taken hostage to Assyria, but his individual repentance could not undo decades of kingdom-wide apostasy; as king, he was accountable.

9. Hananiah (ch. 28) exemplified the politics of false prophecy.

accused God of deceiving both the people—through the false prophets (4:10)—and Jeremiah himself (20:7–18).[10]

In true covenant fashion, God promised measure-for-measure response to their disobedience. The pattern recurs especially around listening, deception, and hard-wired hearts. When God spoke; they did not listen (7:13, 24). Thus, Jeremiah would speak, but God would not listen (7:16; also 7:24). When the people hardened their hearts, God in effect "hardened his heart."[11]

Jeremiah and the Lord in "Conversation"

The voices of God and Jeremiah merge in the early chapters of the book, especially in heart-wrenching laments over the rebellious people.[12] "My anguish, my anguish (*meʿay*—my bowels, inward parts); I writhe; the walls of my heart—my heart thunders; I cannot silence it . . . For my people are fools, they do not know *Me*, they are senseless children. . ." (4:19–22).[13]

The LORD's anger at Judah's rebellion is interspersed with expressions of love for the people and longing for their repentance. Wrath and grace are interwoven even among the admonitions not to pray. "Speak this word to them: 'Let my eyes run down with tears night and day and not cease; for the virgin daughter of my people has been deeply broken—struck with a grievous wound'" (14:17). God's lament over Jerusalem gave hope to Jeremiah to continue to pray.[14]

---

10. The root *patah* means to "be simple." The general sense of the verbal root seems to be openness of the mind, but it most frequently occurs in negative contexts of enticing and deceiving (Pan, "פתה," 714–16).

11. Widmer, *Standing in the Breach*, 383.

12. The prophet gave voice to God's rage at Israel's self-destructive sin. "I am full of the wrath of the LORD; I am weary of holding it" (Jer 6:11). Unless otherwise indicated, all translations are my own.

13. This is not solely Jeremiah's self-description; the same visceral response is expressed specifically by the LORD in contemplating how dear Ephraim was to him (31:20 [19])—"*hamu meʿay*—my innards roar; I will assuredly have compassion."

14. Widmer, *Standing in the Breach*, 371.

SECTION 3: PRAYERS OF PROPHETS

When Did Jeremiah Encounter the Point of No Return?

Here we probe more extensively the immediate historical context. Jeremiah's prophetic ministry apparently began in the thirteenth year of the reign of Josiah (1:1–2).[15] Josiah had already begun to destroy the idols in the twelfth year of his reign, when he was twenty years old (2 Chr 34:3–7). Jeremiah started prophesying the following year, when Josiah would have been twenty-one years old. Jeremiah was also a young man (*na'ar*) when he was called. When Josiah was twenty-six years old (2 Chr 34:8—the eighteenth year of his reign), Hilkiah found the Torah in the temple, Huldah interpreted it, and the full-scale reformation got under way.[16] Nevertheless, as noted above, while Josiah's reform had multiple targets, it apparently did not break through hard-wired hearts.

Josiah did express relief when he heard that the covenant reckoning would not come on his watch, even though it was looming on the horizon. The reprieve was long enough to accommodate the collapse of Assyria and the rapid rise of Babylon.

Josiah's death in 609 BC precipitated a royal crisis. Pharaoh Neco removed Jehoahaz after three months and set up Eliakim in his place, changing his name to Jehoiakim (2 Kgs 23:31–35). That meant there were three kings in the space of that one year. For a brief interval, the text of Jeremiah refers to "kings" of Judah—perhaps Jeremiah's rueful reflection on the unsettled politics.[17] The next four years for Judah were

---

15. There is some disagreement regarding the interpretation of these chronological data. For an alternative chronological reconstruction, see Holladay, *Jeremiah 1*, 1–19.

16. While there seems to be general agreement that the Hilkiah who found the Torah and reported to Josiah (2 Kgs 22) may not have been the same Hilkiah noted as Jeremiah's father (Jer 1:1; Bright, *Jeremiah*, lxxxvii–lxxxviii), nevertheless, Jeremiah was steeped in the prophetic and Sinai covenant traditions. He also echoed Hosea's emphases on God's unfailing *khesed* for his wayward people, their rejection of the knowledge of God, and the profound need for repentance (Thompson, *Jeremiah*, 81–85).

17. "Go and stand in the gate of the people, through which the kings of Judah go in and out; and in all the gates of Jerusalem. Say to them, 'Hear the word of the LORD, O kings of Judah and all Judah and everyone living in Jerusalem who come through these gates" (17:19–20). Shortly thereafter, in the context of Jeremiah's symbolic shattering of the clay jar above the Hinnom Valley, he declared, "hear the word of the LORD, O kings of Judah and people of Jerusalem. . . [Disaster was coming because of the pollution of the Temple, offerings to other gods, and burning sons in

tumultuous with the rapid rise of Babylon vying with Egypt for dominance in Judah. In this context, it seems the fourth year of Jehoiakim (605 BC, the year Babylon defeated Assyria) was a significant juncture; it is specifically mentioned in Jer 36:1 (see also 45:1) as a prelude to the command: "Take a scroll (*megillat-sefer*) and write on it all the words that I have spoken to you against Israel and against Judah and against all the nations from the day I spoke to you, from the days of Josiah to this day" (36:2).

The details that follow are potentially helpful in thinking about dates of the admonitions not to pray. They are also ominous. In this context, Baruch read the scroll, first publicly and then to the officials, who were properly fearful. They were aware of its dangerous nature and sent Baruch into hiding along with Jeremiah while they reported the existence of the scroll to the king who tore up and burned the scroll as it was read to him.[18] Echoing Moses and the second set of tablets, Jeremiah wrote a second scroll with additional words (36:32). It may be that the prohibition(s) should be dated after the scroll was burned; that would have been a tipping point in terms of the king's utter rejection of the Word of the LORD. Once the threat to make Jerusalem like Shiloh (chs. 7 and 26) was activated, there would be no possibility of intercession.[19]

---

the fire as offerings to Baal] . . . they have burned sacrifices in it to gods that neither they nor their fathers nor the kings of Judah ever knew . . ." (19:3–4). "The houses in Jerusalem and those of the kings of Judah will be defiled like this place, Topheth . . ." (19:13). Following that is another, more abbreviated, "Temple sermon" (19:14–15), this time landing Jeremiah in stocks (20:1–2). By the reign of Zedekiah, Jeremiah referred to the king as a single individual (21:1–11; 22:1–2, 6; 27:18).

18. The contents of the scroll were of such a length that Baruch read it to the people (36:10), and re-read it to the concerned leadership (36:15). Whether the king heard it the same day is not as clear. Neither he nor his servants sensed the horror of his desecration of the scroll. How different that reception was compared to his father's only twenty years earlier (2 Kgs 22)!

19. Holladay, *Jeremiah 1*, 252. There are nagging uncertainties about the sequence of events. When Jehoiakim burned the scroll, Baruch was the one who read it in the temple; at that time, Jeremiah did not have the freedom to venture into the public sphere (36:4–5). In other words, this may have been later than the sermons of chs. 7 and 26—if those two are the same—and yet the first prohibition appears in that context. To be sure, the connection of the third prohibition (14:11) with fasting and the drought in the fourth year of Jehoiakim does work.

Section 3: Prayers of Prophets

Although most of Jeremiah's oracles are not tied to a king's name and those that are indicate that the utterances are not all in chronological order, it is nevertheless instructive that the only royal name appearing in the first twenty chapters is that of Josiah. It might be that Jeremiah and the LORD had these exchanges over an undefined period during what turned out to be Josiah's disappointing reign, but they were inscribed as authoritative in the critical fourth year of Jehoiakim. More to our point, the LORD's sobering admonitions not to pray for the people appear only in chs. 1–15. Leading up to the first prohibition are waves of accusations from the LORD about the rebellious nature of the people (2:30; 3:6–10; 5:1–3; 6:16–19) and repeated calls to repentance (3:22–25; 4:1–8; 6:26).[20] From the literary perspective of the completed book of Jeremiah, all of this is the prelude to the first "Temple sermon" (7:1–15),[21] a stinging accusation of deep-seated injustice, flagrant breaking of the Ten Words, and presumptive entitlement. Immediately following is God's first warning not to pray.

---

20. If the temple sermon of ch. 7 was uttered sometime during the reign of Josiah, it could be that the so-called reform had given the people a false sense of security, and Jeremiah was compelled to address that (Bright, *Jeremiah*, xciv–xcv). By the time Jehoiakim was on the throne, any vestiges of the reform had long since dissipated. Interwoven in these first six chapters are also hints of later events. Building siege ramps against Jerusalem (6:6) sounds like a post-Josiah context. The ominous expression *magor missaviv*, "terror on all sides," shifts from the horror of immanent destruction coming from the north (6:25) to the terror wrought by the priest Pashur, whom Jeremiah dubbed *Magor Missaviv* after Pashur thrashed Jeremiah and then put him in stocks (20:1–6).

21. Here we raise the question again: was the "Temple sermon" of 7:1–15 the same event as is recorded in 26:1–6? The latter incident is dated early in the reign of Jehoiakim, probably just before 605 BC. While there are similarities in terms of the reference to Shiloh in each proclamation and the call to repentance and obedience, there are also notable differences. Not least of them is the aftermath in ch. 26, where Jeremiah was accused of treason and brought to trial. Jeremiah appeared in the temple court a third time as well (19:14–15) for an abbreviated warning of the impending disaster. Until his confinement, he very likely was a regular if unwelcome presence at the temple.

"DO NOT PRAY" [22]

This steady admonition from God threads its way among Jeremiah's early laments, and it is a sobering one. It is not, however, without variations. These interest us.

7:16

"And you, do not pray (*'al-tithpallel*), do not lift up for them a cry (*rinnah*) or prayer (*tefillah*) and do not encounter ('touch') me (*ve'al-tifga'-bi*) because I will not listen to you."[23]

This first command is the fiercest of them all. The four prohibitive words ruled out any possible intercession from Jeremiah, and the punchline drove it home. The LORD said he would not listen to *Jeremiah* ("you" is singular). The context reverberates with the deceitful nature of worship conducted as a sham.[24] The word of the LORD through Jeremiah called out the emphatic three-fold repetition of the "temple of the LORD" for what it was—their own self-deception. Their presumption of "safety" in the house that bore the name of the LORD was hollow when their actions were detestable. They thought they could hide there; that was the implication of "cave of robbers" (7:8–11). The reminder of Shiloh's destruction should have given them pause (7:12–15), but it did not. They did not listen to God's instruction (7:13); how could God listen to prayer on their behalf, especially in light of their wholesale, family-style idolatry (7:17–19)? Their history was one long narrative of persistent refusal to listen, ever since the Exodus. Thus, the LORD would abandon this generation (7:20–29).

At the same time, the negation (*'al*) with the jussive suggests a temporary prohibition, one that would be eased after the immediate

---

22. Seitz explores these four admonitions from the LORD to Jeremiah in conjunction with Jeremiah's laments, seeing them as evidence that the prophetic office had broken down with Jeremiah. When the LORD forbade Jeremiah to intercede, that put him in a place where he could not modify God's verdict against the people as Moses had done before him; the office of the prophets who followed in Moses's tradition was no more (Seitz, "The Prophet Moses," 8–11).

23. Widmer (*Standing in the Breach*, 343) renders *paga' bi* as "fall upon," implying pestering or confronting.

24. The LORD had already declared that neither offerings nor incense were acceptable (6:20) and called the people hardened rebels (6:28).

Section 3: Prayers of Prophets

judgment.[25] That fits well with the overarching purpose of covenant sanctions (Lev 26:40–45).[26]

11:14

"And you, do not pray (*'al-tithpallel*) or lift up a cry (*rinnah*) or prayer (*tefillah*) for them, because I will not listen when they call to me in their distress."

The tone this time was slightly tempered. God did not warn Jeremiah against confronting or "touching" him as in the previous admonition. In addition, while the Lord's listening ear would not be attentive to the *people*, Jeremiah was not specifically included. Perhaps that is because Jeremiah had just prayed—powerfully. "I know . . . that a man's life is not his own . . . Correct me, O Lord, but only with justice . . . lest you reduce me to nothing. Pour out your wrath on the nations who do not acknowledge you and who have devoured Jacob . . ." (10:23–25).

The immediate context is important. Chapter 10 is a steady polemic against idolatry. There is also a passing reference to living under siege (10:17), which could suggest some point within Zedekiah's rule.

Having noted those items, the operative concern is listening—or not. This discourse starts with the Lord's command through Jeremiah that the people "listen" to the words of the covenant. The Hebrew imperative, *shema'*, is frequently and properly translated "obey." The history lesson that follows alternates between God's commands that his errant people "listen" and their refusal to do so (11:2–10). Because they did not listen, the Lord would not listen. Even before the admonition to Jeremiah not to pray, the Lord declared: "Behold I am bringing on them disaster (*ra'ah*) from which they will not be able to escape. They will cry out to me, but I will not listen" (11:11). Idolatry, this time offering incense to Baal, was again a primary transgression, and the same refrain follows; the Lord said: "I have forsaken my house; I

---

25. See GKC 152f. The imperfect with *lo'* expresses a more emphatic, even permanent, form of prohibition (GKC 1070).

26. Because later in the text Jeremiah did intercede, this was clearly a temporary restriction. The same verb *hithpallel* is used positively with the people as the object (37:3; 42:2; 42:20). Even more telling, the people were to pray *for* Babylon. In fact, ". . .that the injunction not to pray is so often repeated leads one to suspect that Jeremiah never ceased to pray" (Bright, *Jeremiah*, cii; see also p. 56).

have abandoned my inheritance" (12:7). And yet, there is hope for a future. "After I have uprooted them, I will return and have compassion on them, and return each person to his inheritance and to his land" (12:15).

14:11-12

"Then the LORD said to me: 'Do not pray (*'al-tithpallel*) for them for good (*letovah*). When they fast, I will not listen to their cry (*rinnatham*); though they offer burnt offerings and grain, I will not accept them. I will destroy them with sword, famine, and plague.'"

The immediately prior context provides a possible framework to date this third prohibition. The first six verses of ch. 14 describe the threat of a drought. That might be the undefined "distress" of the second prohibition. In conjunction with impending disaster, it was national practice to declare a fast. Jeremiah rose immediately to the occasion and again *prayed* earnestly—for their good. These were words of confession, but also dismay at God's apparent absence from the scene:

> If our sins answer against us, O LORD, act for the sake of your Name. For our turnings are great; against you we have sinned. O Hope of Israel, the One who saves in time of distress, why are you like a stranger in the land, like a traveler turning (only) to sleep? Why are you like a man who is surprised; like a mighty man not able to save? You are among us, O LORD, and your Name is called upon us; do not forsake us. (14:7-9)

At this point, we revisit the fourth year of Jehoiakim (Jer 36:1; cf. 45:1). The details that follow the command to write on the scroll seem faintly hopeful at first. The LORD expressed a longing that the people would hear of the impending disaster, turn from their wicked ways, and the LORD would forgive (36:1-3; see also v. 7). The text twice mentions fasting. The first was a fast day in that same year (36:6). The second, in the fifth year of Jehoiakim in the ninth month, seems to have been specially called, no doubt in the face of the threats to the national well-being (36:9; cf. Joel 1:1-14).

Judah's wholesale disobedience, however, made the fast pointless (14:10-12). God saw through the trappings of false worship and again adjured Jeremiah not to pray. This time, however, instead of emphasizing the constraints on Jeremiah's prayer life, the LORD focused on those activities that the people thought might bail them out. Not only would the LORD reject the burnt and grain offerings, but he would bring against them sword, famine, and plague—the three-fold devastation that characteristically accompanied a long-term siege.

This third prohibition prompted Jeremiah to appeal on basis of the people's having been led astray by prophets (14:13). God's response was stark. Both the false prophets and the people would perish; the consequences of worthless divination and the "deceit of their own minds" were horrifying beyond words (14:14–16). And yet, the very next verses are God's lament, shared and continued by Jeremiah, weeping over the "virgin daughter" (14:17–18). This morphed seamlessly into Jeremiah's next prayer of confession on behalf of the people:

> We know, O LORD, our evil and the sin of our fathers, for we have sinned against you. Do not despise for the sake of your Name; do not dishonor the throne of your glory. Remember. . . do not break your covenant with us. Do any of the empty (idols) of the nations cause rain? Do the heavens send showers? Is it not you, O LORD our God? We hope in you for you have done all these things (14:20–22).

In spite of the LORD's admonition not to pray and his stated refusal to be moved by their fasting and sacrifices, Jeremiah continued boldly to enter into that prayer space. He echoed Moses's plea in the wake of the golden calf debacle; for the sake of God's Name and God's glory, please forgive.

15:1–4

"And/But the LORD said to me: 'If Moses and Samuel were to stand before me,[27] my soul would not turn to this people. Send them from my presence and let them go!'" (15:1).

The destinations were grim—death, sword, famine, and captivity. Why? Because of Manasseh, son of Hezekiah, and all he did in Jerusalem

---

27. See Ps 99:6. To "stand before" is a technical term for intercession. We see it with Elijah and Elisha as they served God (1 Kgs 17:1; 18:15; 2 Kgs 3:14; 5:16).

(v. 4). Thus, Jeremiah could indeed echo Moses with all his might; he could declare, as Samuel did, "for the LORD will not reject his people for the sake of his great Name ... and I—may it not be that I sin against the LORD by ceasing to pray for you, and teaching you in the good and right way" (1 Sam 12:22–23). Not even those great, selfless intercessors, both of whom appealed to the Name and glory of the LORD of Hosts, could change the course that was required by the covenant sanctions. Likewise, Jeremiah, though he received God's word with joy and was called by the Name of the LORD (15:16), was categorically refused any effective intercessory role, at least for that time. The interwoven fabric of covenant and prayer had been torn apart.

THE AFTERMATH—OF SORTS

And yet, Jeremiah continued to pray, at first for himself, to be sure; in somewhat aggrieved tones, he accused God of being the Source of all his misery (15:15–18). After a stern rebuke by the LORD—accompanied by reassuring words, "I am with you" (15:19–21)—Jeremiah's appeals continued and broadened in scope, even asking for judgment on those persecuting and plotting against him (17:14–18; 18:19–23). In effect, he left his enemies to the judgment of God. At the lowest possible ebb for Judah, the LORD and Jeremiah continued in "conversation." God commanded Jeremiah to purchase land in the tribe of Benjamin, a prophetic-symbolic act demonstrating the long perspective of an anticipated return. Jeremiah's prayer in response was firmly based in the covenant; everything that had transpired was fitting (32:6–25). In time, he again prayed to the LORD in response to a request from king Zedekiah (37:3–17)[28] and on behalf of the people remaining in the land after the destruction of Jerusalem and the temple (42:1—43:7). Never mind that the LORD's responses to those prayers were ignored by the people![29]

---

28. There was a precedent for a prophet's prayer to avert national disaster. Isaiah joined Hezekiah in earnest prayer against the Assyrian onslaught of Sennacherib (2 Chr 32:20; Isa 37:4), even though the earlier words of God through Isaiah had not been encouraging. The people were wicked, godless, destruction was inevitable, and only a remnant would survive the disciplining "rod" (Isa 10; Widmer, *Standing in the Breach*, 340). This may have been the straw at which Zedekiah was clutching.

29. As a bit of a postscript, Jeremiah would be taken into Egypt against his will

SECTION 3: PRAYERS OF PROPHETS

REPRISE: WHEN AND WHY?

Jeremiah's retrospect in 25:3 summed up the wretched spiritual state of the people: "From the thirteenth year of Josiah son of Amon king of Judah until this very day—twenty-three years—the word of the LORD has come to me and I have spoken to you, rising early and speaking, but you have not listened." This was four years after the death of Josiah in 609 BC, and the first year that Nebuchadnezzar was in power. Jeremiah's assessment of the situation was hardly positive.

Later, after the first two deportations (605 and 597 BCE), Jeremiah's (and the LORD's) tone changed significantly. The letter that Jeremiah sent to the exiles in Babylon promised they would return (29:10–14), albeit after seventy years. These hope-filled promises continue through chapters 30–31. However we work through these data, it seems that the destruction of 587 finally canceled the prohibition on prayer.

SUMMARY AND FURTHER REFLECTIONS

Widmer has offered a robust treatment of intercessory prayer in the Old Testament and, as part of that, reflects on the implications of these prohibitions. While there are significant parallels with Moses's four ultimately successful prayers in Exod 32–34, Jeremiah's context was tragically different; the idolatry of the people was far too entrenched, and Jeremiah had to be brought to the point where he would perceive it from God's covenant point of view. That meant praying that God would do justice.[30] Because intercession is powerfully effective, God forestalled Jeremiah's appeal to God's mercy, safeguarding his own obligation to punish.[31] When Jeremiah was adjured not to pray that the people's circumstances would be reversed, his persistent prayer modulated to confession and pleading that the hearts of God's people would be changed.

Jeremiah's prophetic voice reverberates into the New Testament. When Jesus asked the disciples around him how he was being

---

(43:1–7). That may signal the end of the intercessory prophetic office that started when Moses brought the people out of Egypt (Seitz, "The Prophet Moses," 12).

30. Insisting that Jeremiah stop praying brought Jeremiah into line with God's own necessary purposes (Widmer, *Standing in the Breach*, 436–37).

31. Widmer, *Standing in the Breach*, 346–55.

perceived, the responses included, "Jeremiah, or one of the prophets" (Matt 16:13–14). Why single out Jeremiah? Possibly because Jeremiah's unshakable allegiance to God's covenant, even when he was confronted with anguishing circumstances at every turn, stood as a stellar example. This does not mean Jeremiah did not protest; he did so—vehemently.

These observations speak volumes to us. Like Jeremiah, we are called both to trust in God's unfailing covenant love through the grimmest of circumstances, and to invoke God's judgment against deceit and corruption. Following the lead of Jeremiah, the avenues of confession and pleading for radically changed hearts, starting with our own, are always open.

BIBLIOGRAPHY

Bright, John. *Jeremiah*. AB. New York: Doubleday, 1965.

Heschel, Abraham Joshua. *The Prophets: An Introduction*. New York: Harper and Row, 1962.

Holladay, William L. *Jeremiah 1: A Commentary on the Book of the Prophet Jeremiah Chapters 1–25*, edited by Paul D. Hanson. Hermeneia. Philadelphia: Fortress, 1986.

Pan, Chow Wee. "פתח." In *NIDOTTE* 3:714–16.

Seitz, Christopher R. "The Prophet Moses and the Canonical Shape of Jeremiah." *ZAW* 101 (1989) 3–27.

Thompson, J. A. *Jeremiah*. NICOT. Grand Rapids: Eerdmans, 1980.

Widmer, Michael. *Standing in the Breach: An Old Testament Theology and Spirituality of Intercessory Prayer*. Siphrut 13. Winona Lake, IN: Eisenbrauns, 2015.

9

Ask and You Shall Intercede

The Power of a Prayerful Imagination[1]

Steven T. Mann

INTRODUCTION

THIS ESSAY SEEKS TO understand the function(s) of questions when they are used in intercession in order to gain insight into the theological and practical implications of this aspect of the biblical text. Some readers may find this topic surprising, as few of us ask God questions when we pray for other people. We may describe for God how we would like the situation to change, and perhaps direct God on the details for how to accomplish our desired results. While asking God questions might not occur to us, there are numerous intercessory prayers in the Old Testament that utilize questions.[2]

---

1. A previous version of this paper was published as Steven T. Mann, "Ask and You Shall Intercede: The Peculiar Perlocutionary Power of Asking God Questions," *BBR* 29 (2019) 208–24. This article is used by permission of the Pennsylvania State University Press.

2. There are also Scripture passages that display intercessory prayers that do not utilize questions, so this paper does not suggest that questions are always necessary in such prayers.

This investigation will focus on four passages: (1) Abraham's prayer in Gen 18:16–33, (2) Moses's prayer in Exod 32:7–14, (3) Amos's prayers in Amos 7:1–6, and (4) Yahweh's conversation with Jonah in Jonah 4:1–11. The first three passages contain prayers in which an intercessor utilizes questions in petitioning God.[3] The final passage displays a reversal in which Yahweh asks the questions, highlighting Jonah's failure to intercede.

The present study will examine the questions within the prayers in these passages by means of speech act theory (SAT). A philosophy of language that explores the performative function of speech, SAT investigates not only what an utterance means but also what it does. In particular, the investigation will utilize ideas involving two main categories of speech acts: illocutionary acts and perlocutionary acts. An illocutionary act is a speech act that is performed *in saying something*, whereas a perlocutionary act is performed *by saying something*. For example, in saying, "This plate is hot," a server in a restaurant performs at least two illocutionary acts: describing the plate and directing the guests to take care in handling it. However, the perlocutionary act involves the act of persuading guests to take steps necessary to avoid burning themselves. Whereas the illocutionary act(s) can be successfully performed by the speaker alone, the success of the perlocutionary act also depends upon the response by the hearers.

To perform an intercessory prayer is both an illocutionary act and a perlocutionary act. As an illocutionary act, the intercessory prayer is a directive (see figure 1) for Yahweh to act favorably on behalf of an individual or group. The perlocutionary act, the intended result, depends upon God responding in the desired manner.

The taxonomy of illocutionary acts offered by John Searle provides a helpful way to categorize speech acts as assertives, declaratives, directives, commissives, and/or expressives (see figure 1).[4]

---

3. The selected texts are intended to serve as a sample of intercessory prayers that utilize questions as opposed to a complete list.

4. Searle, *Speech Acts*; Searle, *Expression and Meaning*. For further description of this taxonomy of illocutionary acts, see Mann, "Performative Prayers of a Prophet," 21–23.

Section 3: Prayers of Prophets

Illocution-ary act	Example	Performative Function
Assertive	"Today is Monday."	Describe a situation
Declarative	"You're fired."	Impact and describe the situation
Directive	"Leave the building immediately."	Direct someone to do something
Commissive	"I'll leave in a few minutes."	Commit oneself to do something
Expressive	"I hate Mondays."	Express one's feelings

Figure 1

An utterance can be used to perform more than one illocutionary act, and the function(s) of an utterance will often depend upon various aspects of the context, the speech situation.[5] For the present study, it is important to recognize that questions always function as directives because asking a question prompts the hearer to think about the content of the utterance.

One aspect of illocutionary acts that will be important for this study is the concept of "direction of fit." Different illocutionary acts utilize different relationships between one's words and the world (see figure 2).

Illocution-ary act	Function	Direction of fit
Assertive	Describe a situation	Words fit with the world
Declarative	Impact and describe the situation	Words affect the world and fit with the world
Directive	Direct someone to do something	Words affect the world
Commissive	Commit oneself to do something	Words affect the world
Expressive	Express one's feelings	Words may or may not fit with the world

Figure 2

Assertives attempt to describe the world (a "words-to-world" direction of fit), whereas commissives and directives work to affect the world (a "world-to-words" direction of fit). Declaratives operate with both directions of fit, as they both impact and describe the world. Expressives

---

5. Austin, *How to Do Things with Words*, 100. The speech situation is analyzed in detail by Searle and Vanderveken, *Foundations of Illocutionary Logic*, 27–28.

do not utilize a distinct direction of fit with the world as they need only to fit with the speaker's perception of the world. The intercessory prayers in this study are similar to expressives in that the words may or may not fit the world. Moreover, they employ a "world-from-words" direction of fit, which is similar to the way in which storytellers create narrative worlds with their words.[6]

In this study, the questions within the intercessory prayers will be analyzed in regard to their function within the world of the text (which I call the story level) as well as the world of the audience (the storyteller level).[7] On the story level, it will be shown that the questions in these prayers facilitate the success of the prayer (the perlocutionary act) by directing Yahweh's focus away from negative aspects of the situation and toward other aspects to which God is more likely to respond with favor. Operating as directives within the directive, the questions incorporate assertives that utilize what can be called a prayerful imagination.[8] On the storyteller level, the successful use of the prophet's questions as displayed on the story level invites the audience to consider the perlocutionary power that these questions have upon God. This may not only equip believing audiences to utilize questions in their own prayers, but enable them to interact with the world in ways that model God's grace.

ANALYSIS OF INTERCESSORY PRAYERS

Abraham's Prayer to Yahweh in Genesis 18

Questions play an important role in the exchange between Yahweh and Abraham concerning the fate of Sodom. The two main parts of this passage (vv. 16–21 and vv. 22–32) display similar speech situations

---

6. For more on the direction of fit between words and the world, and especially regarding the world-from-words direction of fit, see Mann, *Run David Run!*, 36, 45–49.

7. For an explanation of the story and storyteller levels, see Mann, "Performative Prayers of a Prophet," 23; Mann, *Run David Run!*, 30–57.

8. I am borrowing the term "prayerful imagination" from Camp, "Prayer in the Pentateuch," 31. Camp uses the term to denote an aspect of God's creative activity, specifically the way in which prayer "opens one's eyes to the power of God and the future God is creating" (p. 31). I will use the term as a way to describe the ways in which an intercessor can utilize a world-from-words direction of fit that can open God's eyes to possible aspects of the speech situation.

as well as a similarity in structure when the utterances are viewed as speech acts. On the story level, these similarities may suggest that Abraham constructs his act of intercession parallel to the way in which Yahweh initiates the conversation (see figure 3). Many interpreters have suggested that Yahweh's speech invites Abraham to become involved in the situation.[9] It is possible that Abraham construes Yahweh's speech to also direct the methodology of his participation (see figure 3).

Yahweh's Invitation (vv. 16–21)	Abraham's Intercession (vv. 22–32)
Speech situation: "And the men went out from there and they looked toward Sodom; and Abraham was walking with them on their way" (v. 16).	Speech situation: "And the men turned from there and went toward Sodom, and Yahweh remained standing before Abraham" (v. 22).
A. Question: Directive (v. 17)	A. Question: Directive (+ Assertive) (vv. 23–24)
B. Assertives + Directive (vv. 18–19)	B. Assertives + Directive (v. 25)
A' Yahweh's Response: Assertive + Commissive (vv. 20–21)	A' Yahweh's Responses: Commissives (+ Abraham's Assertives) (vv. 26–32)

Figure 3

The opening to Yahweh's speech is of particular interest for the present study, as Yahweh begins by posing a question to the group (consisting of "the men" and Abraham). Yahweh asks, "Shall I hide from Abraham that which I am doing?" (v. 17).[10] Yahweh's question is not a directive for the members of this audience to provide a response, as the ensuing assertives in vv. 18–19 clearly answer the question in the negative.[11] Yahweh's hearers are thus directed to think. The non-human hearers (ironically called "the men," *ha'anashim*) are to redirect their focus, if only briefly, from Sodom (v. 16) to Abraham (v. 17). The question directs Abraham not only to become involved in the conversation, but reminds him of the purpose of his election.

The assertives that follow the opening question are that "Abraham will become a great nation, and all the nations of the land shall be

---

9. E.g., Goldingay, *Old Testament Theology: Volume Three*, 267–68; Chisholm, "Anatomy of an Anthropomorphism," 8; Fretheim, *The Suffering of God*, 49–50.

10. Unless otherwise noted, all translations are my own.

11. In recognition of this, the NRSV adds the word "No" at the beginning of v. 19.

blessed in him" (v. 18).¹² Yahweh goes on to indicate that Yahweh has known Abraham so that Abraham may direct his kin to keep the "way of Yahweh," which here is identified as "doing righteousness (*tsedaqah*) and justice (*mishpat*)." By Abraham doing this, Yahweh will bring about his promise to Abraham. The clear connection of these utterances to the covenant with Abraham may be a reason that the opening question is not whether Yahweh should reveal these plans to Abraham, but whether Yahweh shall hide them. Abraham is to be involved in Yahweh's dealings in the world, and the way in which he does so specifically involves performing directives on righteousness and justice, the way of Yahweh.

Yahweh then divulges the plan. First, God gives an assertive concerning the greatness of the outcry against Sodom and Gomorrah and the gravity of their sin (v. 20). Then, God issues a commissive by which Yahweh pledges to investigate the matter (v. 21). Many interpreters have assumed that Yahweh is proclaiming judgment and coming destruction against the cities, as if God has already completed the investigation.¹³ This would mean that Abraham's intercession involves changing God's mind from that of bringing destruction to showing mercy.¹⁴ However, this view is well-critiqued by interpreters who note that God has only indicated plans to investigate.¹⁵ Indeed, "What I am doing" (v. 17) in God's question corresponds to the commissive, "I must go down and see . . ." (v. 21). Abraham is invited, not to change God's mind that has been made up already, but to be a part of the decision itself.

Abraham begins his intercession after the men depart for Sodom, leaving Abraham and Yahweh alone together (v. 22). Abraham utilizes four questions, alternating between a general question and one

---

12. I take Gen 18:18 as an indicative (so also NIV, CSB, NET), but, even if it continues the interrogative of Gen 18:17 (NRSV, NKJV, NASB), it nevertheless functions as an assertive that justifies the question.

13. For a helpful overview of this prevailing viewpoint, see MacDonald, "Listening to Abraham," 28–30.

14. E.g., Ben Zvi states, "The conclusion to which Abraham's argument leads is clear from the onset: God should change his/her plans concerning Sodom . . ." ("The Dialogue," 33).

15. E.g., Lyons, *Canon and Exegesis*, 174–76; MacDonald, "Listening to Abraham," 29.

Section 3: Prayers of Prophets

involving a specific number. The fourth question is actually a continuation (or re-articulation) of the second question (see figure 4).

Abraham's Questions to Yahweh
General: "Will you sweep away the righteous with the wicked?" (v. 23b)
Specific: "Will you sweep away and not forgive the place for the fifty righteous who are in it?" (v. 24b)
General: "Shall the judge of all the land not do justice?" (v. 25b)
Specific: "Will you destroy the whole city for lack of five?" (v. 28ab)

Figure 4

Lundbom notes that "Yahweh does not answer every question, only those containing specific numbers for saving the city. Neither of the big questions posed at the beginning of the dialogue is answered (vv. 23, 25b)."[16] The general questions do not require an answer; they serve as directives for Yahweh to think. This will impact Yahweh's answers to the specific questions.

The chiastic structure for the broader conversation identified in figure 4 above can be expanded as shown in figure 5:

Abraham's Speech and Yahweh's Responses (vv. 23–32)
A. Abraham's Questions: Directive (+ Assertive) (v. 23–24)
a. Will you sweep away the righteous with the wicked?"
b. Perhaps (*'ulay*) there are fifty righteous within the city;
a'. Will you sweep away and not forgive the place for the fifty righteous who are in it?
B. Abraham's Assertives (v. 25)
a. Far be it from you
b. such a thing: to kill righteous with wicked,
b'. so that the righteous are like the wicked.
a'. Far be it from you
B'. Abraham's Directive (v. 25)
a. Shall the judge of
b. all the land
a'. not do justice?

---

16. Lundbom, "Parataxis, Rhetorical Structure," 141.

A'. Yahweh's Responses: Commissives (+ Abraham's Assertives) (vv. 26–32)
Yahweh: If I find in Sodom fifty righteous in the city, I will forgive the whole place for their sake.
Abraham: (+Behabitive,[17] v. 27) Perhaps (*'ulay*) five of the fifty are lacking. *Will you destroy the whole city for lack of five?*
Yahweh: I will not destroy it if I find forty-five there.
Abraham: Perhaps (*'ulay*) forty are found there.
Yahweh: I will not do it for the sake of the forty.
Abraham: (+Behabitive, v. 30) Perhaps (*'ulay*) thirty are found there.
Yahweh: I will not do it if I find thirty there.
Abraham: (+Behabitive, v. 31) Perhaps (*'ulay*) twenty are found there.
Yahweh: I will not destroy it for the sake of the twenty.
Abraham: (+Behabitive) Perhaps (*'ulay*) ten are found there.
Yahweh: I will not destroy it for the sake of the ten.

Figure 5

The outer framework follows the specific questions through which Abraham questions Yahweh in light of a potential world in which there are fifty righteous in the city (A), and then Yahweh's initial response followed by responses to Abraham subsequently and continuously reducing the number (A'). Abraham's first two questions serve to direct Yahweh to think about how God will act if there are fifty righteous in the city.[18] The illocutionary force of this assertive is impacted by the word "perhaps" (*'ulay*), allowing it to function more like a directive to consider the propositional content than as an assertive which must be critiqued for its fit with the world.[19] Indeed, the direction of fit for the success of this utterance does not depend upon fitting this world; it must only fit with Abraham's imagination. In fact, neither Abraham nor

---

17. A behabitive is an utterance that relies upon societal conventions, including speeches made with the intention of being polite. Austin, *How to Do Things with Words*, 152. For a study on the politeness of Abraham's intercession, see Bridge, "Abraham's Dialogue with God in Genesis 18."

18. Interpreters are divided on whether Abraham is interceding for the entire city, or only for the righteous. For a discussion of this topic, see Lyons, *Canon and Exegesis*, 197–202.

19. Cf. the translation for *'ulay* here in the NRSV and NASB as "suppose."

Section 3: Prayers of Prophets

Yahweh claim to know how many righteous are in the city of Sodom. Earlier Yahweh had framed the subject of the investigation in terms of the greatness of the outcry and the gravity of the sin of the city; here Abraham is redirecting the search so that the focus is on the righteous in the city.

Before Yahweh responds to Abraham's question concerning the imaginary world, Abraham answers the question. He does so by using the phrase that is often translated "Far be it from you" as an *inclusio* (a, a') for describing the act of killing the righteous with the wicked (b), and treating the righteous like the wicked (b'). Brueggemann points to the manner in which the first word derives from the term meaning "to pollute" or "defile," so that acting in this way would violate Yahweh's holiness.[20] Abraham continues by asking, "Shall the judge of all the land not do justice?" When taken by itself, this question appears to be ambiguous as it conspicuously lacks *tsedaqah* to go with *mishpat*.[21] However, the question functions along with the previous assertive. As Miller states,

> The appeal of this intercessory prayer is to God's own way of being and acting in the world, the way of justice and righteousness. The question appeals to the character and reputation of God, to press the Lord to be and act according to the divine intention and nature.[22]

It can be noted that the chiasm (B) contains the word *tsadiq* and the chiasm B' concerns *mishpat*. Abraham's question directs Yahweh to think about Yahweh's own judgment, which is characterized by righteousness (unlike the judgment of earthly kings).[23]

---

20. Brueggemann, *Great Prayers*, 5–6. Brueggemann points out that the term "'holiness' (*qdš*) is the antithesis of the term 'profane' (*ḥll*)" (p. 5).

21. Lyons states that "the rhetorical question, 'shall not the Judge of all the earth do justice' [is] deeply ambiguous. Obviously, YHWH is that Judge (cf. vv. 20–21) and it is, so Abraham believes, unthinkable that the deity should act unjustly. But it is not clear what Abraham now considers justice to be..." (*Canon and Exegesis*, 193). MacDonald suggests that Abraham "did not rightly understand Yhwh" and points to his omission of "righteousness" as evidence. MacDonald goes on to suggest that Abraham is concerned with judicial procedure ("Listening to Abraham," 37).

22. Miller, *They Cried to the Lord*, 116–18, 269.

23. For a description of a human king's *mishpat*, see 1 Sam 8:11–17.

Persuaded, Yahweh responds by issuing a favorable judgment on behalf of the whole city for the sake of the fifty righteous that exist in Abraham's imagination. Then Abraham decreases the number of possible righteous in the assertive and restates his question. After Yahweh responds in the same manner as before, Abraham reduces the number four more times, each time using the qualifier "perhaps" (*'ulay*). Each time, Yahweh responds in the same way. By reducing the number of righteous in his imaginary city of Sodom and restating his question, Abraham demonstrates that the force of his intercessory question is not in the number of righteous, but the presence of the righteous.[24]

Moses's Prayer to Yahweh in Exodus 32

Yahweh's speech to Moses consists of two parts, one describing the situation involving the Israelites' apostasy and the other involving an imaginary world in which Yahweh commits to consuming the Israelites with divine wrath and starting over with Moses (see figure 6). Both sections start with similar directives for Moses to leave. However, as perlocutionary acts they function in an ironic way: Moses stays and becomes involved. As Childs famously noted, Yahweh's second directive ("Leave me alone") operates paradoxically as an invitation that opens up the possibility of intercession in a manner similar to that made by Abraham.[25]

Yahweh's Speech (vv. 7b–10)	Moses's Speech (vv. 11b–13)
A. Directive ("Go down at once") (v. 7ba)	A. Directive (Question) (v. 11ba)
B. Assertives concerning present situation (vv. 7bb–9): Description of Israelites ("your people"); Summary and description of their apostasy; Description of Israelites as stubborn	B. Assertives concerning present situation (vv. 11bb): Description of Israelites as "your people"
A′. Directive ("Now, leave me alone") (v. 10aa)	A′. Directive (Question) (v. 12aa)

---

24. After God determines that Sodom must be destroyed, angels urge Lot, a righteous man, to take his family far away from the doomed city (Gen 19:12–16; cf. 2 Pet 2:6–8).

25. Childs, *Exodus*, 567. Cf. Camp, "Prayer in the Pentateuch," 27.

Section 3: Prayers of Prophets

B'. Commissives (v. 10ab–10b): Yahweh's wrath against the Israelites; Yahweh's promise to Moses	B. Assertives (world-from-words) of resulting Egyptian speech (v. 12ab)
	A. Directives (12b–13): Yahweh's wrath against the Israelites; Yahweh's promise to Abraham

Figure 6

Moses begins his response to Yahweh with two questions (v. 11b–12a), each starting with "Why?" (*lamah*). These questions are clearly not intended as requests for information; if so, then the first question of why Yahweh's wrath burns against Yahweh's people is positioned immediately after the answer has been given! But as directives to think, these questions invite Yahweh to consider aspects of the situation that differ from the focus of Yahweh's opening speech.

Interpreters have noticed the way Moses uses his first question to counter Yahweh's designation of the Israelites as "your [Moses's] people" and to point out that it was Yahweh who brought them out of Egypt.[26] The Israelites are Yahweh's covenant people. Conspicuously, Moses then offers no assertive regarding the present actions of the Israelites. He removes that aspect of Yahweh's speech and replaces it with the question, "Why should the Egyptians say, 'With evil (*bera'ah*) he brought them out, to kill them in the mountains to consume them from the face of the earth?'" This directive utilizes a prayerful imagination as its accompanying assertive is similar to those offered by Abraham concerning the righteous in Sodom. Unlike Abraham, Moses does not utilize the qualifier "perhaps" (*'ulay*) in the world he creates with his words. Instead, he utilizes Yahweh's own description of the intended action to "consume" the Israelites and imagines how this will be construed by the Egyptians. Thus, Moses uses his second question to direct Yahweh to think about Yahweh's reputation rather than the Israelites' transgression, an approach similar to his intercession in Num 14:13–25. The force of such an appeal to Yahweh is not based on divine vanity,[27] but is tied to God's purpose in the world.[28] Bruckner states that

---

26. Camp, "Prayer in the Pentateuch," 28.
27. Against Propp, *Exodus 19–40*, 555.
28. Cf. Miller, *They Cried to the Lord*, 272.

"the sin of the people had put the reputation of the Lord's salvation at risk."[29] But Moses invites Yahweh to consider that Yahweh's reputation will only be damaged if God acts out of anger.

Amos's Prayers to Yahweh in Amos 7

Whereas most of the book of Amos directs God's message of judgment against Israel, two intercessory prayers by Amos for the nation appear in Amos 7:1–6. The prayers are brief and nearly identical, although the situations differ in the type and scope of calamity facing Israel. The first prayer includes a wide sweeping request to forgive (v. 2b) whereas the second request asks Yahweh to stop the punishment (v. 5b). For both, Amos utilizes the same question ("How can Jacob stand?"), followed by the same assertive, "He is so small" (see figure 7).

Amos's First Plea (v. 2b)	Amos's Second Plea (v. 5b)
Speech situation: vision of the Lord Yahweh forming locusts that ate up the grass of the land.	*Speech situation*: vision of the Lord Yahweh calling to contend by fire, which devoured the great deep and was devouring the plot [of land].
Expressive ("O Lord Yahweh")	Expressive ("O Lord Yahweh")
Directive ("Please forgive")	Directive ("Please cease")
Directive ("How can Jacob stand?")	Directive ("How can Jacob stand?")
Assertive ("He is so small!")	Assertive ("He is so small!")

Figure 7

While there are differences in Amos's argument when compared to the intercession of Abraham and Moses (most conspicuously in length, but also in content),[30] the function of the questions remains consistent. As in the prayers of Abraham and Moses, the question functions as a directive to think about the situation according to the prayerful imagination of the prophet. Interpreters have noticed that this prayer appeals to God's nature, including Yahweh's mercy and tendency to side

---

29. Bruckner, *Exodus*, 284–85.

30. E.g., Paul (*Amos*, 229) notes that in these prayers Amos "does not call upon the traditional guarantees of salvation, nor does he cite the Lord's promises to the patriarchs. The prayer, moreover, is not even motivated by a reminder of Israel's election." Paul goes on to point out that for Amos, Israel's election is actually connected to the punishment (Amos 3:2).

Section 3: Prayers of Prophets

with the weak. Calling the nation by the name Jacob also directs Yahweh to consider the beginnings of God's relationship with this people. When followed by the assertive ("He is so small!") the question also functions as an indirect assertive that presents a case that Israel will not survive the punishment. Apparently, Amos does not think that he must direct Yahweh here to think about God's justice (so Abraham) or God's covenant and reputation (so Moses), but simply to consider the devastating results that the implementation of the visions will have on Israel. Perhaps then Yahweh's mercy will work on its own (cf. the way in which Yahweh's compassion leads God to act mercifully after Yahweh asks questions in Hos 11:8–9).

Yahweh's Dialogue with Jonah in Jonah 4

While the conversations between Yahweh and Jonah do not include an intercessory prayer, a strong case can be made that the story should have included an intercessory prayer! This passage can be set in dialogue with the other passages already discussed due to similarities involving the speech situation and especially the function of questions utilized by Yahweh. Yahweh first asks Jonah questions that attempt to redirect the prophet's perspective of his own response to God's grace toward the city of Nineveh, and then asks the sort of question that Jonah could have (should have?) directed toward Yahweh in an act of intercession for the city.

As with the previous passages, the situation involves Yahweh's judgment and the imminent destruction of an offending party, in this case the city of Nineveh. Yahweh opens up the conversation with the prophet in the beginning of the story by issuing directives (Jonah is to go to Nineveh and cry out against it) and revealing God's plans to respond to the city's wickedness (Jonah 1:1–2). This is a perfect opportunity for Jonah to intercede for the wicked city by directing Yahweh to consider other possible aspects of the situation, for example, that this people cannot stand up to God, that they lack sufficient knowledge, that there as so many humans, or that animals would be affected as well. These ideas do appear in the story but not from the mouth of Jonah (see Jonah 4:11). Jonah responds to Yahweh's directives by fleeing from Yahweh's presence (Jonah 1:3), and later obeys when Yahweh directs him a second time (Jonah 3:1–4). It should be noted that Jonah prays twice in the story (Jonah 2:1–9 [2–10]; 4:2–3).³¹ While both of his prayers utilize questions, neither of them are intercessory prayers but rather attempts to focus God's attention on Jonah.

Unlike the previous passages, this exchange between Jonah and Yahweh occurs after Yahweh has acted on behalf of a sinful group (Jonah 3:10). Jonah's prayer reveals that his knowledge of God's character was the very reason he had initially fled in response to Yahweh's call (Jonah 4:2). The irony of this response to the potential of God's grace, when compared to other discussions of the topic in Scripture, has not been lost on interpreters.³² Yahweh's first question is framed in general terms and directs Jonah to consider whether or not his current anger is appropriate, "Is it right for you to be angry?" (Jonah 4:4). After receiving no verbal response, God appoints a bush to give shade to Jonah and then a worm to kill the bush (Jonah 4:6–7). Yahweh then asks a similar but specific question, "Is it right for you to be angry about the bush?" (Jonah 4:9) This time Yahweh succeeds in prompting Jonah to respond, although Jonah's response shows he has failed to re-think his anger (see Jonah 4:9–10).

After the initial questions, Yahweh contrasts Jonah's lack of commitment to the plant with God's own commitment to the city of Nineveh. Yahweh asks, "Should I not be concerned concerning Nineveh, the great city, in which there are more than a hundred and twenty thousand humans (*'adam*) who do not know their right hand from their left, and also many animals (*behemah*)?" (Jonah 4:11). Yahweh's reference to Ninevites as humans (*'adam*) casts the situation in a way that fits with God's creative act in Gen 1, which celebrates all humanity (*'adam*) as made in God's image. The reference to the animals (*behemah*) in

---

31. For a study of these prayers, see Mann, "Performative Prayers of a Prophet," 20–40.

32. E.g., Simon points out that "the Lord's attributes of mercy and compassion are expressed as a more or less standard trope that is always invoked to praise Him . . . Only Jonah, the proponent of rigid justice, presents them as the reason for his flight from his God and disobedience to His command" (*Jonah*, 35). JoAnna Hoyt remarks that "Jonah, knowing exactly who Yahweh is, decides he does not want Yahweh to be gracious and merciful . . . So Jonah's actions in ch. 1 are an attempt to prevent Yahweh from acting like God" (*Amos, Jonah, & Micah*, 501).

the city not only fits with Genesis 1 but also to the covenant that God makes with Noah (see Gen 9:9–11).[33] With these descriptions Yahweh defends the act of giving grace to Nineveh. Indeed, these are the very questions that Jonah could have used to redirect Yahweh's focus away from the wickedness of the city and toward aspects of the situation that would help God consider responding with grace.

CONCLUSIONS

Conclusions on the Story Level

Patrick Miller suggests that the primary intent of the great intercessors in the Old Testament is "to divert the divine anger [from] the sin of the people, as, for example, Abraham does for Sodom and Gomorrah, Moses for the sinful community in the wilderness, Amos for the sins of the Northern Kingdom."[34] The present study agrees with this assessment, but notes that in all three cases this act of diverting God's anger is one that is prompted by God. Miller goes on to identify the function of motive clauses within these prayers: "In the broadest sort of way, they tend either to draw attention to some feature of God's *nature and character* or to lift up some aspect of *the situation of the petitioner(s)*."[35] The present study suggests that it is the questions in these intercessory prayers that contribute to the aim identified by Miller.

By asking God questions, the intercessor directs Yahweh to think about the situation in ways that guide Yahweh to respond favorably to the petition. Abraham uses his questions to participate in Yahweh's decision concerning Sodom by directing Yahweh's attention to the (possible) righteous rather than the wicked people in Sodom. Moses uses questions to direct Yahweh's focus away from the people's apostasy and toward Yahweh's covenant with them. In addition, by his questions, Moses guides Yahweh to consider one outcome of proceeding with the decision to destroy the Israelites and start over with Moses. Amos uses one question in two prayers, to direct Yahweh to consider the frailty of God's people and thus the need for Yahweh to forgive and to cease. In

---

33. Interpreters have noticed the ways in which the book of Jonah portrays Yahweh as the creator and thus the God of all the earth. E.g., Limburgh, *Jonah*, 34.

34. Miller, *They Cried to the Lord*, 90.

35. Miller, *They Cried to the Lord*, 116 [italics original].

each of these cases, the intercessor prays in response to God's prompting, which suggests that God invites the opportunity to think about aspects of these situations in ways that will lead God to respond favorably to the intercessor. The prophets do not engage in acts of manipulation of God, but of joining with God.[36]

Conclusions on the Storyteller Level (Application)

Many interpreters consider the abrupt ending to the book of Jonah as an invitation for the audience to reflect on God's question. God's directive to Jonah can therefore function as a bridge between the story level and the storyteller level of interpretation. While it is unknown whether Jonah on the story level is aware of the intercessory prayers of Abraham, Moses, and Amos, an audience who knows those stories might also reflect on the similarities of the questions posed to God by these great intercessors. The questions within the intercessory prayers do not simply influence God, but can influence the listening audience in at least a couple of ways.

First, the intercessory prayers in these texts might challenge us to incorporate questions as we pray for others. We might try asking God to consider aspects of their situation that fit with God's purposes for the world and for God's people. In addition to strengthening the force of our prayer, such an act would also serve to remind both us and our communities of God's grace and our mission to the world that God so loves. It also might encourage us to become more familiar with the situation facing the person or group for whom we are praying. Asking God questions in these prayers has the potential to strengthen our prayers as well as our relationship with God and each other.

Second, the questions in these prayers might also transform our own prayerful imaginations as we consider how God attempted to change Jonah's imagination. With Abraham, we might imagine that sin does not automatically have the final word, even in our fallen world. We might be encouraged to live in this world, knowing that the presence of the righteous fosters a hope for repentance and redemption in

---

36. Cf. Camp, who says that "prayer in no way manipulates or forces God to act. Though prayer is relational, it is not a relationship of equals" ("Prayer in the Pentateuch," 29).

Section 3: Prayers of Prophets

the world (cf. Jesus speaking of God's people as the salt and light of the world in Matt 5:13–16). Admittedly, we would also acknowledge that there is eventually a time for God's judgment against the world. With Moses and Amos, we might see a hope of God giving God's people second and third chances, achieving divine purposes even when God's people fall short. Admittedly, we would also be aware, with Moses and Amos, that there is a time for God's judgment against God's people. These prayers do more than teach us how to pray, they can teach us how to live as God's people. The questions in these intercessory prayers might at times redirect our focus away from a purely judgmental attitude to one that first remembers, and appeals to, the gracious character of God.

BIBLIOGRAPHY

Austin, John L. *How to Do Things with Words*, edited by J. O. Urmson and Marina Sbisà. Cambridge, MA: Harvard University Press, 1975.

Ben Zvi, Ehud. "The Dialogue Between Abraham and YHWH in Gen 18:23–32: A Historical Critical Analysis." *JSOT* 17 (1992) 27–46.

Bridge, Edward. "Abraham's Dialogue with God in Genesis 18." *JSOT* 40 (2016) 281–96.

Bruckner, James K. *Exodus*. NIBC. Peabody, MA: Hendrickson, 2008.

Brueggemann, Walter. *Great Prayers of the Old Testament*. Louisville: Westminster John Knox, 2008.

Camp, Phillip G. "Prayer in the Pentateuch." In *Praying with Ancient Israel: Exploring the Theology of Prayer in the Old Testament*, edited by Phillip G. Camp and Tremper Longman III, 21–36. Abilene, TX: Abilene Christian University Press, 2015.

Childs, Brevard. *The Book of Exodus*. OTL. Louisville: Westminster, 1974.

Chisholm, Robert B., Jr., "Anatomy of an Anthropomorphism: Does God Discover Facts?" *BibSac* 164 (2007) 3–20.

Fretheim, Terence. *The Suffering of God: An Old Testament Perspective*. OBT. Philadelphia: Fortress, 1984.

Goldingay, John. *Old Testament Theology: Volume Three: Israel's Life*. Downers Grove, IL: IVP Academic, 2009.

Hoyt, JoAnna M. *Amos, Jonah, & Micah*, edited by H. Wayne House and William D. Barrick. Evangelical Exegetical Commentary. Bellingham: Lexham, 2018.

Limburgh, James. *Jonah*. OTL. Louisville: Westminster John Knox, 1993.

Lundbom, Jack R. "Parataxis, Rhetorical Structure, and the Dialogue Over Sodom in Genesis 18." In *The World of Genesis: Persons, Places, Perspectives*, edited by Philip R. Davies and David J. A. Clines, 136–45. Sheffield: Sheffield Academic, 1998.

Lyons, William J. *Canon and Exegesis: Canonical Praxis and the Sodom Narrative*. London: Sheffield Academic, 2002.

Mann, Steven T. "Ask and You Shall Intercede: The Peculiar Perlocutionary Power of Asking God Questions." *BBR* 29 (2019) 208–224.

———. "Performative Prayers of a Prophet: Investigating the Prayers of Jonah as Speech Acts," *CBQ* 79 (2017) 20–40.

———. *Run David Run! An Investigation of the Theological Speech Acts of David's Departure and Return (2 Samuel 14–20)*. Siphrut 10. Winona Lake, IN.: Eisenbrauns, 2013.

MacDonald, Nathan. "Listening to Abraham—Listening to Yhwh: Divine Justice and Mercy in Genesis 18:16–33." *CBQ* 66 (2004) 25–43.

Miller, Patrick D. *They Cried to the Lord: The Form and Theology of Biblical Prayer*. Minneapolis: Fortress, 1994.

Paul, Shalom M. *Amos*. Hermeneia. Minneapolis: Fortress, 1991.

Propp, William H. C. *Exodus 19–40*. AB. New York: Doubleday, 2006.

Searle, John R. *Expression and Meaning: Studies in the Theory of Speech Acts*. New York: Cambridge University Press, 1979.

———. *Speech Acts: An Essay in the Philosophy of Language*. Cambridge: Cambridge University Press, 1969.

Searle, John, and Daniel Vanderveken, *Foundations of Illocutionary Logic*. New York: Cambridge University Press,1985.

Simon, Uriel. *Jonah*. JPS Bible Commentary. Philadelphia: Jewish Publication Society, 1999.

Section 4

Prayers of Others

10

Prayers of Women in the Old Testament Narratives
A Theological Exploration

PHILLIP G. CAMP

INTRODUCTION

WHILE INSTANCES OF RECORDED prayers abound in the Old Testament, only a few are prayed by women. In his *They Cried to the Lord*, Patrick Miller finds only twelve prayers of women, eleven in the narratives and one psalm, out of nearly three hundred prayers in the OT.[1] This study focuses on the prayers of women in the OT narratives listed by Miller, though with expansions or modifications to his textual boundaries.[2]

---

1. Miller, *They Cried to the Lord*, 233. On p. 413n2, Miller lists the following prayer texts: Gen 21:16–17; 25:22; 29:35; 30:24; Exod 15:21; Judg 5:1–31; Ruth 1:8–9; 4:14; 1 Sam 1:10, 12–15; 2:1–10; 1 Kgs 10:9; Ps 131 (often attributed to a mother). Whether Ps 131 is, in fact, written by a woman is far from certain. See, e.g., Goldingay, *Psalms: Volume 3*, 543, and DeClaissé-Walford, *Psalms*, 932.

2. One could expand the sample by including the prayers of women in the Apocrypha (Tob 3:10–17; 8:4–7; Jdt 8:31; 9; 12:8; 13:7, 14; 16:1–17; Add Esth 14:3–19; Sus 13:42–45), but a study of these texts goes beyond the scope of this chapter.

Section 4: Prayers of Others

While men likely composed the OT narrative books and at times adapted the prayers in these stories to fit their narrative and theological purposes,³ it is reasonable to conclude that women's prayers in the narratives represent their authentic prayers, or the *ipsissima vox* of such prayers. At the very least, the prayers represent the *kinds* of prayers women prayed in ancient Israel. That is, the writers would have wanted their audiences to consider the prayers as plausibly coming from women.

THE TEXTS

Hagar (Genesis 16:7–14; 21:16–19)⁴

16:7–14

In Gen 16:7–14, Hagar encounters "the angel of the LORD" after she flees from Sarai. Through the angel, God initiates contact by asking Hagar where she has come from and where she is going. Hagar's response is not really a petition. She simply replies that she is fleeing from Sarai. The text, however, indicates that God understands what stands behind her response because the name she is to give her son, Ishmael, means "God has heard." The second part of v. 11 then indicates what God has heard is her affliction (*'oni*). The shocking thing here is that, rather than alleviating her immediate suffering, Yahweh has just commanded her to return and "submit to" or "be afflicted" (*'anah*) by her mistress (v. 9; cf. v. 6). Perhaps God did so because at least it gave Hagar the more protective environment of a home, rather than being on her own in the wilderness of northern Sinai on the way to Shur, which would have been a recipe for disaster for a lone, pregnant woman. Hagar also receives the promise of an uncountable multitude of descendants through Ishmael (v. 10), echoing the promise just given to Abram (Gen 15:5).

Hagar's response is to give Yahweh a new name, a praise name, El-roi, which can be translated "God of seeing" (i.e., the "all-seeing God"), "God of my seeing" (i.e., "whom I have seen"), or "God who sees me."⁵

---

3. Some have proposed that women produced, at least at the oral stage, the story of Ruth. E.g., Tischler, "Ruth," 158–60; Dijk-Hemmes, "Ruth," 134–39.

4. For discussions of women's prayers in the Pentateuch, see also my "Prayer in the Pentateuch."

5. Sarna, *Genesis*, 121. Sarna says all of these meanings were likely to have been

Despite the translation difficulties, the point is that Hagar recognizes that she has encountered God personally. Furthermore, even when God compels her to return to a situation of affliction and forces her to bear up under it for a time, God is aware and offers her hope for the future. Hagar's new appellation for God shows that she understood God in this way.

21:16–19

In Gen 21, Abraham, at the demand of Sarah and at God's instruction, sends Hagar and Ishmael from his camp. After their water runs out, Hagar puts her son under a bush and moves off a distance so she will not have to watch him die. Verse 16 says that "she[6] lifted up her voice and wept."[7] The text says that God responds, not to her cry (at least not explicitly in the text), but to the boy's cry (twice noted in v. 17).

So, is there a prayer by Hagar here? Miller argues that there is. He notes that her statement in v. 16, "Do not let me look on the death of the child" is a request rather than a statement. He adds, "Her weeping is typical of those who cry out to God in affliction."[8] What follows, particularly the oracle of salvation addressed to Hagar, further supports the claim that God also heard a prayer from Hagar.[9] The responses include a promise that God will make Ishmael into a great nation and God delivering Hagar and Ishmael from the current distress by pointing her to a source of water.

Rebekah (Genesis 25:22–23)

In Gen 25:22, Rebekah laments concerning her pregnancy, "If it is to be this way, why do I live?" Or, more literally, she says, "If thus, why this, I" (*'im ken lammah zeh 'anokhi*), perhaps reflecting her utter confusion. She inquires of Yahweh and receives the answer that she is carrying twins, the progenitors of two nations. Their struggles in her

---

heard in this name.

6. The LXX has "they lifted up their voice, and the boy cried."
7. Unless otherwise noted, all citations of the Bible are from the NRSV.
8. Miller, *They Cried to the Lord*, 235.
9. Miller, *They Cried to the Lord*, 235.

womb anticipate the struggles between her sons and the nations that will come from them. In this case, she gets no relief from Yahweh, but, rather, a remarkable insight into Israel's future geo-political affairs with its dominance over its neighbor Edom. Prayer opened insights into God's plans for the near and distant future.

Leah and Rachel (Genesis 29:35; 30:6, 17–18, 22–24)

In the rivalry for children between Leah and Rachel in Gen 29–30, some of the sons' names are direct responses to a plea of the mother to God. Judah's name means "praise" because, in light his birth, Leah says, "This time I will praise (*yadah*) the LORD" (29:35) Thus, Judah's name reflects an address to God, who is exalted for granting her yet another son.

Joseph's birth comes because God finally remembers and hears Rachel, and God opens her womb (30:22–24). What did God hear? Rachel indicates the nature of her prayer in her claim, "God has taken away my reproach." Thus, God has removed the shame of not having a son. In naming her son Joseph, a play on "add" or "continue" (*yasaf*), her prayer goes on, "May the LORD add to me another son." This prayer will be answered in the birth of Benjamin (35:16–20).

Other namings by Leah and Rachel recognize that God has acted. The accounts of the names given to Dan and Issachar indicate that God responded to direct pleas, though their contents are not recorded. In Gen 30:6, Dan receives his name in light of Rachel's plan to raise up children through her servant Bilhah. Rachel exclaims, "God has judged (*din*) me[10] and also heard my voice and given me a son." Thus, she understands the son as God's response to her voice and God's vindication of her over against her sister. Issachar's name is linked to the story of Leah's exchange of her mandrakes for Rachel's night with Jacob (Gen 30:14–18). "God heard (*shamaʿ*) Leah" and she has another son. His name, Issachar, is a praise name that plays on "hired" (*sakhar*) because "God has given me my hire because I gave my maid to my husband." The impression here is that Leah had requested another child and God responded.[11]

---

10. Or perhaps better, with the NASB and NIV, "vindicated me."

11. See also Gen 29:32–33. Leah invokes God's seeing (*ra'ah*) and hearing

These prayers arise out of the women's personal or socially debilitating circumstances. Leah seeks from God the only thing she can think of to win her husband's love, the one thing Rachel cannot offer for a long time, children. Rachel seeks from God removal of the cultural shame that she endures by not bearing children ("my reproach" in 30:23). She appeals to God, who alone, in her view, opens and closes wombs and so is responsible for her situation (29:31; 30:2, 22).

It appears that God take sides between the sisters, particularly favoring Leah at first, and their prayers suggest this may be how they interpreted the situation at times. However, God meets a need of both Leah and Rachel, for love and to remove shame, respectively. God shows compassion on both, though not necessarily as they would have preferred, particularly Rachel, who has to wait a long time to give birth to her first child. The prayers associated with their sons' names indicate their gratitude to God and become a praise and witness to the God who has heard and responded.

Miriam (Exodus 15:21)

In Exod 15:21, after God defeats the Egyptian army at the Red Sea, Miriam leads the women in a victory celebration and sings to them, "Sing to the LORD, for he has triumphed gloriously; horse and rider he has thrown into the sea."

While some argue that Miriam wrote the longer song in 15:1–18,[12] v. 1 says only that "Moses and the Israelites sang this song to the LORD," with no attribution of authorship. In the literary context, her song in 15:21 repeats the opening line (v. 1b) of the longer song. In doing so, she calls to mind the whole song. Thus, her praise evokes the full range of the song in 15:1–18. Miriam's praise, therefore, recognizes Yahweh as a defender, savior, and warrior, who overcomes those who foolishly oppose him. It also acknowledges Yahweh as the unmatched God who

---

(*shama'*), respectively, when she names Reuben (*re'uven*) and Simeon (*shim'on*), because she believes God saw her affliction and heard that she was hated. In these cases, there is no indication of a previous address to God, but simply that God is aware and responds.

12. E.g., Carol Meyers says, "The accumulated weight of literary, textual, historical, sociological, musicological, and feminist research on Exodus 15 indicates that Miriam is the more likely author" (*Exodus*, 116).

redeems his people because of his covenantal love (*khesed*; v. 13). The song portrays Yahweh's victory over Egypt through the unleashing of Yahweh's power over creation. Furthermore, Yahweh's victory has "universal effect"[13] because the "peoples heard, they trembled." Miriam's brief praise reminds readers of how Yahweh's actions have affected the people of Israel as a whole and have implications for the world.

Deborah (Judges 5)

In Judg 5, Deborah, along with Barak, sings a song as praise to Yahweh in light of the victory recounted in Judg 4. Though both Deborah and Barak are named, Deborah is likely the one responsible for the song.[14] Beyond the recitation of Yahweh's actions that serve as praise, there are two specific calls to "bless" (*barakh*; vv. 2, 9) and the imprecation "so perish all your enemies, O Lord!" (v. 31).[15]

Deborah praises Yahweh as a warrior who defeats the enemies of Israel, a fact that reverberates beyond Israel. The praise celebrates an actual victory for Israel, particularly through the roles of Deborah (vv. 7, 12–15) and Jael (vv. 24–27). Beyond the immediate victory, the song-prayer gives insights into the social, political, and religious world of Israel[16] and indicates the creation-wide effects of Yahweh's action. The earth shakes and the heavens pour out their water in light of Yahweh's coming (vv. 4–5). The stars join the battle against Sisera (v. 20). Furthermore, kings and princes are instructed to "hear" (v. 3). Thus, Deborah's song-prayer celebrates Yahweh's deliverance of God's covenant people, prays that Yahweh will deal with future enemies and

---

13. Fretheim, *Exodus*, 168.

14. The verb in v. 1, is third person feminine singular (cf. the similar construction in Num 12:1). Furthermore, in v. 7, the verb (*shaqqamti*) in the MT is most naturally read as a first person common singular, pointing to Deborah as the author/speaker: "I, Deborah" (so the NIV, ESV, NASB). However, some read it as an archaic second person feminine singular form: "You, Deborah" (so the NRSV). Given that Deborah is identified as one of the singers, the first person common singular makes sense (Webb, *Judges*, 195n44). For a list of arguments supporting Deborah's authorship, see Block, *Judges, Ruth*, 214–15.

15. Webb refers to v. 31a as the "closing prayer" of the song (*Judges*, 217).

16. Block, *Judges, Ruth*, 216–17.

uphold those who love (obey) him, and expresses the effects of Yahweh's action beyond Israel.

Naomi's Blessings (Ruth 1:8b–9a; 2:20)

1:8b–9a

In Ruth 1:8b–9, Naomi offers a brief prayer on behalf of her daughters-in-law as she tells them to return home: "May the LORD deal kindly with you, as you have dealt with the dead and with me. The LORD grant that you may find security, each of you in the house of your husband." It may be that Naomi believes that, in her own destitute state, she cannot repay the daughters'-in-law kindness towards her, so she invokes Yahweh's kindness or covenantal love (*khesed*) on their behalf.[17] She further prays for their "security" (*menukhah*), defined as finding new husbands. From Naomi's perspective, Yahweh's *khesed* toward these widowed women can find expression only through the security offered within a man's household. Naomi's prayer also shows that she believes that Yahweh cares about these foreign women[18] and that Yahweh can act on their behalf because Yahweh's "authority and presence extended to lands outside Israel."[19]

2:20

In Ruth 2:20, when Ruth returns from gleaning in Boaz's field, she says, "Blessed be he by the LORD, whose kindness (*khesed*) has not forsaken the living or the dead!" (v. 20a). Naomi recognizes Yahweh's *khesed* in the providential events that led Ruth to the field of her husband's near relative. How Yahweh has shown kindness to the living, Ruth and Naomi, is obvious. Through Boaz, Yahweh had provided food for them. How Yahweh has shown kindness to the dead is less obvious, until Naomi identifies Boaz as one close to them, from among their redeemers (*go'el*) (v. 20b).

---

17. Sakenfeld, *Ruth*, 24–25.
18. Block, *Judges, Ruth*, 633–34.
19. Hubbard, *Ruth*, 103.

Section 4: Prayers of Others

The Women of Bethlehem (Ruth 4:14)

In Ruth 4:14, after Yahweh enables Ruth to conceive and she gives birth to Obed, the women speak to Naomi and proclaim praise to Yahweh in the form of a blessing: "Blessed be the LORD, who has not left you this day without a redeemer; and may his name be renown in Israel!" (ESV).[20] With respect to Naomi, the praise acknowledges that God has provided her with what she needed for well-being, a kinsman-redeemer. The redeemer referred to here could be Boaz, but more likely it is the child, since he will receive Elimelech's inheritance and take care of Naomi in her old age.[21] The reason for the praise is elaborated in v. 15a, "He shall be a restorer of your life and a nourisher of your old age."

Ruth's son is also likely the one whose name the women pray will be renowned, though the phrase could be praise to Yahweh. The fact that the son is the subject of v. 15, which flows from v. 14, makes the son the most likely antecedent of the pronoun in "his renown."[22] Or, as Brittany Kim suggests, "The ambiguity may be intentional, and the book fulfills both aims, extolling Yahweh for his gracious deliverance of Naomi and perpetuating the name of her grandson, Obed."[23]

The women address their praise toward Yahweh, whom they see as the one who was both willing and able to provide the widowed Naomi with what she needed for survival. Yahweh's care works itself out through natural processes: a devoted daughter-in-law, a redeemer who is willing to step up, and the birth of a child.[24]

Hannah (1 Samuel 1:10–16; 2:1–10)

First Samuel presents two prayers of Hannah, both linked to her desire for a son.[25] The basis for her predicament is the shame that a married woman in her culture experienced by not having a child, a situation

---

20. The NRSV's translation of *goʾel* as "next-of-kin" obscures the functional aspect of the role.
21. Hubbard, *Ruth*, 271; Bush, *Ruth/Esther*, 253–54.
22. Campbell, *Ruth*, 163–64; Hubbard, *Ruth*, 271.
23. Kim, "Prayer in Ruth and Esther," 122.
24. Kim, "Prayer in Ruth and Esther," 122–23.
25. Hannah is the only woman in the OT said specifically to pray (*pll*, 1:10, 12, 26–27; 2:1). See Bergen, *1, 2 Samuel*, 67.

exacerbated by a rival wife who taunts her and a seemingly oblivious husband (1:6–8). As in the case of Leah and Rachel, the text indicates that Yahweh had closed her womb (1:5, 6) and would eventually "remember" her (1:19). Thus, Yahweh has put her in this situation, so she must appeal to Yahweh for relief.[26]

1:10–16

In 1:10–16, Hannah comes to Yahweh as a lamenter. She is, literally, "bitter of soul" (*marath nafesh*, v. 10) and she weeps intensely while she silently prays (v. 10, 12–13). The prayer includes both a vow (v. 11) and an interior struggle, which she describes to Eli as "pouring out my soul before the LORD" (v. 15) and "speaking out of my great anxiety and vexation" (v. 16). In her vow, she addresses Yahweh as "LORD of hosts," one with cosmic power, while deferentially referring to herself three times as "your servant" (*'amatekha*). She appeals to Yahweh as the one who can see her affliction, remember her, and grant to her what she believes she needs to relieve her affliction, a son. She does so from the acknowledged position of dependence of a servant who turns to her caring master for relief.

2:1–10

In 2:1–10, Hannah prays (*pll*) and says (*'mr*) her response to God, who has answered her previous prayer by "remembering her" and giving her a son, Samuel.[27] Thus, she celebrates the victory over her "enemies" (v. 1), including no doubt the mocking Peninnah (1:6). Her experience of the answered prayer leads her to declare that Yahweh is exceptional; there is no other like him (v. 2). In vindicating her, Yahweh stops what may have been the proud boasting of Peninnah, as the only child-bearing wife (v. 3). The reversals she describes in vv. 4–8 include the barren woman having seven children, though Hannah stops just short with five more beyond Samuel (v. 21).

---

26. Evans, *1 & 2 Samuel*, 16.

27. While Hannah could have composed the prayer in 2:1–10, it is also possible that she made use of an existing hymn to express her praise and thanksgiving. Evans, *1 & 2 Samuel*, 20.

Section 4: Prayers of Others

Hannah couches her own experiences of God within the larger framework of displays of God's power throughout the earth and for her nation. Hannah's recognition in her own life that "not by might does one prevail" (v. 9) allows her to commend this truth to others. According to David Firth, testimonies like Hannah's "insist that the experience of the one who prays is not unique, but rather representative of something more typical" with respect to Yahweh's working.[28] So much in her prayer expands beyond the birth of Samuel and extends to God's actions, set in cosmic terms, on behalf of a king (v. 10) who has yet to appear in the narrative. She speaks of Yahweh defeating warriors, killing and making alive, seating the poor with princes, and judging the ends of the earth (vv. 4, 6–8). Yahweh can do all of this for Hannah and others, including the anticipated king, because Yahweh is the incomparable Rock (v. 2), who owns the earth's pillars and set the world on them, thunders from heaven, and has jurisdiction over the ends of the earth (v. 10).

The Queen of Sheba (1 Kings 10:9)

In 1 Kgs 10:9 (cf. 2 Chr 9:8), the queen of Sheba witnesses for herself Solomon's wisdom and prosperity and the happiness of his court, and she bursts into a brief praise of Yahweh:

> Blessed be the LORD your God, who has delighted in you and set you on the throne of Israel! Because the LORD loved Israel forever, he has made you king to execute justice and righteousness.

In this praise, she acknowledges God's favorable disposition toward Solomon, which resulted in God placing him on the throne.[29]

While her assessment and praise no doubt arise from a royal perspective, her focus on the happiness of the court does not necessarily imply, as Walter Brueggemann asserts, that she has no regard or care for the average Israelite.[30] First, because the people are not mentioned as "happy" in the lead-up to her prayer does not necessitate Bruegge-

---

28. Firth, *1 & 2 Samuel*, 60.
29. Cf. 2 Sam 12:24–25.
30. Brueggemann, *1 & 2 Kings*, 133–34, 139.

mann's conclusion that "others do not count" and "nobody cares" about their happiness.[31] He argues from silence. Second, she states that Yahweh's purpose in making Solomon king was Yahweh's love (*'ahavah*) for Israel so that the king could work for the well-being of Israel, that is, "to execute justice and righteousness." The queen's praise echoes and confirms the observation of the people, following Solomon's wise decision in the case of the two prostitutes and the baby, that Solomon had wisdom from God "to execute justice" (1 Kgs 3:28; cf. 3:9–11). Furthermore, the praise demonstrates that Yahweh's actions have provided testimony to—indeed have elicited testimony from—foreigners about Israel's God.[32]

SUMMARY OBSERVATIONS ON WOMEN'S PRAYERS IN THE OT

This brief study of women's prayers in the OT suggests the following conclusions. First, we must be careful in thinking of a "typical" woman in Israel and, therefore, of "typical" prayers of women. There are common features of women's lives in that world, particularly that they were subjected to the constraints of a patriarchal society and their primary roles were as wives and mothers. Indeed, several of the prayers of women in the OT relate to concerns of having children and status within the household. Yet the OT narratives containing these prayers show that women in Israel are not uniform in status and experiences. There is a difference between a matriarch of a household like Sarah and a slave woman within the household like Hagar. The experiences of a lone wife like Rebekah differ from households with competing wives in polygamous marriages, like those of Rachel and Leah and of Hannah and Peninnah. The Queen of Sheba's situation is surely not as precarious as that of a widow like Naomi. Miriam, the prophet, and Deborah, the prophet and judge, occupy roles normally held by men in Israel, giving them more authority than the other Israelite women. So, as we consider these prayer texts, it becomes apparent that treating the

---

31. Brueggemann, *1 & 2 Kings*, 133–34.

32. Fretheim, *First and Second Kings*, 59, sees the queen's praise as a fulfillment of Solomon's prayer that Yahweh would care for him and Israel "so that all the peoples of the earth may know that the LORD is God; there is no other" (1 Kgs 8:60).

women as a monolithic entity is problematic. They represent a range on the socioeconomic spectrum and with respect to their roles and experiences.

These varying social locations and experiences affect what and how the women pray in their stories. Hagar's and Naomi's prayers come in response to situations of desperate need for personal survival. Leah's and Rachel's prayers reflect longing for what the other has, Leah's desire for Jacob's love and Rachel's desire for freedom from the shame and stigma of not having children. So, their prayers revolved around the same basic theme of children, but arise out of different motivations. As leaders within the community, the prayers of Miriam and Deborah are responses to what God has done and will do for the community. Hannah's prayer ventures into this territory as well. The queen of Sheba offers praise to God from her own perspective, one with a top-down view, seeing God's blessing through a royal lens.

Second, in light of the first point, it is a mistake to assume a limited or unique set of concerns for which women prayed in Israel. Having children or issues related to their children provide the grounds for many of the prayers of women in the OT. Thus, Leah, Rachel, and Hannah pray to have children and in response to having children. Rebekah inquires of God concerning the distress she has in her pregnancy, and Hagar prays for the well-being of her dying son. The women of Bethlehem praise God concerning the birth of Ruth's son and its benefit for Naomi. But men also prayed concerning children, including Abraham (Gen 15:1–21; 17:15–21) and Isaac (Gen 25:21). Like Hagar, David prays for his dying son (2 Sam 12:16–23). Admittedly, with respect to children, the motivations of women's and men's prayers can differ. The women are often moved by the desire for acceptance in the households and a sense of self-worth, while the men are concerned about the perpetuation of their family line.

Furthermore, women's prayers in the OT extend beyond children and matters related to the household. Their prayers reveal an awareness of and concern for God's activity within the national, international, and cosmic spheres. Miriam's, Deborah's, and Hannah's prayers move into these realms. They make theological claims about God's work in their immediate circumstances but also identify what God has done or will do on behalf of Israel or against the enemies of Israel. They also assert how those actions of God will reverberate into the larger creation. Miriam and Deborah pray about war and victory. The prayers of Hannah and the queen of Sheba speak, respectively, to the future and present political life of Israel in their contexts. The women who pray in the OT have a vested interest in the broader issues of life in Israel and the world and in the reputation of their God.

Third, prayers are offered within specific theological and social parameters whose effects the women feel. In his discussion of women's prayers, Miller focuses on Hagar's and Hannah's prayers, ones "that arise out of the affliction of women"[33] Even more, he says, their affliction not only arises out of the patriarchal system they are caught in but also "their suffering is ordained by God," who is therefore their only "recourse and help in their suffering." Miller further notes that recognizing this situation does not minimize the joy of Hannah's and Hagar's prayers, but it does reveal both how Israel thought of God and why they turned to God in their plights.[34]

In similar ways, other women who pray to God suffer because of what God has done. Rebekah's distressed confusion over her pregnancy is a result of God answering Isaac's prayer on her behalf (Gen 25:21). God opens Leah's womb (Gen 29:31) but has closed Rachel's for a long time (Gen 30:2; cf. 30:22), inflaming their rivalry. Ruth 1:6 says Yahweh "had considered his people and had given them food," implying that it was in God's hands whether or not there was famine, a root cause of Naomi's distress. The angel of Yahweh sends Hagar back to Sarai to be afflicted, and God later instructs Abraham to send Hagar and Ishmael away (Gen 16:9; 21:12–13). Thus, in keeping with Miller's point, they must appeal to the God whose sovereignty means, in some sense at least, that God is responsible for the predicaments that lead them to prayer. However, this situation is not unique to women's prayers. Laments from men in the OT also claim or recognize that God is responsible for their circumstances (e.g., Ps 22:1, 15; Jer 20:7–10; Job 6:4; 7:11–21; 9:13–18).

---

33. Miller, *They Cried to the Lord*, 233.
34. Miller, *They Cried to the Lord*, 239.

Section 4: Prayers of Others

Fourth, we should note more positive aspects of women's relationships with and understandings of God, as reflected in their prayers. God responds to the prayers of the barren, the widow, and the slave, who in turn respond to God. The women repeatedly offer praise as the response to God's action on their behalf, especially but not exclusively with respect to children. Leah praises God at the birth of Judah, and the townswomen on account of Ruth's son Obed, but Naomi also praises God's *khesed* in leading Ruth to Boaz's field. And Miriam, Deborah, and the queen of Sheba praise God for his actions on behalf of the people of Israel. While men may disregard them, women pray to and praise the God who sees (Gen. 16:13; 1 Sam 1:11) and hears them (Gen 16:11; 30:17, 22), the God who acts on their behalf. In Hagar's case, God opens before her an unexpected third way through her son Ishmael and his future. While, again, these types of prayers are not unique to women in Israel, their situations in society may make them all the more appreciative of the God who responds to them in these situations that may cause others to look down on or overlook them.

Fifth, access to God in prayer is not limited to channels that might exclude women. The prayer texts demonstrate that women are not obligated to go through men, whether their husbands or the exclusively male Israelite priesthood, to address God. They have immediate recourse to the Authority over these other authorities in their lives. Granted, Rebekah's inquiry may have been through a prophet or oracle.[35] If so, we are not told whether that person was male or female.[36] In any case, Rebekah's inquiry, if it was through a prophet or oracle, would be the exception rather than the rule in the stories of women's prayers. Nor do Hannah's prayers at the sanctuary contradict the claim. Hannah offers her own prayer. In fact, it is Hannah who has to correct the

---

35. Inquiring (*drsh*) of the Yahweh usually involves a prophetic figure or oracle (e.g., Exod 18:15; 1 Sam 9:6–9; 2 Kgs 22:13–20). See Wenham, *Genesis 16–50*, 175. Arnold, however, refers to Rebekah's inquiry as a prayer (*Genesis*, 232).

36. Such an intermediary could have been a woman, as indicated by Josiah's inquiry of the Yahweh through Huldah in 2 Kgs 22:13–20; 2 Chr 34:19–28. If prophets like Moses (Exod 32:9–14, 30–34; Deut 5:23–29) and Samuel (1 Sam 7:5–9; 9:5–10) are an indication of the prophetic role, then Deborah, as a prophet, may have, in fact, served in the role as intermediary for Israel's prayers in her time.

priest's Eli's misperceptions, since he is unable to recognize anguished prayer when he sees it.

WOMEN'S PRAYERS IN THE OT AND THE CHURCH

The prayers of women in the OT remind the church that there is not a sharp divide between the prayers of women and men with respect to their concerns. I suspect this is what we witness in our churches on a regular basis as prayer requests are made by church members. Women and men alike are concerned about God's activity in their families, their communities, their nations, and their world. Both pray to God when trapped or harmed by the circumstances they find themselves in. Both trust in the sovereignty and power of God to respond, and, when God does respond, both express thanksgiving and praise.

Yet, though society and culture have changed greatly since the days of ancient Israel, circumstances particular to women continue because of their social location and cultural expectations that may trap them or create pain, anxiety, and despair. As with the women of the OT, these circumstances can elicit prayers unique to women. As the prayers of women in the OT demonstrate, in these times prayer becomes a means to engage and wrestle with God but also to trust in the sovereignty of God in the midst of those circumstances. However, the prayers of women in the OT remind us as well that socioeconomic and cultural differences exist among women that affect their experiences of the world, of men, and of other women. Thus, studying these women and their prayers can help the church become aware of the differences, the needs, and the concerns of women today that arise from their situations. Likewise, the church can join women in prayer for these concerns.

Finally, the women's prayers teach the church to praise God in those situations where the marginalization of women has been overcome, where their hurts have been healed, and where their needs have been met. Furthermore, knowing that church and society are not yet where we need to be with respect to how women are treated, the women's prayers in the OT can help us recognize that God reigns over the cosmos, bringing about the wholeness and healing that God intends for all creation and that God has initiated through the death and resurrection of our Lord Jesus Christ.

BIBLIOGRAPHY

Arnold, Bill T. *Genesis*. New Cambridge Bible Commentary. Cambridge: Cambridge University Press, 2009.

Bergen, Robert D. *1, 2 Samuel*. NAC. Nashville: Broadman & Holman, 1996.

Block, Daniel I. *Judges, Ruth*. NAC. Nashville: Broadman & Holman, 1999.

Brueggemann, Walter. *1 & 2 Kings*. SHBC. Macon, GA: Smyth & Helwys, 2000.

Bush, Frederic. *Ruth/Esther*. WBC. Dallas: Word, 1996.

Camp, Phillip G. "Prayer in the Pentateuch." In *Praying with Ancient Israel: Exploring the Theology of Prayer in the Old Testament*, edited by Phillip G. Camp and Tremper Longman III, 21–36. Abilene, TX: Abilene Christian University Press, 2015.

Campbell, Edward F., Jr. *Ruth: A New Translation with Introduction and Commentary*. AB 7. Garden City, NY: Doubleday, 1975.

DeClaissé-Walford, Nancy. *The Book of Psalms*. NICOT. Grand Rapids: Eerdmans, 2014.

Dijk–Hemmes, Fokkelien van. "Ruth: A Product of Women's Culture?" In *A Feminist Companion to Ruth*, edited by Athalya Brenner, 134–39. Sheffield: Sheffield Academic, 1993.

Evans, Mary J. *1 & 2 Samuel*. NIBC. Peabody, MA: Hendrickson, 2000.

Firth, David G. *1 & 2 Samuel*. AOTC. Downers Grove, IL: InterVarsity, 2009.

Fretheim, Terence E. *Exodus*. IBC. Louisville: John Knox, 1991.

———. *First and Second Kings*. Westminster Bible Companion. Louisville: Westminster John Knox, 1999.

Goldingay, John. *Psalms: Volume 3: Psalms 90–150*. BCOTWP. Grand Rapids: Baker, 2008.

Hubbard, Robert L., Jr. *The Book of Ruth*. NICOT. Grand Rapids: Eerdmans, 1988.

Kim, Brittany D. "Prayer in Ruth and Esther." In *Praying with Ancient Israel: Exploring the Theology of Prayer in the Old Testament*, edited by Phillip G. Camp and Tremper Longman III, 117–33. Abilene, TX: Abilene Christian University Press, 2015.

Meyers, Carol. *Exodus*. New Cambridge Bible Commentary. Cambridge: Cambridge University Press, 2005.

Miller, Patrick D. *They Cried to the Lord: The Form and Theology of Biblical Prayer*. Minneapolis: Fortress. 1994.

Sakenfeld, Katharine Doob. *Ruth*. IBC. Louisville: John Knox, 1999.

Sarna, Nahum M. *Genesis*. JPSTC. Skokie, IL: Jewish Publication Society, 1989.
Tischler, Nancy M. "Ruth." In *A Complete Literary Guide to the Bible*, edited by Leland Ryken and Tremper Longman III, 151–64. Grand Rapids: Zondervan, 1993.
Webb, Barry G. *The Book of Judges*. NICOT. Grand Rapids: Eerdmans, 2012.
Wenham, Gordon. *Genesis 16–50*. WBC. Dallas: Word, 1994.

11

Getting It Right While Getting It Wrong
Joshua's Prayer in Joshua 7

DAVID G. FIRTH

INTRODUCTION

THE BOOK OF JOSHUA is not noted as a major resource for a biblical theology of prayer.[1] Indeed, it only reports two prayers: Joshua's prayer after the initial failure of Israel to capture Ai (Josh 7:6–9) and his citation from the Book of Jashar in his southern campaign (Josh 10:12–14). In the latter case, although it is said that Joshua spoke to Yahweh and that Yahweh heeded him, the actual content of the prayer is far from clear since the words he cites are not actually directed in the first instance to Yahweh but rather to the sun and moon. The difficulties surrounding the interpretation of this passage means its contribution to a biblical theology of prayer will inevitably be contested. The same is not true of the earlier prayer which contains both words addressed

---

1. One might note that Miller's *They Cried to the Lord* provides only scattered references to Joshua and offers no sustained treatment of any passage from it. Brueggemann's *Great Prayers of the Bible* is admittedly a selective work, but one in which Joshua receives no mention. Balentine mentions this prayer (*Prayer in the Hebrew*, 121–23), though he does not consider it a major resource.

to Yahweh (Josh 7:6–9) and a response from Yahweh (Josh 7:10–15). If prayer is regarded as a form of dialogue with God, then it is only appropriate to consider both Joshua's words to Yahweh and Yahweh's words to Joshua as a specific case of how a prayer was answered, albeit in a way which is distinct from what Joshua seems to imply in the prayer.

Indeed, it will be argued in this essay that the distinctive contribution that this passage makes to a biblical theology of prayer is that it demonstrates the possibility that an authentic answer to prayer may not reflect the expected outcomes of the one who prays. Rather, God takes the intent of the one who prays into account so that, even though the prayer itself may be grounded in a wrong understanding of reality, God can restructure the understanding of those who pray so that God's answer is understood as appropriate for the circumstances. Within Josh 7, the narrative demonstrates this by providing a context that makes clear that Joshua's prayer is based on a false understanding of reality. It is this understanding that triggers the prayer. Yet, in spite of this wrong understanding, the prayer properly understands the character of God as foundational to prayer so that it can still be presented as an appropriate prayer. Accordingly, this essay will work through each major section of the text in order to situate the prayer and explore its main features before providing some concluding reflections on the distinctive contribution of this passage to the biblical theology of prayer.

THE NARRATIVE CONTEXT—JOSHUA 7:1–6

The book of Joshua is notable for some important shifts in narrative technique. It moves from external focalization in Josh 1:1—5:12, a technique in which the narrator withholds important information necessary for interpretation, to (mostly) zero focalization, a technique in which the narrator discloses key information for interpretation in Josh 5:13—11:23.[2] This change is clearly marked at Josh 7:1, which announces key information about Israel's sin and therefore Yahweh's anger before recounting the defeat at Ai. Here, even before any Israelites have gone to Ai, the narrator declares that Israel had acted treacherously (*ma'al*) with regard to those items that had been placed

---

2. See Firth, "Disorienting Readers."

Section 4: Prayers of Others

under the ban (*kherem*) at Jericho. Joshua 6:18 had made clear that a particularly strict interpretation of the ban was to be applied at Jericho. Subsequent application of it in the book allowed Israel to keep some booty—a tragedy that is particularly marked here by the fact that Israel was permitted to keep spoil from Ai (Josh 8:27). But not only had Israel acted treacherously, the treachery could be traced back to Achan, an Israelite of a clearly significant standing since his genealogy is traced back through four generations. When Achan is exposed as the source of Yahweh's anger against Israel, this genealogy is traced in reverse. But at this point in the narrative readers know considerably more than Joshua and the rest of the Israelites.[3]

This background knowledge means that readers know that all is not well when Joshua is then reported to have sent some spies to scout out the land. Unlike the two spies who had gone to Jericho and met Rahab (Josh 2), these spies appear to have done what Joshua asked. Moreover, they brought back what seems like militarily significant information about Ai.[4] Readers might subsequently deem their estimate of the numbers needed to take Ai to be rather optimistic in that the spies suggested to Joshua that a force of only two to three thousand was needed, arguing that because it was only small and difficult to reach there was no point in sending all the people. By contrast, when Yahweh later prepared a battle plan for the city's capture, he sent all the fighting men with Joshua, including a force of thirty thousand in his ambush alone (Josh 8:1–3).[5] On the other hand, as they journeyed to the city, the Israelites were unaware of the circumstances they were facing. As such, because Joshua's initial actions followed those employed at Jericho, the spies' confidence is understandable, even if it is later revealed to be hubris. The extent of their hubris becomes clear in Josh 8. They had

---

3. Source critics have often separated out an "Achan" story from an "Ai" narrative, but it is better to see Achan's story as an embedded element within the larger Ai story. See Winther-Nielsen, *Functional Discourse Grammar*, 216.

4. For the purposes of this essay, the contested questions about the location of Ai and how best to interpret the archaeological evidence are not addressed.

5. These numbers raise the inevitable question about how they are to be read. My own view is that "thousand" refers to the largest of Israel's military units, though the actual size of such a group was most likely considerably less than a thousand men. See Wenham, "Large Numbers." Fortunately, this issue does not bear directly on the interpretation of the prayer.

completely misjudged the situation, and it is reported immediately that a force of three thousand Israelites was defeated at Ai, with thirty-six killed. There are no reports of Israelite casualties at Jericho, making this statement even more shocking. Indeed, not only was Israel defeated, but they fled before the men of Ai to some local quarries.[6]

Faced with an unexpected defeat, the narrator reports that Israel's hearts melted, becoming like water. Attentive readers should recognize this language from elsewhere in the book. It was pivotal to Rahab's confession in Josh 2:11, describing the response of the Canaanite population to the exodus and the later defeats of Sihon and Og. Likewise, the hearts of the Canaanite kings are said to have melted when Yahweh dried up the waters of the Jordan (5:1), permitting Israel to enter the land of Canaan. In both instances, it refers to an inability to resist what Yahweh was doing through Israel. But now, it is Israel whose hearts melt, becoming like water. Indeed, this statement becomes a pivot that changes the response of the Canaanite peoples to Yahweh within the book of Joshua. Subsequently, when Canaanite kings hear about Israel, instead of their hearts melting, they gather to fight (Josh 9:1–2; 10:1–5; 11:1–5). The phrasing of these subsequent statements deliberately evokes the observation at Josh 5:1, except that they now are subverted precisely because of the fact that Israel's heart has melted here. What Israel does not know (though readers do) is that this defeat is not a failure on Yahweh's part. Rather, the failure of the spies' mission (however appropriate it initially seemed) and the subsequent defeat at Ai are to be understood as an expression of Yahweh's anger against Israel. Israel's treachery, enacted by Achan, has brought Israel to this point, though this is not something that Israel yet knows.

THE PRAYER—JOSHUA 7:6–9

The narrative setting thus generates a clear disconnect between what has been disclosed to readers and what the characters within the story know. Readers know that Israel's failure to capture Ai is not a result of a military failure but is rather the result of sin. But Israel and Joshua,

---

6. *Shebarim* could be a proper noun, coming from a root meaning "break." But, given that names of places were often descriptive of what happened there, then even if this is a proper noun it probably indicates the presence of some quarries.

Section 4: Prayers of Others

in particular, are unaware of this. Their perspective, like that of any believer who engages in prayer, does not have the luxury of looking back to align a perceived reality with the actual one. That is, the narrator of Josh 7 has carefully placed Joshua as he prays in response to this defeat into a setting that is typical of the experience of all who pray, indicating that there is vastly more to know about any context in which prayer is offered. Moreover, Joshua's personal position here matches that in which readers were placed in Josh 1:1—5:12, where how God was acting can be known only after the event. All of this means that there is a marked disconnect between Joshua's narrated understanding of his prayer and what the narrator is reporting about prayer because the basis on which Joshua prays is in fact contrary to what is happening, while yet being true to what Israel believed was happening.

The prayer itself is presented in two parts. In Josh 7:6 the focus shifts away from Israel's national response to the defeat to Joshua's personal one. It is immediately noticeable that, although Joshua shares some of the nation's perceptions, the simple fact of his prayer means that he is at least capable of doing something in response. Nevertheless, that "something" is not an overtly military response unless we understand "military" here to include invoking Yahweh. While it is true that Yahweh war[7] generally included prayer as a standard feature of preparation for battle,[8] it is notable that there is nothing in Joshua's preparation or the prayer itself which would indicate that this was intended as preparation for war. Rather, his actions—tearing his clothes, prostrating himself and throwing dust on his head—are typical marks of mourning (e.g., Gen 37:34; 2 Sam 13:31; Ezek 27:30).

The one possible exception to this is the mention of the ark, since it could be included in preparations for battle.[9] The ark has a range of functions within the Old Testament.[10] Although sometimes associated with war, its primary function in Joshua to this point has been as a physical symbol of Yahweh's presence that Israel can follow. For

---

7. This is a better label than the widely used "holy war."

8. See Longman and Reid, *Warrior*, 33–35, on preparations for legitimate Yahweh war.

9. See Longman and Reid, *Warrior*, 40–41.

10. See Shin, *Ark of Yahweh*.

example, in crossing the Jordan, the ark was carried by the priests to mark the way Israel should go (Josh 3:7–17), while also symbolizing Yahweh's presence. Likewise, in the Jericho narrative Joshua directed the priests to take up the ark (Josh 6:6), though this was not an element included in Yahweh's command. Rather, Joshua himself deployed the ark as a means of pointing to Yahweh's presence, consistent with the fact that, although Yahweh presented the outline of the battle plan for Jericho, Joshua was free to work out details himself. That the ark is elsewhere associated with warfare (Num 10:33–36) means it is not possible to disentangle all the elements involved in its use here (nor in the crossing of the Jordan), but it does mean that we should not restrict its use to warfare, especially if its main function in both prior narratives in Joshua is to point to divine presence. The ark is mentioned only one other time in Joshua, in the ceremony on Mount Ebal (Josh 8:30–35). It is difficult to identify any specifically military connotations there, and the fact that all Israel stood on opposite sides of the ark (Josh 8:33) would suggest that it was understood there as pointing to Yahweh's presence. Thus, in Joshua, the ark's primary function is to point to Yahweh's presence with Israel. This does not mean that it has no military connotations, but these are secondary. In light of this, it seems best to understand Joshua's prostrating himself before the ark as an expression of prostration before Yahweh, much as others might prostrate themselves before the altar. In these instances, the item before which suppliants prostrate themselves belongs to Yahweh and can thus be understood by metonymy as the equivalent of prostration before him.[11] Joshua thus mourns and falls before Yahweh (as symbolized by the ark). He is joined in this by the elders of Israel until the evening, though it is not entirely clear how long this was since it could either be the rest of the day of the battle or virtually the whole of the following day. But, in either case, it is intended to show how seriously Joshua took the defeat at Ai. His mourning was serious and sustained and also showed leadership in bringing others to be a part of it.

Although Joshua was present with the elders, the prayer that is reported in vv. 7–9 is his alone. It is here that we come to the heart of

---

11. This receives an ironic twist when Dagon falls down before Yahweh (1 Sam 5:1–4), with language almost identical to that used here.

Section 4: Prayers of Others

his response, as his words give shape to the mourning that was reported in the previous verse as he raises the issue of Israel's defeat with Yahweh. The prayer itself is structured as an initial interjection ("Alas"), and then a series of three questions with some expansions:

1. Why did Yahweh bring Israel across the Jordan rather than Israel being content to dwell across the Jordan? (v. 7)

2. What can Joshua say in light of Israel turning their back to their enemies? (v. 8)

3. A declaration of the future action of the Canaanites against Israel before asking what Yahweh would do for his reputation. (v. 9)

Rhetorically, the prayer manages to do two different things through this structure. At a literal level, it functions to ask for information from Yahweh in a context of lament, as is clearly indicated by the opening "Alas, Lord Yahweh" (Josh 7:7a). That is, one could read the prayer as a series of questions that are asking God to provide information. However, the opening question is counter-factual because it knows that Yahweh has indeed brought Israel across the Jordan, and the form of the question acknowledges this. Within the larger narrative of the book, Josh 1:1–9 has effectively answered this question already. Yahweh was giving the land to Israel, and with this came the promise that Yahweh would therefore defeat those already in the land. This was made clear in Josh 1:5, where the declaration that no one could resist Israel is clearly military in tone. But it is this background that informs the opening question, the focus of which is not really a request for information (even if it allows that Yahweh might indeed respond in this way). Rather, at a second level it functions to accuse Yahweh since he has indeed brought Israel across the Jordan, but, as far as the prayer is concerned, only to give Israel into the hand on the Amorites so that Israel would be destroyed. Hence, the form of a question is used, but the prayer does not really ask for information. Rather, it accuses Yahweh of not doing what had previously been promised,[12] which is why Joshua

---

12. Hall, *Conquering Character*, 121, argues that Joshua should have known that the problem was sin on Israel's part because he was present in the events recounted in Num 13–14, the last time Israel was defeated. Although this is not impossible, it is worth noting that the narrative is careful to refrain from allusions to those chapters

suggests that it would have been better for Israel to have remained east of the Jordan.

Verse 8 continues this double level strategy. Grammatically, it employs the form of a question, with the interrogative following a vocative, though where the opening question is prefaced by a formal lament, this time the focus is on Joshua's own position. Nevertheless, this can again be interpreted grammatically as a request for information, as if Joshua were asking for some public relations guidance. But again, the question is actually accusing Yahweh, noting that Israel has fled from before a group of people that were supposed to have been unable to resist them.[13] There is therefore nothing really that can be said, because the implication is once again that Yahweh has failed.

Verse 9 varies the structure from the previous two verses by opening with a direct assertion: the Canaanites and other inhabitants of the land would hear and cut off Israel's name from the land. The statement itself deliberately reverses two earlier statements about the Canaanites "hearing," namely, Rahab's declaration (Josh 2:10) and the report of the response of the Amorite kings following the crossing of the Jordan (Josh 5:1). In both these cases, Canaanites "hearing" about Israel leads to their fear, whereas from this point on their "hearing" will lead to them gathering to oppose Israel (Josh 9:1–2; 10:1–5; 11:1–5), picking up the allusion to these passages already noted in Josh 7:5. Joshua's assertion about the Canaanites being emboldened will thus turn out to be correct, but though they do indeed attempt to cut off Israel, they do not succeed. Within the prayer, however, Joshua is not really assigned a prophetic role, since this statement is simply preparatory for the question "What will you do for your great name?" Once again, this could be construed as a request for information, but rhetorically it assumes that no such information is available. If Yahweh has brought Israel across the Jordan only for them to be defeated by a minor enemy such as Ai,

---

here, and neither does it make any direct criticism of Joshua beyond the points noted in Yahweh's response.

13. The interrogative *mah* can be used to infer blame, and we find this usage also in Josh 22:16, the opening of another series of questions which build to a climactic reference back to the events of this chapter. That it can be used to infer blame is why some translations (e.g., ESV) render this verse as an exclamation rather than a question.

Section 4: Prayers of Others

then the implication is that there is in fact nothing that Yahweh can do. Once again, the grammatical form of the question is deployed in order to make an accusation.[14]

It is notable that Joshua's prayer, though phrased as a set of questions functions instead as a series of accusations, all of which can to some extent be tied back to the promise in Josh 1:5. As a prayer, it is rhetorically quite similar to Ps 44:9–22 [10–23], even if the grammatical form is quite different. There too, God is accused of having failed Israel, with the result that they were defeated by their enemies. But that psalm makes the accusation quite directly through a series of second person singular verbs. Here, the accusation is more indirect, but the effect is the same. Yahweh is accused of having failed Israel. However, the presence of prayers like Ps 44 within the Psalter indicates a tradition of complaint in Israel in which it was legitimate for God to be both the object of the complaint and the one to whom the complaint was made.[15] There is no sign within the Psalter that such prayers were unacceptable, though there may be signs that the editorial structure of the book serves to limit their applicability.[16] However, limiting their applicability does not mean they were no longer acceptable. Perhaps more importantly, the narrative context to this point has made clear that Joshua's prayer is a faithful response to what he genuinely believed to be the problem. Bear in mind that readers know about Israel's sin through Achan at Jericho, but at this point Joshua does not. The narrative has thus carefully presented Joshua's prayer so that, as it is focalized through him, it reports what Joshua believes to be an appropriate prayer even though the narrator has already made clear that it is not. Joshua's prayer is sincere, and rooted within a tradition of complaint in prayer, but readers also know that his assessment of Israel's circumstances are incorrect.

YAHWEH'S RESPONSE—JOSHUA 7:10–15

Although Joshua's prayer was cast in the form of a series of questions, its rhetorical goal does not really ask for any specific action from Yahweh.

---

14. On the broader possibility of using this form, see GKC §148c.
15. More fully, see Broyles, *Conflict of Faith*.
16. Firth, "Reading Psalm 46."

It is intended to express complaint, but in doing so it does not specify any action from Yahweh. The task of the narrator in reporting Yahweh's response is then to bring together the horizons, one established for readers in setting the context for the prayer and the other from which Joshua is reported to have prayed. This is achieved by having Yahweh respond to the prayer's rhetorical goal, explaining why complaint against him is not appropriate. That is, it is only after Joshua has prayed that Yahweh makes clear to him that the failure is Israel's. Moreover, the information provided for readers in Josh 7:1 provides the frame for Yahweh's response, thus bringing together the horizon of the reader and that of Joshua within the narrative. What is striking, however, is that although Yahweh corrects Joshua's understanding of the events, at no point does he criticize him for his prayer.

In that our main goal is to understand the prayer itself, we can pass over the response more quickly, though some comment is still required. We will concentrate in particular on Josh 7:10–12, since these are the verses where Joshua's horizon is brought into line with that of the reader. By contrast, Josh 7:13–15 outlines the steps necessary for the problem to be resolved. Rhetorically, the two halves of the response are marked by the imperative "stand up" (*qum*) being addressed to Joshua.

The first part of the response, requiring Joshua to stand, seems to assume that Joshua has indeed prostrated himself before Yahweh, while indicating that it is not appropriate. It mirrors Joshua's strategy by using a question to indicate that his action is misplaced. As with the prayer, Yahweh's question does not require information. Rather, it makes clear that Joshua should not be prostrate. The reason for this is precisely that Israel has sinned. Here, Yahweh uses a different verb for "sinned" than v. 1 (*khata'* rather than *ma'al*), but the nature of the sin is explored more thoroughly because it is also a transgression of covenant that was expressed through the taking of items which had been placed under the ban. Reference to items under the ban thus joins this statement with the narrator's introduction, whilst at the same time explaining the sin more fully as a combination of theft and deceit, since the items under the ban were apparently placed with Israel's belongings. The description of the sin is thus more extensive than that of v. 1, though it is evidently referring to the same act. It was this sin that meant Israel

Section 4: Prayers of Others

was unable to stand before its enemies. In explaining this, Yahweh even picks up on Joshua's language of Israel turning their backs before their enemies. That is, the promise of Josh 1:5 cannot apply in a circumstance where the Israelites have placed themselves under the ban.[17] Israel's future always depended on Yahweh's presence. Unless they destroyed the items under the ban that they held, they could not rely on the promise of Josh 1:5 because they had placed themselves outside of the setting where it could be experienced. The first half of Yahweh's response thus aligns Joshua's awareness of the situation with that of readers in order to demonstrate that Joshua's prayer, though sincerely offered, was based on a thoroughly flawed awareness of the circumstances. Once this has been done, the second half of the response can provide a mechanism for addressing the problem. Although we will not consider it here, it is notable that the solution is also closely tied to the statements in vv. 1 and 11 through mention of possession of the items under the ban and transgression of covenant, while also adding that the offender had committed something outrageous (*nevalah*, v. 15) in Israel.

In neither phase of Yahweh's response is Joshua criticized for the content of his prayer. Indeed, Yahweh actually responds quite precisely to the words of Joshua's prayer even while rejecting their rhetorical goal. That is, although Joshua has used the form of the question to suggest that Yahweh has acted inappropriately, Yahweh in fact gives Joshua exactly what he has asked for, an explanation of why it is that Israel was defeated at Ai. Indeed, the response takes up some of the language of both vv. 7 and 8 though with some key changes in emphasis. In v. 7, Joshua had inferred that Yahweh had brought Israel across (*'br*) the Jordan in order to destroy (*'bd*) them. But now Yahweh (Josh 7:11–12) points out that Israel has transgressed (*'br*) the covenant, and that Israel must destroy (*shmd*) the banned items. Key words such as "back" (*'oref*) also occur in both the prayer and the response (vv. 8, 12), showing that these elements belong together. So, throughout the first half of the response Yahweh takes up Joshua's own language to demonstrate that he has misconstrued the situation.

---

17. Mitchell, *Together in the Land*, 75, points to the analogy of Deut 13:12–18 as allowing for the possibility that a part of Israel might be placed under the ban.

In spite of this, there is one important gap. Joshua's final question asked what Yahweh would do for his "great name" (v. 9). Unlike the other elements of the prayer, this one is not taken up directly in the response. In part, this is because the basis of Joshua's prayer has been shown to be wrong; Yahweh had not failed or acted inappropriately towards Israel. One might suggest, therefore, that there was no need for Yahweh to respond to the final question since it was raised from what has now been shown to be a demonstrably false premise. It was Israel, not Yahweh, who needed to act. Nevertheless, it is also possible that the absence of language directly responding to this question, unlike the other two, is important. Joshua may have asked the question on the basis of a misreading of the circumstances, but it remained an appropriate question to ask. As with the other questions in the prayer, it was not really asking for information, but it certainly challenged Yahweh to act because of his great name. Yahweh's reputation mattered. And though the second part of the response focuses on what Israel is to do, one can also suggest that the very fact that Yahweh provided Israel with a mechanism for addressing their sin and restoring their relationship with him means that he has indeed acted for his great name. Once again, the form of the response is not really what Joshua sought, but it is there, because concern for Yahweh's name is indeed an important element in prayer, even when that prayer is effectively complaining about a failure on Yahweh's part.

JOSHUA 7 AND A BIBLICAL THEOLOGY OF PRAYER

One cannot, of course, construct a biblical theology of prayer on the basis of a single text, especially one that represents a comparatively unusual prayer. Nevertheless, some observations are in order as we tie the various threads here together. Three key observations can be made.

First, this story recognizes an important truth about prayer that is not widely represented elsewhere in the Bible, and that is that when we pray it is always on the basis of a partial understanding of reality, and that understanding may be so partial that it may in fact express itself in ways that are a serious misreading of what is happening. That the majority of texts in the Bible report prayer from the perspective of an omniscient narrator means that we most often also know God's

Section 4: Prayers of Others

perspective as the prayer is reported.[18] But here the narrator chooses a different strategy in order to highlight the important gap between what is known by God and by those who pray. We may, at times, know enough that even when our knowledge of a situation is partial it might still fairly represent circumstances. But this is not always the case, and no doubt many other prayers have been offered from the perspective of knowledge which is so partial that it leads to an erroneous interpretation of the context.

Second, prayers which actually complain about God are deemed perfectly acceptable. The presence of prayers in the Psalter that do this is well recognized, but we can also note that Hab 1:2–4 also represents a prayer in this tradition.[19] Although Morrow has argued that this tradition was gradually eclipsed within the Bible,[20] its presence in a relatively early tradition such as Josh 7 and later ones such as Habakkuk and a number of Psalms would suggest that it remained a vibrant part of Israel's prayer life. That a similar form of prayer is reported in Rev 6:10 would indicate that this remained an important part of the New Testament's theology of prayer.[21] It is, of course, entirely likely that many prayers that complain about God are also prayers that are operating from an erroneous understanding of the situation that triggered the prayer, but this does not make the prayer invalid.

Third, God accepts Joshua's prayer even though wrongly it accuses him of failing to keep his promises. However, although God's response is not the one which is implicitly sought by the prayer, it is one which actually addresses the substance of the prayer. That is, God honors the intent of the prayer—which is for his honor—by reshaping Joshua's perspective. In the end, Joshua can no longer complain because he knows the actual circumstances (or at least enough of them) to interpret the situation appropriately. Unlike Habakkuk, where the prophet must ultimately learn to trust God even where circumstances are not what he

---

18. See, for example, Ezra's prayer about mixed marriages in Ezra 9.
19. See Firth, "Habakkuk," 541–42.
20. Morrow, *Protest against God*.
21. In Rev 6:10, the martyrs under the altar cry out, "Sovereign Lord, holy and true, how long will it be before you judge and avenge our blood on the inhabitants of the earth?" (NRSV)

would choose (Hab 3:16–19), or the various psalms of complaint for which no answer is recorded, Joshua is brought to a new level of insight into his circumstances. The prayer may have sought to provoke God so that he would change, rather as Moses had done in Exod 33:12–13, but in this case it is Joshua who is changed through the practice of prayer. This is a comparatively uncommon element in biblical prayers, though there are traces of it in Jer 15:10–21, where Jeremiah complains but is told that he is the one who needs to repent. In Josh 7, the change in Joshua leads to a change in the nation so that they are restored to participate in God's purposes.

Joshua is not a book much studied on the topic of prayer, and both its prayers stand somewhat outside the mainstream. Nevertheless, Joshua's own prayer here is an important contribution to a theology of prayer and to the church's understanding of prayer. It demonstrates that we who pray may well get prayer right, even when we have our facts wrong and the content of the prayer is misdirected. When that happens, then God corrects the one who prays, while the appropriate response for the person praying is to act in light of God's correction.

BIBLIOGRAPHY

Balentine, Samuel E. *Prayer in the Hebrew Bible: The Drama of Divine-Human Dialogue*. Minneapolis: Augsburg Fortress, 1992.

Broyles, Craig C. *The Conflict of Faith and Experience in the Psalms: A Form-Critical and Theological Study*. LHBOTS 44. Sheffield: JSOT, 1989.

Brueggemann, Walter. *Great Prayers of the Bible*. Louisville: Westminster John Knox, 2009.

Firth, David G. "Disorienting Readers in Joshua 1.1–5.12." *JSOT* 41 (2017) 413–30.

———. "Habakkuk." In *ESV Expository Commentary*, Vol. 7, edited by Iain M. Duguid et al., 533–60. Wheaton, IL: Crossway, 2018.

———. "Reading Psalm 46 in its Canonical Context: An Initial Exploration in Harmonies Consonant and Dissonant." *BBR* 30 (2020) 22–40.

Hall, Sarah Lebhar. *Conquering Character: The Characterization of Joshua in Joshua 1–11*. LHBOTS 512. London: T. & T. Clark, 2010.

Longman III, Temper, and Daniel G. Reid. *God is A Warrior*. Grand Rapids: Zondervan, 1995.

Miller, Patrick D. *They Cried to the Lord: The Form and Theology of Biblical Prayer*. Minneapolis: Fortress, 1994.

Section 4: Prayers of Others

Mitchell, Gordon. *Together in the Land: A Reading of the Book of Joshua.* LHBOTS 134. Sheffield: JSOT, 1993.

Morrow, William S. *Protest against God: The Eclipse of a Biblical Tradition.* Sheffield: Sheffield Phoenix, 2007.

Shin, Deuk-Il. *The Ark of Yahweh in Redemptive History: A Revelatory Instrument of Divine Attributes.* Eugene, OR: Wipf & Stock, 2012.

Wenham, John W. "Large Numbers in the Old Testament." *TynBul* 18 (1967) 19–53.

Winther-Nielsen, Nicolai. *A Functional Discourse Grammar of Joshua.* Stockholm: Almqvist & Wiksell, 1995.

12

A House of Prayer for All Nations?
Temple, Prayer, and Xenophobia in Ezra 9 and 1 Kings 8

KEVIN J. YOUNGBLOOD

A NUMBER OF THE Hebrew Bible's most beautiful and pious prayers are jarringly juxtaposed to narratives portraying those who prayed them in ethically problematic, if not offensive, ways.[1] Among these are Ezra 9 and 1 Kgs 8, both preserving beautiful, theologically rich prayers, but both also surrounded by actions on the part of Ezra and Solomon that grate the sensibilities of contemporary readers.

Indeed, many scholars find the treatment of the "foreign wives" recorded in Ezra 9–10 so draconian that they cannot renounce the mass coercive divorce proceedings emphatically enough.[2] Such responses are understandable, especially considering the many contemporary

---

1. Examples include Exod 15, uttered immediately following the drowning of the Egyptian army in the Reed Sea, Jonah 2, uttered after Jonah's blatant disobedience to the divine commission due to his hatred of the Ninevites, and Neh 9, a beautiful prayer of confession preceded by a number of Nehemiah's ugly imprecations and followed by the forced dissolution of marriages to foreigners.

2. A couple of recent examples make the point. David Janzen, for instance, compares the incident to a witch hunt ("Scholars, Witches, Ideologues," 49–69), while Julia O'Brien suggests that the incident evinces a community slipping into increasing sexism and racism ("From Exile to Empire," 213).

Section 4: Prayers of Others

examples of harm caused by racism and sexism of various kinds. Even those who read Ezra–Nehemiah sympathetically cannot help but wince at the text's severity. Furthermore, the tension is palpable between the xenophobia on display in this text and the rather different attitude one finds in passages like Isa 56:6–8, where foreigners are promised full access to the new temple—a temple envisioned as a house of prayer for all nations.

What follows is an attempt to read Ezra 9–10 both critically and sympathetically in the light of the very similar text found in 1 Kgs 8. Of particular interest is Ezra's confessional prayer that serves as the centerpiece of the text and functions as a kind of distillation of the traditions and concerns that led to the austere divorce proceedings that follow in Ezra 10. Ezra's confessional prayer can be viewed as standing in a similar relationship to the second temple as did Solomon's dedicatory prayer to the first temple. Each of these prayers encapsulates the nature and agenda of the communities formed around these sacred centers as well as the function of the temples themselves. The challenge is to discern the theological function of these prayers within their disturbing contexts. What is their relationship to the surrounding narrative, to the temple that is at the heart of their concerns, and to the apparently disenfranchised foreigners who were supposed to be the beneficiaries of Israel's prayers and temple?

KEY INTERPRETIVE ISSUES

A number of interpretive issues related to Ezra's prayer and its immediate context should be addressed before proceeding with a comparison of Ezra 9 and 1 Kgs 8:22–53. First, the presentation of the intermarriage issue in Ezra 9:1 seems abrupt. One wonders what motivated the officials to approach Ezra with a report regarding the pervasiveness of mixed marriages in the community. Torrey appears to have been the first to suggest that Ezra 9–10 fits more naturally as the sequel to Ezra's reading of the law in Nehemiah 7:73b [72b]—8:18 and that the latter text originally preceded the former.[3] Ezra's public reading of the law, therefore, originally provided the narrative rationale for bringing the

---

3. Torrey, *Ezra Studies*, 268–70. Cf. Blenkinsopp, *Ezra-Nehemiah*, 174.

issue to Ezra's attention. This view has been adopted by most commentators since and is assumed in this study.

Regardless of its original arrangement, however, the task before the interpreter is to make sense of the text as we have it. The question, therefore, is how the episode functions in its current form. If the text has been rearranged, what motivated the relocation of Neh. 7:73b [72b]—8:18? A number of suggestions have been offered, but a compelling explanation can be found in the narrative's portrayal of the return to the land as a new exodus. The book of Ezra thus develops an extensive typology between postexilic events and episodes from Israel's national epic.[4]

This typology is established early on when the Persian neighbors of those determined to return to the land supply them with everything necessary for returning and rebuilding the temple (Ezra 1:6), thus recapitulating the "plundering of the Egyptians" recorded in Exod 12:36. With this typology in mind, one can understand the dismissal of "foreign wives" and the children born to them as tantamount to a new conquest paralleling the *kherem* warfare prescribed in Deut 7 and executed in Joshua.[5] In fact, the foreigners dismissed from the community are compared to Israel's ancient Canaanite enemies in terms of their abominable practices and potential for defiling the sacred community (Ezra 9:1).

In its current arrangement, therefore, the report of the mixed marriage crisis, complete with its allusion to Deut 7:1, follows on the heels of the departure from the new "Egypt" and the reentry to the land, thus strengthening the connection between the *kherem* warfare waged under Joshua and the separation ritual performed under Ezra.[6]

---

4. Blenkinsopp, *Ezra-Nehemiah*, 37, and Throntveit, *Ezra-Nehemiah*, 15–18.

5. Contra the suggestion that the author of Ezra–Nehemiah, under the influence of the Priestly tradent, omitted any parallel to the conquest, moving immediately to the establishment of the sanctuary at Shiloh and the distribution of the tribal territories. See Blenkinsopp, *Ezra-Nehemiah*, 37. Note also that the term used in Ezra 10:8 for the confiscation of property that served as penalty for missing this solemn assembly is *yakharam* a cognate of *kherem*.

6. One may object to associating the dismissal of the foreigners with the original conquest on the grounds that the temple is built in Ezra 3–6, thus disrupting the expected parallel sequence: exodus, conquest, settlement, temple construction. My response would be that Ezra 3 associates the second temple with the construction

Section 4: Prayers of Others

Furthermore, it sets the separation from foreign wives as the first in a series of reforms instituted by Ezra and Nehemiah culminating in the climax of Ezra's reading of the law and renewing the covenant in Neh 8–10.[7] As it stands, Ezra's reading and renewal of the covenant forms a nice parallel with Joshua's renewal of the covenant at Shechem (Josh 23–24).

A second issue impacting the interpretation of the text is the identification of the "people(s) of the land(s)" ('*am ha'arets*) with whom members of the *golah*[8] community intermarried. Though traditionally interpreters have taken this designation to indicate that the wives in question were foreigners,[9] recently the designation has been taken to refer to anyone who did not belong to the post-exilic community.[10] Thus, in anthropological terms, Ezra 9–10 is an example of ethnic exclusivism in which ethnicity has less to do with racial distinction than it does with boundary maintenance of a cohesive group that has formed an identity on the basis of a shared history or heritage. Southwood explains the concept well.

---

of the tabernacle in the wilderness rather than with the first temple. This is evident in the fact that its construction is facilitated by materials donated by the returnees' foreign hosts (Ezra 1:6) as is similarly suggested of the Tabernacle's construction vis-à-vis Israel's "plundering" of the Egyptians (Exod 12:35–36). Furthermore, a celebration of the Feast of Booths (Sukkoth) occurs upon the completion of the altar of whole burnt offering in Ezra 3:4, clearly recalling the wilderness period. This association is further supported by the statement in Ezra 3:3 that the construction of the altar was motivated in part by the community's fear of the "peoples of the land," a situation more akin to their wilderness wandering (cf. Num 14:9) and an indication that the second "conquest" had not yet occurred.

7. Throntveit, *Ezra-Nehemiah*, 50.

8. The Hebrew term *golah* means "deportation" or "exile" and is traditionally used in biblical scholarship in reference to this particular community that repatriated in waves their ancestral land after Cyrus' decree allowing such repatriation in 539 BCE. This convention is retained throughout the chapter.

9. Myers, *Ezra-Nehemiah*, 77. Myers represents this traditional view though helpfully nuanced by Würthwein's thesis that the term '*am ha'arets* designates not only that they are foreign but that they are landholders who took over after the exile. See Würthwein, *Der 'amm ha'arez*, 51–71.

10. Redditt, *Ezra-Nehemiah*, 191–92. It is interesting that Redditt takes it for granted that the excluded persons are fellow Hebrews who remained in the land during the exile without even discussing the alternative view of their being foreign or of mixed blood.

During times of upheaval, conspicuous forms of boundary maintenance occur in conjunction with an increased focus on ethnicity. This provides a form of continuity and stability when all the familiar structures of existence are uprooted. However, ironically, in such times of uncertainty where ethnicity is necessitated, it is often those who are most similar, the proximate Others, rather than the profoundly different, that constitute the greatest perceived threats.[11]

While one can see how this would be an apt description of the *golah* community under Ezra's leadership and how it is helpful in understanding the group dynamics at work, some scholars take this anthropological approach too far by denying any ethnic difference to the group under expulsion. The text's own description of "the people(s) of the land" indicates that they were in fact the product of ethnically mixed unions that carried with them syncretistic religious connotations. A prime example is their adversaries' offer to help build the temple in Ezra 4:2. They state, "Let us build with you, for we worship your God as you do, and we have been sacrificing to him ever since the days of Esarhaddon king of Assyria who brought us here."[12] In 4:4 this group is clearly identified as "the people of the land" (*'am ha'arets*), and the self-description clearly refers back to 2 Kgs 17:24–29. It seems best to identify these "people(s) of the land" as descended from mixed parentage resulting from the Assyrian policy of deportation and assimilation.

One final interpretive issue to resolve is the nature and function of the list of nations to which the people(s) of the land are compared in Ezra 9:1. According to the Masoretic Text eight nations are mentioned: Canaanites, Hittites, Perizzites, Jebusites, Ammonites, Moabites, Egyptians, and Amorites. The first four of these are derived from Deut 7:1–3, where Israel is prohibited from intermarrying with the occupants of the land they are about to inherit. The Ammonites and Moabites are added to this list from Deut 23:3 [4], where they and their descendants are banned from the congregation. The inclusion of the Egyptians and the Amorites in this list has baffled interpreters. The Amorites are

---

11. Southwood, *Ethnicity*, 30. Southwood identifies this with the ethnic theory of Frederic Barth.

12. All translations are the author's unless otherwise noted.

Section 4: Prayers of Others

mentioned in Deut 7:1, but one wonders why they are separated from the other nations derived from the traditional seven originally slated for annihilation. Egypt simply seems out of place.[13]

It is precisely these two anomalies in the list that launch the investigation that will be the focus of the remainder of this paper. First, the Masoretic Text's "Amorites" is likely a corruption of what originally read "Edomites." In fact, this variant appears in Esd A 8:66.[14] This would bring the list into alignment with Deut 23:7-8 [8-9], where the Edomites and Egyptians are mentioned shortly after the Ammonites and Moabites as being allowed into the assembly after the third generation.[15] Further confirmation of this reading may be found in the abundant archeological evidence of a thriving Idumean culture located a short distance from Jerusalem at Maresha during the late exilic and early post-exilic era.[16] This suggests that this remnant of Edom could well have been a source of the foreign women accused of contaminating the *golah* community via intermarriage.

Though nothing is said in Deut 23:7-8 [8-9] regarding intermarriage with an Edomite or an Egyptian, the same two ethnicities are mentioned as being among the foreign wives Solomon took for his harem in 1 Kgs 11:1. As 1 Kings points out, it was precisely Solomon's foreign wives that were his undoing. This is the first of a number of allusions to the Solomonic tradition that punctuate Ezra 9-10 and that help to explain the zealous aversion to such intermarriages that threaten the *golah* community in our text.

---

13. Throntveit, *Ezra-Nehemiah*, 51.

14. Esdras A 8:66 has *kai Idoumaiōn*. Hanhart notes only one variant in his critical apparatus: the omission of *kai Idoumaiōn* in the Syriac translation. See Hanhart, ed., *Esdrae Liber I*, 130.

15. The MT's reading is easily explained as a case of metathesis and *resh/daleth* confusion thus understandably deriving "Amorite" from "Edomite" (*'mri* vs. *'dmi*). Alternatively, one could argue that an original "Edomite" was changed to Amorite to align this text with Deut 23:7 [8] which prohibits abhorrence of Edomites, thus falling in line with the scribal practice of harmonization. See Van der Toorn, *Scribal Culture*, 7.

16. Kloner, "The Identity of the Idumeans," 563-73.

SOLOMONIC ALLUSIONS IN EZRA 9

Nehemiah indicts Solomon as having sinned with regard to his intermarriage to foreign women. In fact, he points to him as an illustration of the fact that even one who enjoys unprecedented divine favor and wisdom is not exempt from the dangers posed by assimilation via intermarriage (Neh 13:26).

Solomon's precedent profoundly influences the attitudes and actions that unfold in Ezra 9 in more subtle ways as well. To begin with, Ezra extends the prohibition of intermarriage beyond the strict confines of the Mosaic law insisting that intermarriage with any non-Israelite constitutes a breach of Torah. The only other text in the Hebrew Bible to adopt a similar stance is 1 Kgs 11:1–2, where all of Solomon's intermarriages with various foreigners are condemned. First Kgs 11:1–2 extends this prohibition and, thus, grants Ezra a precedent for his interpretation and application of this prohibition in his own context. Ezra's "Torah," therefore, seems to include this tradition preserved in 1 Kgs 11:1–2.

COMPARISON AND CONTRAST OF EZRA 9 WITH 1 KINGS 8 AND THEIR CONTEXTS

This connection encourages a rereading of Ezra's prayer and its immediate context in light of the Solomon tradition, particularly his dedicatory prayer in 1 Kgs 8. For example, the officials indict the community leaders as particularly at fault for initiating and encouraging the practice of intermarriages like Solomon's near the beginning of the Davidic dynasty. Ezra's prayer, therefore, is preceded and followed by the same threat that frames the account in 1 Kings of the temple's construction and dedication culminating in Solomon's prayer (cf. 1 Kgs 3:1; 7:8; 11:1).

It is also instructive to notice the postures that both Ezra and Solomon adopt in preparation for their respective petitions. Ezra 9:3 portrays Ezra as sitting desolate until the time of the evening sacrifice, while the most pious among the Israelites gathered around him. A similar, though larger, assembly gathers around Solomon during the dedication of the first temple. The mood, however, is completely different. In 1 Kgs 8 there is a tremendous spirit of celebration as opposed to the contrite mood of Ezra 9.

Solomon prays before the assembly with his palms spread outward heaven (1 Kgs 8:22). Ezra similarly spreads his hands to YHWH (Ezra 9:5). The idiom in both cases is the same. In fact, these are the only two instances in the Hebrew Bible where this ritual hand gesture is immediately followed by the content of the prayer.[17] In both cases the extended open palms facing heaven appear to indicate supplication—empty hands ready to receive whatever the deity is inclined to offer.[18] Solomon's gesture seeks divine favor and forgiveness for any who pray at or in the direction of the temple (1 Kgs 8:28–30). Ezra's gesture is much more urgent and immediate, grasping for the favor and forgiveness for which Solomon prayed.

Perhaps even more significantly, this posture for prayer is included in one of Solomon's explicit petitions for divine pardon for Israel's sins: "And will spread his hands toward this house" (1 Kgs 8:38). Ezra's adoption of this posture recalls Solomon's petition and perhaps in Ezra's mind strengthens his appeal on its basis. At the same time, however, the connection underscores the ironic tension of the fact that it is the very sin for which Solomon was condemned that necessitates the pardon that Ezra now seeks on the basis of Solomon's petition.

In light of this irony, perhaps it is not insignificant that the terminology in Ezra 9:5 differs in one detail from the very similar terminology in 1 Kgs 8:38. Whereas Solomon speaks of spreading the palms toward "this house" referring to the temple, Ezra indicates that he spread his palms "toward YHWH, my God." Ezra's omission of temple language may reflect a chastened assessment of the temple and its role in the community's relationship with YHWH. It is no guarantor of divine mercy. Its mere existence should not be taken as an indication of YHWH's unequivocal support of the *golah* community and its actions.

The attention that both texts give to the posture adopted and the similarity of their postures strengthens the relationship between the two prayers. Ezra adopts a kneeling posture throughout his prayer (Ezra 9:5) while Solomon is portrayed as standing at the beginning of

17. Callabro, "Ritual Gestures," 246.
18. Callabro, "Ritual Gestures," 657.

the prayer (1 Kgs 8:22) but kneeling at the end (1 Kgs 8:54). Kneeling in prayer is an indication of self-abasement before YHWH in recognition of his kingship. For Ezra, it is a physical manifestation of the sentiment he expresses in Ezra 9:6. He states, "O my God! I am too ashamed and humiliated to lift, my God, my face to you." The posture is also in keeping with the preponderance of servile language in Ezra's prayer. It simultaneously indicates Judah's position under Persia and the underlying theological reason for her subjection to foreign domination—the ongoing judgment of God (Ezra 9:9).[19]

For Solomon, the posture may be more ritualistic. Cogan has persuasively argued on the basis of ANE iconography and royal inscriptions that standing and kneeling are appropriate for different moments in liturgical or ritual prayers.[20] It is conceivable that, as Solomon's prayer turns toward appeals for divine mercy regarding Israel's future sins, he adopts the more contrite posture. In so doing, however, he anticipates precisely the kind of scenario described in Ezra 9. The irony is that, despite Solomon's contrite posture, he proceeds to enter into mixed marriages, thus setting Israel on a course of apostasy and judgment. Ezra picks up where Solomon left off, on his knees head bowed before YHWH, but not as a ritual act. Ezra's posture is ad hoc and spontaneous in response to the revelation of the mixed marriages.

A key aspect of Solomon's prayer is his request that YHWH would ever be attentive and responsive to the prayers offered toward the temple, particularly supplications for pardon (1 Kgs 8:30). Ezra seems to presume this divine disposition toward his holy dwelling when he states in his prayer "But now for a short while . . . God has given us a stake in his holy place" (Ezra 9:8). Ezra's emphasis on the brevity of the window of opportunity represented by the *golah* community's return to the land and resumption of temple worship reflects a humility and tentativeness noticeably absent in Solomon's prayer. Ezra seems to view the *golah* community's situation as gracious but probationary and, therefore, vulnerable (Ezra 9:13–15).

---

19. For the significance of kneeling vis-à-vis reverence for God and the relationship between such reverence and subordination to a dominating power in the ancient Near East, see Strawn, "Fear of the LORD."

20. Cogan, *I Kings*, 288.

Section 4: Prayers of Others

On the other hand, Solomon seems to anticipate Ezra's situation when he requests that YHWH give the exiles favor in the eyes of their captors (1 Kgs 8:50). Ezra acknowledges in his own prayer that this is precisely what YHWH did (Ezra 9:9). Thus, the two prayers connect in terms analogous to prophecy and fulfillment as though Solomon were proleptically interceding for the *golah* community. Part of the divine favor acknowledged by Ezra is the fact that the exiles' Persian overlords allowed the exiles to return and funded the rebuilding of their temple.

An interesting difference between the two prayers, however, regards their respective attitudes concerning the temple's future. Solomon seems not to entertain the possibility of the loss of the temple (see especially 1 Kgs 8:48) though he does envision the possibility of exile (1 Kgs 8:46–53). This may explain the reason for the divine address to Solomon in 1 Kgs 9:1–9, in which YHWH emphasizes the destruction of the temple as a possible consequence of apostasy. For Ezra, however, the possibility of the loss of the temple is very real (Ezra 9:8, 15).[21] It appears that Ezra is eschewing the very presumption that led to Solomon's disconnect between his prayer and the consequences of his marital practices.

The two prayers also share an interesting and significant structural feature. Ezra's prayer turns on two occurrences of a significant transitional phrase marking critical junctures in the logic of his confession. The phrase is "but now" (*ve'attah*), and the two instances occur together in succession at Ezra 9:8–10.[22] Together they draw a pair of contrasts that stand in dramatic tension and form the central spiritual conundrum of the confession. The first of these occurrences (9:8) introduces a contrast between the present and surprising respite of grace that led to the *golah* community's return to the land and Israel's long history of sin and judgment culminating in the exile. The second occurrence (9:10) introduces the contrast between God's gracious provision of a fresh start and the community's utterly inappropriate response to that new beginning—their defiling practice of intermarriage with foreigners.

---

21. Brueggemann, *Great Prayers*, 94.
22. Brueggemann, *Great Prayers*, 93–94.

Embedded within this second contrast is a third occurrence of "but now" (*ve'attah*) in Ezra 9:12. This one introduces a conflated paraphrase of Deut 7:3 and 23:6 [7], warning of the danger of defilement in the land. The appeal to Deut 7:3 and 23:6 [7] forms the core of Ezra's confession, serving to define the precise nature of their sin and the threat that such an infraction poses to the community's future in the land. It also, however, lays the foundation for the drastic measures taken in Ezra 10 in an attempt to remedy the breach of covenant.

Each of these critical moves in Ezra's prayer marked by "but now" (*ve'attah*) responds in some way to the logic of Solomon's prayer and its surrounding context. For example, the appeal to Deut 7:3 and 23:6 [7] applies to Ezra's situation only if Ezra and his community are assuming the extension of these prohibitions to all foreigners first found in the account of Solomon's apostasy in 1 Kgs 11:1–8.

Similarly, Solomon orients his petitions around two statements beginning with "but now" (*ve'attah*). As in Ezra, they occur in immediate succession in 1 Kgs 8:25–26. In Solomon's prayer, the two statements beginning with "but now" introduce a series of petitions based on the Davidic covenant. The effect of these petitions is to project optimism about the future by presenting the completion of the temple and YHWH's filling it with his presence as a first installment on the promises of the Davidic covenant. What Solomon requests is confirmation of the Davidic covenant in the form of a divine guarantee closely associated with the temple and the enduring nature of its structure and rituals (1 Kgs 8:26).

Ezra, on the other hand, while recognizing the completion of the second temple as an overture of grace and the opening of a door to a more hopeful future for Judah, seeks no guarantee of divine blessing on this basis. To the contrary, he underscores how tentative this new beginning is, how precarious the *golah* community's situation is in this repatriation of their ancestral land that is now home to a very foreign culture. The backdrop of the second temple, in fact, exacerbates in Ezra's mind the severity of the offense, since it potentially quarantines the implicated members of the community from sacred space.

The issue of ritual purity and sacred space brings us to the most crucial contrast between Solomon's and Ezra's prayers. In 1 Kgs

Section 4: Prayers of Others

8:41–43, Solomon asks that YHWH treat the foreigner who comes and makes petition at the temple as he does the Israelite—that he would hear and grant the foreigner's request. By contrast, Ezra appears to seek the exclusion of foreigners from this assembly (9:11–12). The very issue raised by intermarriage has to do with the purity of the community and who may participate in the sanctity of land and temple (Ezra 9:10–12).

At the same time, however, Solomon concludes his prayer with the recognition that Israel has been set apart from the other nations (1 Kgs 8:53). It is this aspect of Israel's vocation that occupies Ezra's prayer perhaps to an extreme. The contrast between the two texts, however, points to a perpetual dilemma faced by God's people. On the one hand Israel is called to be a light to the nations and to adopt an inclusive stance toward them so that the temple can be "a house of prayer for all nations" (Isa 56:7; Mark 11:17). On the other hand, Israel cannot do this if she assimilates to the surrounding culture and compromises the leverage of her holiness.

The unqualified openness to foreigners expressed in Solomon's prayer is laudable for its embrace of Israel's ultimate calling. In the larger context of 1 Kings, however, it is also followed by Solomon's apostasy largely due to the influence of his foreign wives (1 Kgs 11:3–9). It is to this last concern that Ezra responds in his prayer and in the separation from foreign wives that he oversees (Ezra 10).

A possible precedent for the expulsion of the foreign women and children carried out in Ezra 10 may be found in 1 Kgs 9:24, on the heels of Solomon's prayer. Here the reader is informed that Pharaoh's daughter was removed from the City of David, after the temple's construction, to her own palace. The Chronicler expands on this note in a most intriguing manner, including Solomon's rationale for his wife's relocation: "My wife shall no longer live in the city[23] of David, King of Israel; for holy are the places to which the Ark of YHWH has come" (2 Chr 8:11). Is the Chronicler reflecting a tradition, known also to Ezra, that indicated that even Solomon recognized the need to distance his foreign wives from the sacred precincts of the temple? If so, Ezra

---

23. The MT literally says "in the house of David" (*beveth david*) but I, along with most commentators, have opted for the OG rendering "in the city of David" (*en polei David*). See Japhet, *1 & 2 Chronicles*, 626.

and the community he led may have felt that Solomon did not go far enough. After all, this action did not prevent his apostasy due to the influence of his foreign wives.

An even more significant connection that may shed considerable light on Ezra 9–10 is that Solomon's foreign wives appear to be interpreted as political marriages, unions formed for the sake of securing Israel's upward mobility and national security (1 Kgs 3:1). In anthropological terms, this constitutes the phenomenon of hypergamy—the practice of marrying into wealthy, established families for the purposes of greater political and economic advantage.[24]

Smith-Christopher has argued convincingly that this was precisely the phenomenon occurring in the *golah* community in Ezra 9–10.[25] The "people(s) of the land(s)" with whom members of the *golah* community intermarried were probably landholders of mixed ethnicity who took over control of the land after the exile.[26] It is understandable that many in the *golah* community would have seen intermarriage with these as a means of regaining a foothold in power and property within the land,[27] but at what cost? Solomon attempted a similar strategy with regard to enriching and securing his kingdom, and look what happened.

This view, if correct, may mitigate some of the ethical concerns surrounding Ezra's prayer and the separation ritual described in Ezra 10. It is often assumed that this action jeopardized the economic well-being of the women and children in question. If, however, hypergamy à la Solomon, and not just exogamy, is the issue in the text, then the separation ritual could well have been to the *golah* community's disadvantage economically and politically speaking.[28]

---

24. Note how the larger Solomonic tradition often critiques Solomon for this practice. For example, Song 8:11–12 may well be alluding to this practice metaphorically when negatively comparing Solomon's vast and numerous "vineyards" compared to the lover's one vineyard. See Longman, *Song of Songs*, 219–20.

25. Smith-Christopher, *A Biblical Theology*, 152–55.

26. This view was first argued by Würthwein, *Der 'am ha'arez*, 51–71.

27. Eskenazi demonstrates that land tenure and inheritance were major concerns in post-exilic times and further demonstrates from the Elephantine papyri that even women could inherit land. See Eskenazi, "Out of the Shadows."

28. Smith-Christopher, *A Biblical Theology*, 146. Smith-Christopher helpfully

Section 4: Prayers of Others

The similarities and differences between Ezra's and Solomon's prayers noted above are numerous and varied. The table below provides a convenient summary for review before proceeding to draw some pertinent conclusions.

Feature	Solomon's Prayer (1 Kgs 8 and Context)	Ezra's Prayer (Ezra 9 and Context)	Comment
Expands the prohibitions of intermarriage in Deut 7 and 23 to include all foreigners.	YES	YES	These are the only two passages that explicitly expand the Deuteronomic prohibitions.
Framed by comments/concerns regarding intermarriage with foreigners	YES	YES	Ezra 9:1; 10:1–44; 1 Kgs 3:1; 7:8; 11:1
Person praying adopts kneeling posture with palms spread toward heaven	YES	YES	Solomon begins his prayer in a standing posture but, at some point, kneels (1 Kgs 8:22, 54)
Emphasizes the temple as focal point for prayer and evidence of divine favor	YES	NO	Ezra has a much soberer assessment of the temple and its role in YHWH's relationship w/Israel than does Solomon
Emphasizes favor in the eyes of Israel's captors as a manifestation of divine grace and fidelity	YES	YES	Ezra's mention of the favor shown by the Persian king functions as a fulfillment of Solomon's request that YHWH grant such favor
Structured around two statements beginning with "But now" (ve'attah)	YES	YES	Though both prayers have this feature, the feature functions very differently in each.

points out regarding the proper framework for reading Ezra 9–10, "The second, and wider, circle within which Ezra must be read is not only other biblical examples of priestly attitudes and ideologies but also in the context of minority and refugee behaviors in circumstances of subordination."

Displays an openness to foreigners sharing sacred space with Israel	YES	NO (OR BETTER, NOT YET)	This is the key difference. Many interpreters have perhaps too hastily read Ezra 9–10 as a hard "no." I think it is fairer to read it as a soft "no" (i.e. not yet) though admittedly, Ezra is silent on this issue.
Argues for the need to separate foreigners from the assembly and sacred space	YES (SUBTLY)	YES (EMPHATICALLY)	I am thinking here of the separation of Pharaoh's daughter from Jerusalem (1 Kgs 9:24; cf. 2 Chr 8:11)
Engages in or reacts to hypergamy	YES	YES	Given the Chronicler's interpretation of this action, this could be the point of the series of Solomonic allusions, serving as a precedent for the separation of Ezra 10

CONCLUSIONS

Solomon's prayer displays a remarkable openness to foreigners' participation in prayers directed toward the temple. This attitude is consistent with the cosmopolitan nature of Solomon's reign. Arguably, however, it was an undisciplined openness that jeopardized Israel's holiness and risked the loss of her positive influence on the nations. Thus, Ezra's prayer emphasizes the opposite dynamic in Israel's complex relationship with other nations—separation for the sake of ritual purity and access to the temple rituals.

The suggestion that, like Solomon, members of the *golah* community practiced a kind of hypergamy potentially alleviates some of the tensions felt between these two prayers and their contexts. First, it calls into question the common assumption that the members of the *golah* community were the powerbrokers in the situation whose xenophobia disadvantaged the expelled wives and children. Much of the sociological and anthropological evidence points in the other direction. The *golah* community was more likely the disadvantaged minority seeking reentry into landholding and inheritance by means of these marriages.

This illegitimate means of regaining the promise was modeled by Solomon whose hypergamy stands in stark contrast to the reliance on YHWH suggested by his dedicatory prayer. Solomon prays as though the security of David's dynasty, of the temple, and of Israel rests in God's hands. He rules, however, as if such security rests in his own hands, making repeated compromises in the interest of securing foreign alliances through marriages that ultimately led to his apostasy.

Ezra's prayer, on the other hand, parallels Solomon's only to highlight a crucial difference, indeed a theological "about face." Recognizing the grace that YHWH has shown the *golah* community, and recognizing the community's utter dependence on the continuation of that grace, Ezra renounces the Solomonic hypergamy into which they've fallen. The *golah* community's future cannot be secured by "marrying up," thus repeating the sins of previous generations that resulted in their present servitude. This ultimately serves neither God's people nor the nations YHWH seeks to reach through his people.

This comparison between the prayers of 1 Kgs 8 and Ezra 9 highlights two fundamental theological truths regarding prayer in general. First, prayer by its very nature is an act of radical dependence on God that must be followed by an equally radical rejection of the kind of security offered by the defiling power structures of the current world order. Second, prayer is an acknowledgement of and participation in God's universal sovereignty and love that propels us into the world with sanctifying power.

Ironically, these two truths often stand in almost unbearable tension both in Scripture and in the life of faith. It is a tension, however, with which the people of God must live and wrestle if we are to draw the nations into sacred space for an encounter with the divine. Jesus himself simultaneously insists that the temple be a house of prayer for all nations and that his disciples remain distinct from the world (Mark 11:17; John 17:14). The tension thus continues, indeed intensifies, in the new covenant—a tension that Christ and every faithful follower of Christ embody as they come together to form a house of prayer for all nations (Eph 2:19–22).

BIBLIOGRAPHY

Blenkinsopp, Joseph. *Ezra-Nehemiah*. OTL. Philadelphia: Westminster, 1988.
Brueggemann, Walter. *Great Prayers of the Old Testament*. Louisville: Westminster John Knox, 2008.
Callabro, David Michael. "Ritual Gestures of Lifting, Extending, and Clasping the Hand(s) in Northwest Semitic Literature and Iconography." PhD diss., University of Chicago, 2014.
Cogan, Mordechai. *I Kings*. AB 10; New York: Doubleday, 2001.
Eskenazi, Tamara. "Out of the Shadows: Biblical Women in the Post-exilic Era," *JSOT* 54 (1992) 25–43.
Hanhart, R., ed. *Esdrae Liber I*. Vol. VIII/1. Göttingen: Vandenhoeck & Ruprecht, 1991.
Janzen, David. "Scholars, Witches, Ideologues, and What the Text Said: Ezra 9–10 and Its Interpretation." In *Approaching Yehud: New Approaches to the Study of the Persian Period*, edited by Jon L. Berquist, 49–69. Atlanta: SBL, 2007.
Japhet, Sarah. *1 & 2 Chronicles*. OTL. Louisville: Westminster John Knox, 1993.
Kloner, Amos. "The Identity of the Idumeans Based on the Archeological Evidence from Maresha." In *Judah and the Judeans in the Achaemenid Period*, edited by Obed Lipschits et al., 563–73. Winona Lake, IN: Eisenbrauns, 2011.
Longman, Tremper III. *Song of Songs*. NICOT. Grand Rapids: Eerdmans, 2001.
Myers, Jacob M. *Ezra-Nehemiah*. AB. New York: Doubleday, 1965.
O'Brien, Julia M. "From Exile to Empire: A Response." In *Approaching Yehud: New Approaches to the Study of the Persian Period*, edited by Jon L. Berquist, 209–14. Atlanta: SBL, 2007.
Redditt, Paul. *Ezra-Nehemiah*. SHBC. Macon, GA: Smyth & Helwys, 2014.
Smith-Christopher, Daniel. *A Biblical Theology of Exile*. Minneapolis: Fortress, 2002.
Southwood, Katherine. *Ethnicity and the Mixed Marriage Crisis of Ezra 9–10: An Anthropological Approach*. Oxford: Oxford University Press, 2014.
Strawn, Brent A. "'The Fear of the LORD' in Two (or Three) Dimensions: Iconography and *Yir'at Yhwh*." In *Iconographic Exegesis of the Hebrew Bible/Old Testament*, edited by Izaak J. de Hulster et al., 295–311. Göttingen: Vandenhoeck & Ruprecht, 2015.

Section 4: Prayers of Others

Throntveit, Mark A. *Ezra-Nehemiah*. IBC. Louisville: John Knox, 1992.
Torrey, Charles C. *Ezra Studies*. New York: KTAV, 1910.
Van der Toorn, Karel. *Scribal Culture and the Making of the Hebrew Bible*. Cambridge, MA: Harvard University Press, 2009.
Würthwein, Ernst. *Der 'amm ha'arez im Alten Testament*. BWANT, Band 69; Stuttgart: Kohlhammer-Verlag, 1936.

13

Recycled and Reclaimed
God's Words as Echoed in Nehemiah's Prayer (1:5–11)

Sheri L. Klouda Sharp

INTRODUCTION

WHEN I PROPOSED A thesis that sought to examine the relationship between Moses' prayers and the prayer of Nehemiah in 1:5–11, my original goal was to establish a connection between the prayers of these two leaders and demonstrate Nehemiah's dependence on Moses in the composition of his prayer. However, what I discovered after a careful analysis was not that Nehemiah employed elements from Moses' prayers, but rather, that Nehemiah drew on the words of Yahweh himself as recorded by Moses. His appropriation and recontextualization of Yahweh's words, representative of those who were so steeped in Scripture that familiar expressions colored their petitions and speech, lends credibility to Nehemiah's petition, providing a model for a prayer that draws its authority through the reappropriation of God's words. The reclamation of God's words and the incorporation of those words in personal prayer shape the petitions of the faithful, not only reminding them of their imperfections,

Section 4: Prayers of Others

but also reassuring them of God's immanence, mercy, and compassion in answering those prayers.

Later biblical writers drew on earlier texts in the composition of their messages. They did so for a variety of reasons, whether to evoke the memory of an earlier event, or to draw on the authority of a previous text in order to reaffirm the credibility of the new message. Earlier texts are often adapted for the needs of the new audience. It makes sense then, that petitionary prayers of people in the Old Testament would appropriate the words and expressions used by prominent Old Testament individuals from the past in the composition of their petitions and prayers. After all, if God heard and responded favorably to those earlier petitions and prayers, why not adapt a successful model from the past?

At the time of his first recorded prayer to God, Nehemiah served in the critical role of the cupbearer for the king. Nehemiah's position gave him unusual access to the king on a regular basis. He pleads to God on behalf of the people in a prayer that shares elements with other intercessory prayers in the Hebrew Bible. In particular, Nehemiah's prayer draws heavily on cultic language, contextual models, and themes from the words of Yahweh as recorded by or repeated by Moses. This literary dependence on divine speech as conveyed to Moses suggests that Nehemiah sought to reproduce past patterns of expression of prominent Israelites as a means of establishing authoritative grounds for their current petition. This chapter examines the thematic and verbal links between the prayer of Neh 1:5–11 and divine speech in Exod 32–34 and passages in Deuteronomy,[1] especially Deut 30, and aims to demonstrate the continued impact and profound influence of *earlier texts of significant individuals on later petitions* by common people in the Old Testament, and how those appropriations influence the prayers of God's people.

DISCERNING INTERTEXTUALITY

Intertextual relationships among biblical texts are typically determined from the following generally accepted criteria: chronology, familiarity, contextual affinities, linguistic correspondence, formulaic or repetitive language, and the history of interpretation.[2]

---

1. Myers, *Ezra-Nehemiah*, 95–96.
2. See Hays, *Echoes of Scripture in the Letters of Paul*, 29–32, where Hays presents

Textual dependence assumes a clearly discernible diachronic relationship, establishing one text as historically preceding the other.³ While it is easier to establish a linear timeline when discussing Old Testament and New Testament interdependence, the process is often more difficult when determining the historical provenance of two or more Old Testament texts. In the case of Nehemiah's prayer and the prayers of Moses, the historical trajectory clearly identifies Moses' words as the literary predecessor. In an unusual twist, Nehemiah employs a rare citation formula, clearly identifying the source of his words (v. 8).

Similarly, we can affirm the availability of the texts from Exodus and Deuteronomy and their familiarity to the post-exilic audience, who would not only recognize Moses' words and the events surrounding his prayers and conversations with Yahweh, but who also as a community already historically understand those texts as authoritative, and thus, to some degree, canonical. It is incumbent upon us to discern in our analysis, however, whether Nehemiah's prayer intentionally quotes from a specific earlier text, a *biblical allusion*, or if Nehemiah's prayer draws from a collection of texts sharing a corresponding theme, commonly known as *biblical echo*.⁴

In addition, a comparison of the contextual elements of potentially interdependent texts endeavors to establish thematic correlations that indicate that the two or more passages share elements that would link them together in the minds of the reader. We acknowledge that the context of a literary predecessor plays an interpretive role when it is adopted and appropriated in a later text.⁵ The Jewish audience or reader would import the contextual significance of a familiar, historically pivotal set of passages, which then exert an interpretive influence on the later text

---

seven criteria to determine the presence of biblical echoes: availability, volume, recurrence, thematic coherence, historical plausibility, history of interpretation, and satisfaction. Hays does not use the term "echo" as this study defines it, since the scope of his study does not strive to establish lines of continuity between interpretive strategies in the Old Testament as much as it seeks to discuss the imaginative discontinuities and stunningly creative "mis-readings" by which Paul departs from his textual precursor.

3. Fishbane, *Biblical Interpretation*, 335.
4. Hollander, *The Figure of Echo*, 64.
5. Schultz, *The Search for Quotation*, 212–14.

Section 4: Prayers of Others

for the contemporary audience. As we will see, Nehemiah's prayer draws on contextual similarities from select passages from Exodus and Deuteronomy by quoting the words of Yahweh as recorded by Moses.

A careful linguistic analysis of literary pretexts with later compositions often identifies the degree of terminological correspondence between two or more passages, providing evidence that argues in favor of or against a specific literary relationship. A comparison of verbal affinities includes identifying rare or eclectic terminology that occurs in only two possibly related texts, noting specific or intentional word deviations or omissions in potentially dependent passages, and exploring the use of formulaic, or cultic, expressions which typically occur in the Old Testament corpus. Consequently, the absence of distinctive terminology limited to two texts presents a formidable argument against the later writer's reuse of a specific literary precedent. However, the lack of unique or rare terms does not negate the possibility of biblical echo, in which the writer awakens in the reader the recognition of a specific group of literary pretexts familiar to the audience. As we will see, a comparison of Deut 30:1–4 and Neh 1:7–9 reveals the usage of at least one relatively rare term, and a shared concentration of verbal links.

In addition, determining how often later biblical authors allude to or echo an earlier text and in which contexts contributes to our understanding of Nehemiah's purpose for quoting the divine attribute formulary. Nehemiah 1:5 employs portions of the divine attribute formulary from Exod 34:6–7, which is adapted multiple times in Old Testament prayers.[6] In addition, Neh 4:5 reuses unusual language from the intercessory prayer of Moses in Exod 32:31–33. Finally, in Nehemiah's later prayer (Neh 9:17), he employs a fuller form of the divine attribute formulary as he recollects Yahweh's response to the Golden Calf incident in Exod 32.

THE PRAYER

As the catalyst for Nehemiah's initial recorded prayer, an entourage travels from Jerusalem to Susa and reports to Nehemiah that the defensive wall of the city is heavily damaged, leaving the capital vulnerable

---

6. Pss 86:15; 103:8–10; 111:4; 116:5; 145:8; Nah 1:3; Joel 2:13; Neh 9:17, 31; Jonah 4:2; 2 Chr 30:9; 2 Kgs 13:23; Mic 7:18–20; Jer 32:18.

to predators and enemies. Nehemiah's proximity as a servant to King Artaxerxes enables him to ask the king's permission to travel to Jerusalem and oversee the work on the wall. In addition, Nehemiah asks for letters of permission issued by the king to government officials instructing them to permit the rebuilding to take place.

In order to accomplish this goal, Nehemiah prays a petitionary prayer to Yahweh, which has the following form, based loosely on the outline of an individual lament:

1. Introductory Address and Appeal (v. 5)
2. Petition (v. 6ab)
3. Repentance and Confession (6cd–7)
4. Confession of Trust (v. 8–9)
5. Reminder (v. 10)
6. Petition Proper (v. 11)

Nehemiah employs the term "servant" or "servants" eight times in his prayer, suggesting a potential keyword that provides the central emphasis of the prayer. Nehemiah refers to Moses twice as Yahweh's servant at the end of v. 7, and again in v. 8. If we look at the overall structure of the passage, we note a loose chiastic or parallel arrangement based on the significance of the term "servant."

A. Your *servant* (Nehemiah) v. 6a

  B. Your *servants* (Israel) v. 6c

    C. Your *servant*, Moses, v. 7d

    C¹ Your *servant*, Moses, v. 8a

  B¹ Your *servants* (Israel) v. 10

A¹ Your *servant* (Nehemiah) v. 11a, AND

  B¹ Your *servants* (Israel) v. 11b

A¹ Your *servant* (Nehemiah) v. 11c

The chiastic structure emphasizes Yahweh's commands to Moses (vv. 7d, 8a), evoking for the reader not only Moses himself, but pivotal

Section 4: Prayers of Others

events and terminology associated with the Exodus.[7] Furthermore, the term "command" and its derivatives are concentrated in vv. 7b–9a, occurring four times, and forge another connection between Nehemiah's prayer and Exodus, as well as Deuteronomy. Moses served as prophet par excellence, and enjoyed a unique relationship with God, speaking with him "face to face" as friends do.[8] He mediated the counsel of God to the Israelites. That unique privilege was reserved for Moses alone, in a different time and place in Israel's early developmental history. Physical manifestations of the presence of God and direct communication between God and humanity ceased long before Nehemiah's time.[9] Thus, there is no direct exchange between Nehemiah and Yahweh. Nevertheless, Nehemiah appeals to the form and words used by Moses in formulating his own prayer, anticipating a more favorable response from Yahweh in light of Moses' unique relationship with God. In addition, Nehemiah employs prior revelation, or God's own words, to address the current crisis in a specific way. Nehemiah represents himself as a servant in his approach to God in order to demonstrate his obedience and his submission to God's response.

Nehemiah introduces his prayer with the praise of Yahweh's name, referring to Yahweh as the God of the heavens (or God of heaven), an address typical of the Ezra-Nehemiah corpus.[10] He then echoes the divine attribute formulary, Yahweh's self-revelation of his character in Exod 34:6–7, which Nehemiah later quotes in his prayer in ch. 9. The fullest form of this expression occurs first in Exod 34, and the Old Testament writers adapt and reuse the formula frequently though never in its entirety. Each biblical writer appropriates those parts of the formula which best fit the specific context of his message, often emphasizing the positive attributes of Yahweh in times of distress.[11]

---

7. See, in particular, Exod 32:13 where Moses exhorts Yahweh to remember his servants.

8. Exod 33:11; cf. Deut 34:10.

9. See Friedman, *The Disappearance of God*, 19–26.

10. E.g., Ezra 1:2; Neh 1:4, 5; 2:4, 20.

11. Widmer, *Standing in the Breach*, 83–92. Widmer considers Exod 32–34 as the most "detailed and intense treatment of intercessory prayer in the entire Old Testament." In fact, Widmer believes that Moses' prayers provide an authoritative prayer model upon which to build later prayers. He further observes, in particular, that the

> Yahweh, Yahweh, God of compassion and mercy, slow to anger and *abounding in covenant love* and faithfulness, *extending covenant love to thousands,* forgiving sin, transgressions and iniquity, but he does not leave the guilty unpunished, visiting the punishment of the fathers upon children and grandchildren unto the third and fourth generation. (Exod 34:6–7)

> Know, therefore, that Yahweh your God is God; he is a faithful God, *keeping his covenant of love to a thousand generations of those who love him* and keep his commands. (Deut 7:9)

> Then he said, "I ask please, Yahweh, God of the heavens the great God and one to be feared, *the one who keeps the covenant and covenant love, to those who love him and to those who keep his commandments*" (Neh 1:5a).[12]

Nehemiah's first prayer hints at the formula, reminding God of his covenant love or loyalty (*khesed*). While affirming an inherent tension between Yahweh as a holy, wrathful God and a God of covenant love and loyalty, he presumes the dominance and permanence of Yahweh's merciful and compassionate maintenance of the covenant as superseding God's individual acts of judgment. Divine wrath is temporary (cf. Mic 7:18), but God's *khesed* prevails. Nehemiah prays the words of God back to him.

Key to understanding Nehemiah's prayer model and why he invokes Exod 34 centers on the definition of the Hebrew term *khesed*. While the term is often simplistically translated as "lovingkindness," the concept is actually too complex to translate with a single English word. The term *khesed* denotes a voluntary, not obligatory, love.[13] When Yahweh established the bi-lateral or conditional Mosaic Covenant, each party agreed to certain responsibilities. However, Israel almost immediately abrogated the covenant, essentially breaking the agreement. The other party, Yahweh, was no longer contractually obligated to keep his promises based on the covenant alone. Yet, Yahweh's essential character

---

divine attribute formulary in Exod 34:6–7 describes how God's name is related to "sin, divine judgment, intercessory prayer, and covenant renewal."

12. All translations are the author's own unless otherwise specified.

13. For a full discussion, see Glueck, *Hesed in the Bible*; Sakenfeld, *Faithfulness in Action*; and Clark, *The Word "Hesed" in the Hebrew Bible*.

Section 4: Prayers of Others

and nature are immutable, and, as the result of the nature of his covenant love or loyalty, he voluntarily continues to maintain his promises to Israel despite her continued malfeasance. Nehemiah's prayer serves as a conduit through which he and the people see the outworking of God's covenant love towards them in a practical way. Yahweh's intervention ensures a favorable answer from King Artaxerxes, and his covenant loyalty expresses itself as he acts providentially towards the returning exiles as they face challenging opposition from other leaders.

Nehemiah once again appropriates the divine attribute formulary from Exod 34:6–7, though more fully, in the dedicatory prayer in Neh 9:17: "But you are *a forgiving God, gracious and compassionate, slow to anger and abounding in covenant love.*" In the midst of a historical summary of Yahweh's gracious acts towards Israel, the prayer in Neh 9 recollects Israel's worship of the golden calf and Yahweh's response. Yahweh chose to continue his relationship with his people, despite their unfaithfulness. Nehemiah's understanding of Yahweh's propensity to forgive and his appreciation for the divine attribute formulary provide the foundation of his petition, and these clearly influence his prayer in ch. 1.

In fact, vv. 6b–7a acknowledge Israel's continued sinfulness as a potential impediment to Yahweh's positive response. Nehemiah identifies with his people and understands himself as equally guilty in their irresponsible behavior. This bond intrinsically equips him to intercede on their behalf, just as Moses demonstrates his inextricable bond to the Israelites by offering to have his name "blotted from Yahweh's book (Ex 32:32–33)."[14] Nehemiah expresses repentance on his behalf and on behalf of the people in an effort to remove any obstacle that would hinder Yahweh's intervention.

A comparison of Deut 30:1–4 and Neh 1:7–9 reveals the usage of at least one relatively rare term, and a shared concentration of verbal links. Note that the content in vv. 8b–9 derives from Moses' speech in

---

14. Interestingly, we see a stunning reversal expressed in the short imprecatory prayer of Neh 4:4, in which he requests that the insults of the officials fall back on them, so that their "guilt would not be removed and their sins would not be blotted" from Yahweh's sight.

Deut 30:1–4, and reinforces a linguistic and contextual literary relationship that appears intentionally to allude to this specific text:

> If you are disloyal, *I will scatter you among the peoples*, but if you return to me and observe my commandments by performing them, *then those who have been scattered to the edges of the heavens, from there, I shall gather them* and bring them to a place which I chose for my name to dwell (Neh 1:8b–9).

> When all these blessings and curses I have set before you come upon you and *they return* to your heart among all the nations where Yahweh God dispersed you there, and *when you return* to Yahweh your God and *obey him* with one voice regarding all that which *I am commanding* today, you and your children, with all your heart and all your soul, then Yahweh your God will restore your fortunes and have compassion on you and *gather you again from all the peoples where he scattered you. Even if you have been scattered to the edges of the heavens, from there Yahweh your God will gather you and bring you back.* He will bring you to the land ... (Deut 30:1–4)

From a linguistic perspective, the two passages share the rare Hebrew verb *nadakh*, which means "disperse." The term occurs only twice in the Pentateuch with reference to people, once in the Hiphil form in Deut 30:1, and again, in the Niphal stem in v. 4.[15] In addition to the passage in Nehemiah, Jeremiah employs the term in connection with God's people frequently.[16] Other occurrences of the term are limited to late exilic and post-exilic literature. In addition to the rare use of a citation formula,[17] which identifies the following words as a quotation, we can conclude that the use of a rare term from Deut 30 in Nehemiah's prayer indicates that Nehemiah intentionally alluded to this specific passage. The correlation of contexts (sin and forgiveness lead to restoration) serves to remind the audience of Yahweh's promises. In addition, there is also a unique concentration of phrases shared by these two passages alone:

15. *HALOT* 673.
16. Jer 30:17; 40:12; 43:5; 49:5, 36.
17. "Remember the word you gave your servant Moses, saying ..." (v. 8).

those who *have been scattered* (*nadakh*) to the *edges of the heavens, from there I shall gather them* (Neh 1:8b–9)

where Yahweh God *scattered* (*nadakh*) you there . . . even if you *have been scattered* (*nadakh*) *to the edges of the heavens, from there Yahweh your God shall gather you* (Deut 30:1–4).

It appears that Nehemiah recollects God's speech from Deut 30 and reuses it in his prayer in order to remind Yahweh of his promise to rescue and restore Israel. He adopts terminology, context, and distinctive phrases, as well as adopting a citation formula. He invokes the past words of God and prays the words of God back to him.

Nehemiah formally connects his prayer with Yahweh's words to Moses, not only the authoritative basis for Israel's eventual captivity and dispersion, but also as the grounds upon which Nehemiah seeks a positive response of deliverance from God. He appeals to the God of promise, acknowledging Israel's sinfulness as the cause of her exile, but also reminding Yahweh of his commitment to the ongoing process of national restoration. Nehemiah prays God's words back to him here in this context, much as Moses used God's words in his prayer in Exod 32:13. In both instances, a failure on God's part to act would ratify Yahweh's anger and abandonment of his people and minimalize Yahweh's covenant love, his mercy and compassion.

In my final example, the phrase "your great power and your mighty/strong hand" (Neh 1:10) at first suggests a familiar cultic or formulaic expression that recurs frequently in praise of Yahweh. In fact, we find this particular verbal combination only in Exod 32:11 and Neh 1:10. The phrases "mighty hand" and "great power/strength" stand separately in other contexts. Compare:

with great power and a mighty hand (*bekhoakh gadol uveyad khazaqah*) (Exod 32:11)

by your great strength and your mighty hand (*bekhokhakha haggadol uveyadkha hakhazaqah*) (Neh 1:10)

As we have already noted, Exod 32 plays a significant contextual role in Nehemiah's prayers, forging a connection between the events and words surrounding the Golden Calf incident and the guilt of the returning exiles who have "acted corruptly." The interplay of texts in Nehemiah's prayer conflates the events and words from Exod 32–34 and Deut 30, indicating that he and his audience would recognize a particular corpus of material associated with the Golden Calf incident in Exodus and Moses' mediating role as the one who speaks God's words to the people. Perhaps the audience understands these texts as all parts of one seamless story, particularly since Nehemiah refers again to Israel's idolatry in his later prayer (Neh 9). In any case, Israel's sin of idolatry provides the contextual backdrop to Nehemiah's petition, since it was idolatry and covenant abrogation that led to Israel's dispersion and exile.

CONCLUSIONS

Our observations lead to the conclusion that Nehemiah's petitionary prayer shares language and contextual features that both allude to and echo texts from Exodus and Deuteronomy. Nehemiah's use of a rare citation formula introducing a quote from Deut 30:1–4 indicates that he intentionally sought to evoke a specific earlier text in his prayer, praying God's words back to him as they were recorded by Moses. In addition, the verbal correspondence of the two passages and the use of a rare term suggest literary borrowing. Moreover, the structure of Nehemiah's prayer indicates that Moses plays a central role in how the prayer is fashioned in an effort to connect the circumstances of the returning exiles with the Israelite situation during the Exodus. Contextually, both Moses and Nehemiah petition God on behalf of the people, associate themselves with the sinful behavior of the nation, and seek the Lord's forgiveness and his merciful and compassionate deliverance. A portion of the self-revelatory formula spoken by Yahweh describing his character in Exod 34 recurs in Deut 7:9, which Nehemiah reuses along with Deut 30 to remind Yahweh of his covenant loyalty and his deliverance of Israel in the past. Yahweh's positive response toward his people in the past provides the basis for his current intervention for the post-exilic community. The shared terminology between Neh 1:11 and Exod 32:11 further reinforces Nehemiah's appeal for Yahweh's divine intervention on Israel's behalf as an outworking of Yahweh's covenant love or loyalty.

Section 4: Prayers of Others

WHAT NEHEMIAH'S PRAYER TEACHES US ABOUT PRAYING

Oftentimes, God's people will rely on the words of God himself in the formation of personal prayer, praying those prayers back to him. Jesus' prayer in the Sermon on the Mount (Matt 6:9–13) remains the iconic and most popular model. The faithful perceive the divine authority inherent in God's spoken word, which provides the foundation upon which they can form personal prayer consisting of their specific concerns. Individuals appropriate the words themselves and internalize their relevance in their conversations with God, seeking connections between the source prayer and its application to their particular circumstances.

The use of God's words in personal prayer serves to remind the petitioner of certain theological truths shared commonly among the faithful (such as God's immutability and power), while concomitantly assisting in the most beneficial formulation of prayer by providing prompts to guide petitioners in presenting themselves in humility and obedience. Nehemiah acknowledges the sinfulness of the people and their need for repentance as a precursor to a positive response from God by echoing Yahweh's words from the past and pointing towards God's propensity for forgiveness and deliverance.

Scriptural prayer models also draw on God's historical dealings with his people in the past as a paradigm for contemporary expectation that God remains aware and merciful and answers prayers. This adaptation and reuse of Scriptural prayers by individuals, in which meaning can be subjective through Scriptural application (rather than interpretation), often differs from Scripture's appropriation of earlier texts in later writings, where the meaning of the original text is not relative but unaltered and imported in some way into the later context.

Challenges to the recitation of confessional or formulaic prayer suggest that prayers that are generated externally and reused by individuals or in a community context are somehow inadequate or less authentic. However, value lies in group recitation of formulaic prayer as believers draw strength from one another through shared beliefs and shared struggles.

Although confessional and formulaic prayers serve to link the faithful together, they cannot totally replace the need for personal reflection and the brutal honesty that derives from our personal, heartfelt, unique conversations with God.

BIBLIOGRAPHY

Clark, Gordon R. *The Word "Hesed" in the Hebrew Bible.* JSOTSup 157. Sheffield: JSOT, 1993.

Fishbane, Michael. *Biblical Interpretation in Ancient Israel.* Oxford: Clarendon, 1985.

Friedman, Richard Elliott. *The Disappearance of God: A Divine Mystery.* New York: Little, Brown & Company, 1995.

Glueck, Nelson. *Hesed in the Bible.* New York: KTAV, 1968.

Hays, Richard. *Echoes of Scripture in the Letters of Paul.* New Haven, CT: Yale University Press, 1989.

Hollander, John. *The Figure of Echo.* Berkeley, CA: University of California Press, 1981.

Myers, Jacob. *Ezra-Nehemiah.* AB 14. New York: Doubleday, 1965.

Sakenfeld, Katherine Doob. *Faithfulness in Action: Loyalty in Biblical Perspective.* OBT. Philadelphia: Fortress, 1985.

Schultz, Richard. *The Search for Quotation: Verbal Parallels in the Prophets.* JSOTSup 180. Sheffield: Sheffield Academic, 1999.

Widmer, Michael. *Standing in the Breach: An Old Testament Theology and Spirituality of Intercessory Prayer.* Siphrut 13. Winona Lake, IN: Eisenbrauns, 2015.

14

Agur's Prayer (Proverbs 30:7–9)
An Everyday Response to Extraordinary Revelation

JOANNA GREENLEE KLINE

THE ONLY PRAYER IN the book of Proverbs is found in an enigmatic collection of sayings introduced as "the words of Agur" (30:1). In his brief supplication, Agur makes two requests: to be kept far from deceit and to be given neither riches nor poverty (30:7–9). While the text of the prayer itself is clear, its placement in the collection of Agur's sayings, as well as in the book of Proverbs as a whole, raises the question of whether the prayer relates in an integral way to the material surrounding it, or whether it is simply an independent tradition that has been inserted. Answering this question is complicated by the fact that Agur's speech is one of the most textually difficult and hermeneutically perplexing passages in the book of Proverbs. Interpreters have debated issues such as the delimitation of textual units in Prov 30, the meaning of certain words and phrases, and the tone of the passage, all of which have implications for understanding the prayer. In this essay, I will examine the prayer of vv. 7–9 in its context, arguing that it is an integral part of Agur's discourse and that it offers a resolution to the difficulties of the human predicament addressed at the beginning of Agur's speech.

Joanna Greenlee Kline—Agur's Prayer (Proverbs 30:7–9)

In his prayer, Agur provides a model of a faithful response to revealed wisdom and divine transcendence through his position of utter humility and simultaneous boldness in asking God for what he needs.

THE EXTENT OF AGUR'S WORDS

In order to understand the function of Agur's prayer, it is necessary to determine how much of Prov 30 can be understood as Agur's words. The content of the chapter can be summarized as follows: v. 1 contains a heading and a nearly untranslatable line; vv. 2–4 consist of a confession of human ignorance and limitations; vv. 5–6 are an affirmation of the trustworthiness of God's words; the prayer is found in vv. 7–9; v. 10 is a proverb about not slandering a servant to his master; vv. 11–14 are adages about an evil generation; and vv. 15–33 contain mostly numerical sayings. Proposals about how much of Prov 30 is Agur's words range from the first three verses to the entire chapter (a new heading at Prov 31:1 shows that Agur's words do not extend beyond the chapter).[1] Those who argue that Agur speaks only the first three or four verses typically characterize his speech as a pessimistic evaluation of the human quest for wisdom, which is answered in vv. 5–6 or vv. 5–9 by a pious interlocutor who provides a corrective teaching to counter Agur's skeptical assertions.[2] Against those who see a debate between a pessimistic Agur and an orthodox believer, some commentators have pointed to other biblical and deuterocanonical texts, such as Job 28, Ps 73, and Bar 3:29—4:1, that contrast human limitations with divine power and wisdom.[3] Since there are no explicit markers of a dialogue in Prov 30:1–9, it is best to read this passage as the statement of one speaker, who proceeds from despair at his own ignorance to a statement of trust in God's words, concluding with a prayer.[4]

---

1. For a summary of opinions on the extent of Agur's words, see Fox, *Proverbs 10–31*, 851.

2. See Crenshaw, *Old Testament Wisdom*, 75, 205; Scott, *Proverbs, Ecclesiastes*, 175–77; Toy, *Book of Proverbs*, 517, 523. André Barucq attributes vv. 1–3 to Agur and v. 4 to God (*Le livre des Proverbes*, 219).

3. See Clifford, *Proverbs*, 257; Fox, *Proverbs 10–31*, 861–62; Franklyn, "Sayings of Agur," 244–45, 251–52; Waltke, *Proverbs 15–31*, 466–67.

4. See Fox, *Proverbs 10–31*, 850–51; Franklyn, "Sayings of Agur," 251.

SECTION 4: PRAYERS OF OTHERS

While Prov 30:1–9 can be read as a unit, the same coherence cannot be found throughout the rest of the chapter. Although there are some verbal and conceptual links between Agur's sayings in vv. 1–9 and the proverbial wisdom of vv. 10–33,[5] it is difficult to discern a logical progression of thought after the end of Agur's prayer. It may be the case that the whole of Prov 30 should be considered a collection of Agur's sayings; nevertheless, because the first nine verses exhibit a coherence that is not found in the rest of the chapter, these will be considered a unit for the purposes of the present analysis.

TEXTUAL AND INTERPRETIVE PROBLEMS IN VERSE 1

If Prov 30:1–9 is to be understood as the words of Agur, as I have just argued, then Agur's prayer forms the conclusion of his speech. In order to understand the prayer, however, it is necessary to understand the material that precedes it. This task is especially difficult in the case of v. 1, which contains many textual ambiguities. Given the opaque nature of this verse, some of its interpretive problems will remain unresolvable. Nevertheless, the text requires close examination, both because v. 1 contains a number of connections to Agur's prayer and because the very difficulties in this verse may be a part of how it communicates its message.

Some minor interpretive issues appear in the first half of v. 1 ("The words of Agur son of Yaqeh. The oracle. The utterance of the man"),[6] inasmuch as the names Agur and Yaqeh are not found elsewhere in the

---

5. Verbal connections include the following: the construction "do not . . . lest" appears in vv. 6, 8b–9 and v. 10; the verb "sated" (*s-b-ʿ*) appears in v. 9 and vv. 15–16, 22; the same verb appears in the phrases "lest I become poor (*'ivvaresh*)" (v. 9) and "a maidservant when she displaces (*tirash*) her mistress" (v. 23); and the verb "to grasp" (*t-f-s*) appears in v. 9 and v. 28. As for conceptual links, vv. 7–9 have been associated with the numerical sayings of vv. 15–31 because Agur asks for "two things" (v. 7) but adds a third request ("feed me my apportioned food," v. 8), which gives his prayer an implicit similarity to the x/x+1 structure of the numerical sayings (see O'Dowd, *Proverbs*, 405). In addition, a first-person voice reappears in v. 18, with a tone similar to Agur's in vv. 2–3. Finally, Leo G. Perdue identifies "the sin of exalted self-pride" as the unifying theme of ch. 30, although he attributes only the first four verses to Agur (*Proverbs*, 256).

6. All biblical translations are my own unless otherwise noted.

Bible[7] and the words "the oracle" and "the utterance" are locutions typically found in prophetic contexts.[8] It is the final clause of v. 1 (*le'ithi'el le'ithi'el ve'ukhal*), however, that is the most textually difficult in the passage. According to the Masoretic pointing, these words are proper names (with a prefixed preposition or conjunction): "to Ithiel, to Ithiel and Ukal."[9] This interpretation is evidenced in the Syriac[10] and the targum and is used in the KJV, NASB, NIV (1984), and NJPS translations, but it is not followed by many modern commentators.[11] Another option is to divide the first and second words in two, reading *la'ithi* (from the root *l-'-h*) *'el*: "I am weary, O God, I am weary, O God" (cf. NRSV, ESV).[12] The last word in the clause (*ve'ukhal*) can be read "and I have wasted away," from the root *k-l-h* (cf. ESV, "and worn out"),[13] or

---

7. Ancient interpreters made sense of the names by associating them with related Hebrew words. In rabbinic midrash, for example, both names are said to refer to Solomon, who "girded (*'agar*) his loins for wisdom" and was "a son who is innocent (*naqi*) of sin" (*Midrash Proverbs* on Prov 30:1).

8. Some commentators emend the word "the oracle" (*hammassa'*) so that it becomes a gentilic ("the Massaite"). See Scott, *Proverbs, Ecclesiastes*, 175–76; Clifford, *Proverbs*, 260. On the terms "oracle" and "utterance" in prophetic contexts, see Fox, *Proverbs 10–31*, 852–53. The phrase "the utterance of the man" is unusual, as the word "utterance" is almost always followed by a name for God. The only other times the word is used in the context of a non-divine speaker are in the cases of Balaam (Num 24:3, 4, 15, 16), David (2 Sam 23:1), and personified "transgression" speaking to the wicked (Ps 36:1 [2]).

9. The name Ithiel is attested in Neh 11:7, but Ukal is unknown outside this passage.

10. The Syriac treats only Ithiel (not Ukal) as a proper name, and it appears only once (Fox, *Proverbs 10–31*, 1060–61).

11. Fox lists four reasons that this reading is unlikely: (1) the word *ki* (v. 2) indicates the continuation of a sentence, (2) it is strange for a name to be repeated twice, (3) similar headings include the words "his sons" after personal names, and (4) nowhere else in the Hebrew Bible is an oracle or pronouncement spoken to a named person (*Proverbs 10–31*, 853–54). O'Dowd is an exception to those who reject the reading of the MT (*Proverbs*, 402–3).

12. A related solution is to read the first instance of *le'ithi'el* as a name ("to Ithiel") and the second as a verb plus a vocative ("I am weary, O God") (cf. NIV [2011]; Waltke, *Proverbs 15–31*, 455, 467–77).

13. See Franklyn, "Sayings of Agur," 243–44 for a survey of other options. Franklyn (244), Fox (*Proverbs 10–31*, 853–54), and Longman (*Proverbs*, 519–20) prefer the reading from *k-l-h*, and LXX and Aquila also reflect this verb. In support of this reading, Fox notes that David is near death when he pronounces his "utterance" (*ne'um*) (cf. 2 Sam 23:1) and that the author of Ps 73 (a text similar in some ways to

Section 4: Prayers of Others

alternatively, "yet I am able" or "yet I can prevail," from the root *y-kh-l* (cf. NIV [2011]).[14] It is difficult to decide between the two readings, neither of which requires emending the consonantal text.[15] An entirely negative statement ("I am weary, O God, and I have wasted away") provides a logical introduction for the confession of human limitations in vv. 2–3. On the other hand, the reading "I am weary, O God, yet I can prevail" fits with the two-sided message of Agur's whole speech (vv. 1–9): humans are limited, but they can receive what they need with God's help.

For the purposes of the present analysis, it is significant that either reading produces a structure in which Agur's words begin and end with a prayer. The cry "I am weary, O God" introduces Agur's problem in an address to God, while the prayer at the end provides a measure of resolution. A second important point to be made about this ambiguous verse is that its textual difficulties may be a way of communicating the limitations of human understanding that Agur comments on in vv. 2–3. Perhaps the text of v. 1 works to initiate its readers into a feeling of helpless incomprehension similar to Agur's state in v. 2, so that the obscurities of the text embody its meaning.[16] The following verses also include several interpretive ambiguities, as we will see.

HUMAN LIMITATIONS (VV. 2–4)

Agur's anguished expression "I am weary, O God" is developed in vv. 2–3: "For I am more brutish than any man, and I do not have human understanding. I have not learned wisdom, nor do I have knowledge of the Holy One."[17] Agur's statement of ignorance has difficulties both

---

Prov 30:1–9, including a claim of ignorance in v. 22) has flesh that "is wasting away" (*kalah*) (v. 26); see *Proverbs 10–31*, 853.

14. See Waltke, *Proverbs 15–31*, 468.

15. Fox argues against the *y-kh-l* reading because "the writing of the sg. impf. of this verb without a *waw* would be aberrant" (*Proverbs 10–31*, 854); see, however, the evidence provided for this reading by Waltke, *Proverbs 15–31*, 468n102.

16. For other biblical examples of literary form reinforcing content, see Rendsburg, *How the Bible Is Written*, 128–54, 539–49.

17. The word translated "Holy One" is in the plural ("holy ones"). It could refer to holy things, angels, or God, but the fact that the phrase "knowledge of the Holy One" appears in parallel with "the fear of Yahweh" in Prov 9:10 is evidence that the

on the level of grammar and with regard to the role of such a confession in a wisdom book. First, as Fox notes, there is a double entendre in v. 2a, which can be read "I am the most ignorant of men" or "I am more beast than man."[18] A more difficult ambiguity is presented by v. 3, which has a negative particle only in the first clause: "I have not learned wisdom." Most interpreters understand the second clause as negative ("nor do I have knowledge of the Holy One") by extending the force of the negative particle to both clauses.[19] The alternative is to read the verse as presenting a contrast: "I have not learned wisdom, but I have knowledge of the Holy One." As was the case with the translational options in v. 1 ("I am weary, O God, and I have wasted away" and "I am weary, O God, but I can prevail"), both options can be understood as consistent with Agur's message. According to the majority reading with two negative clauses, Agur presents himself as utterly ignorant; his lack of knowledge is later contrasted with God's perfect words (vv. 5–6). If v. 3 is read with only one negative clause, however, the contrast between human knowledge and divine wisdom is present here as well: Agur has not received knowledge from other people—his wisdom comes from divine revelation. While the traditional rendering is probably to be preferred,[20] the ambiguity presented by the grammar of the verse should not be overlooked. As in other difficult parts of vv. 1–4, more than one meaning may be intended.

Despite the ambiguities of vv. 2–3, it is clear that Agur's statement is an extraordinary claim of ignorance, one that is especially striking at the end of a book whose purpose is to teach wisdom. As O'Dowd points out, the words Agur uses here—"understanding" (*binah*), "wisdom" (*khokhmah*), and "knowledge" (*da'ath*)—recall the introduction to the book of Proverbs, which explains the goal of the book: "To know wisdom (*lada'ath khokhmah*) and instruction, to discern words of

---

word refers to God here (see Fox, *Proverbs 10–31*, 855).

18. Fox writes, "The root meaning of *ba'ar* is 'beast,' and it retains that connotation here" (*Proverbs 10–31*, 854).

19. See Fox, *Proverbs 10–31*, 854–55.

20. Fox, whose earlier interpretation of v. 3 limited the force of the negative particle to the first clause, changed his opinion due to a consideration of the statement in its wider context: "It seems unlikely that Agur would lay claim to such knowledge, since in the next verse he insists on human limitations" (*Proverbs 10–31*, 855).

understanding (*binah*)" (1:2).[21] Agur's words thus appear to portray a sage who has not absorbed the instruction found in the book of Proverbs. Or perhaps he has. Agur's statement of ignorance is probably not intended to undermine the whole pursuit of wisdom, but is meant as a mature appraisal of the limits of human understanding. The tension between wisdom as both obtainable and unobtainable is found earlier in the book of Proverbs and in other biblical wisdom books.[22] A careful study of a wisdom text such as the book of Proverbs should produce humility; the extreme nature of Agur's words may show that he has been zealous in his search for wisdom, and wearied by it (cf. Eccl 7:23–24; 12:12).

Agur's questions in v. 4 are a continuation of his statement of human limitations: "Who has ascended to heaven and come down? Who has gathered the wind in the hollow of his hand? Who has wrapped up the waters in a garment? Who has established all the ends of the earth? What is his name, and what is the name of his son, if you know?" These questions serve to universalize the position of ignorance expressed by Agur in vv. 2–3.[23] There, Agur expressed his own lack of knowledge; here, he challenges his audience to recognize the chasm that separates humans from God. As with the statements in vv. 1–3, these questions may operate as a multivalent riddle, giving rise to different interpretations. Some commentators argue that the answer to Agur's first four questions is, in Fox's words, "No one, of course."[24] According to this

---

21. O'Dowd, *Proverbs*, 403; see also Waltke, *Proverbs 15–31*, 469.

22. The premise of the book of Proverbs, as seen in its introduction (1:1–7), is that wisdom *can* be learned. On the other hand, the book warns against relying on one's own understanding (3:5) and it counsels humility (11:2) (see O'Dowd, *Proverbs*, 403). Agur's statements are even closer to texts from Job (chs. 28, 38–42) and Ecclesiastes (3:11; 7:23–24; 8:17), however.

23. See Fox, *Proverbs 10–31*, 856–57.

24. Fox, *Proverbs 10–31*, 856–57; see also Clifford, *Proverbs*, 262. Fox argues, "The scope of the questions is implicitly confined to humanity, because Agur is speaking about the inadequacy of human wisdom" (856). This makes the emphasis of Agur's questions different from the emphasis of God's questions to Job in Job 38, which "call for the answer 'God, of course'" (Fox, *Proverbs 10–31*, 857). The final clause of Prov 30:4, "if/surely you know" (*ki theda'*), is also found in Job 38:5, leading some interpreters to understand Agur's words here as similarly sarcastic (see, e.g., Toy, *Book of Proverbs*, 519). In the context of Agur's speech, however, it is more likely that the question simply emphasizes the lack of knowledge about these matters that

reading, the goal of the questions is to highlight human limitations, and the challenge to name the one who has done these things (and to name his son) cannot be met, because no one fulfills these criteria. This message certainly fits with Agur's previous statements in vv. 2–3. Other commentators, however, argue that the answer to the first four questions is, basically, "God," and that the final questions *can* be answered: God's name is Yahweh, and his son's name is Israel.[25] Both interpretations of v. 4 highlight the contrast between human limitations and divine ability expressed in Agur's questions, and the answers "no one" and "God" are really two sides of the same coin. The second reading uncovers an additional, implicit message, however: that God has a special relationship with the people of Israel and communicates divine wisdom to them.[26] This interpretation flows well into vv. 5–6, which counsel trust in God's revealed words. The questions of v. 4 may therefore be Janus-faced: when read looking back to vv. 1–3 their emphasis is on human limitations, and when read looking forward to vv. 5–6 their emphasis is on God's sovereign power and God's relationship with Israel.[27]

THE TRUSTWORTHINESS OF GOD'S WORDS (VV. 5–6)

Although the questions of v. 4 may lead in a way to Agur's address in vv. 5–6, the latter verses nevertheless represent a remarkable turning

---

Agur and his audience have in common.

25. See O'Dowd, *Proverbs*, 403–5; Waltke, *Proverbs 15–31*, 471–75; Skehan, *Studies in Israelite Poetry*, 42–43.

26. Advocates of this position have pointed to a parallel in Bar 3, which contains similar questions and makes explicit the idea that God transmitted divine wisdom to Israel: "Who has gone up into heaven, and taken [wisdom], and brought her down from the clouds? . . . No one knows the way to her, or is concerned about the path to her. But the one who knows all things knows her, he found her by his understanding. . . . This is our God; no other can be compared to him. He found the whole way to knowledge, and gave her to his servant Jacob and to Israel, whom he loved" (3:29, 31–32, 35–36 NRSV). See O'Dowd, *Proverbs*, 397–98, 404; Waltke, *Proverbs 15–31*, 472–73.

27. Waltke applies the term "janus" to v. 4 but interprets the text differently than I do. He advocates the second interpretation of v. 4 as outlined above (see nn. 25 and 26), calling the text "a janus verse" because it points "to a personal relationship with the wise Sovereign as the means to overcome the human predicament of ignorance and death" (*Proverbs 15–31*, 467).

point in Agur's speech: "Every word of God is purified; he is a shield to those who take refuge in him. Do not add to his words, lest he rebuke you and you be proved a liar." Given the fact that ambiguities are found throughout vv. 1–4, the textual clarity that meets the reader in these verses is striking. If the sometimes garbled, ambiguous, and multivalent text of vv. 1–4 helps to underscore the limitations of human understanding, the lucidity of vv. 5–6 reinforces their message that God's speech is trustworthy. Despite the change in tone here, however, it is not necessary to see these words as so radically discontinuous with vv. 1–4 that they must be spoken by another person, as some interpreters argue. Rather, Agur's message in vv. 5–6 follows logically from his preceding expressions of despair and statements of ignorance. If human knowledge and ability are limited, only God's words can be trusted. Those who trust in God will be protected, but those who try to supplement God's wisdom with their own will be put in their place.

The message of vv. 5–6 is reinforced further by the fact that these verses are made up of references to other biblical texts. Verse 5 appears to quote Ps 18:30 [31] // 2 Sam 22:31, with minor differences: the word "every/all" (*kol*) appears in the first clause of Prov 30:5 ("every word of God") but in the second clause of Ps 18:30 ("all who take refuge in him"), and Prov 30:5 uses the name Eloah for God where Ps 18:30 has the personal name Yahweh.[28] The use of Eloah in Prov 30:5 may have been inspired by its appearance in the next line of the psalm as part of a question that overlaps with Agur's focus on God's identity and name: "Who is Eloah but Yahweh?" (Ps 18:31 [32]).[29] Another biblical allusion is found in v. 6, where Agur's admonition "Do not add to his words" appears to be a reference to Deut 4:2: "You shall not add to the word that I am commanding you."[30] The warning about adding to God's words in Deuteronomy relates to God's laws, and the allusion to

---

28. In addition, the beginning of Ps 18:30, "As for God, his way is perfect," is not quoted in Prov 30:5.

29. The name Eloah occurs in Proverbs only here and is rare in Psalms, occurring only in Pss 18:31, 50:22, 114:7, and 139:19. The parallel text 2 Sam 18:32 uses the name El rather than Eloah.

30. The language used in Prov 30:6 and Deut 4:2 to prohibit adding to God's words (*y-s-f* + *'al davar*) does not occur elsewhere in the Old Testament except in Deut 12:32 [13:1].

Deuteronomy in Prov 30:6 probably carries this idea with it, especially since several of the Ten Commandments are alluded to in the words of Agur, as I will discuss below.

Agur's clear statement of trust in God's words in vv. 5–6 provides the first resolution to the problem of weariness and ignorance that is laid out in vv. 1–4. The allusions to Ps 18 and Deut 4 convey the implicit message that God's words are to be found in written scripture, especially given the fact that the admonition "Do not add to his words" is a formula typically used with regard to authoritative written texts.[31] These allusions also reinforce concepts that are expressed elsewhere in Agur's speech, such as God's power and the importance of trusting God and following God's law. The message of vv. 5–6 is therefore an antidote to Agur's weariness and ignorance as well as a segue to his prayer.

AGUR'S PRAYER (VV. 7–9)

Agur's prayer of vv. 7–9 represents the second resolution to his dilemma: "Two things I ask of you; do not withhold them from me before I die: keep falsehood and lying words far from me; do not give me poverty or riches; feed me my apportioned food. Lest I be sated and act deceptively and say, 'Who is Yahweh?,' or lest I become poor and steal and profane the name of my God" (vv. 7–9). In his direct appeal to God,[32] Agur's speech comes full circle, with prayers forming an *inclusio* around his address to a human audience.

Although at first glance this simple prayer may seem unrelated to Agur's speech that precedes it, upon closer examination it demonstrates several verbal and conceptual connections with that material. Agur's desire that his requests be fulfilled "before I die" (v. 7) fits with his exhausted state in v. 1.[33] Furthermore, Agur's request that "falsehood and lying words (*devar kazav*)" be kept far from him (v. 8) recalls his warning about adding to God's words in v. 6, which uses the same

---

31. See Fox, *Proverbs 10–31*, 858–59; Waltke, *Proverbs 15–31*, 475; Toy, *Book of Proverbs*, 523.

32. Although God is not named explicitly as the addressee of Agur's plea in vv. 7–9 (contra the NIV, which supplies "Lord"), his requests could not be granted by other people (see Fox, *Proverbs 10–31*, 859).

33. See similarly Franklyn, "Sayings of Agur," 249.

root: "lest you be proved a liar (*venikhzavta*)." In addition to this echo, the focus on "lying words" presents a contrast with God's "purified" word that should not be added to (*'al tosp 'al devarayv*) (vv. 5–6). Agur's appeal to be kept far from human falsehood and lies thus complements his reliance on God's true words.

Agur's second entreaty is given both a negative and a positive formulation—to be given neither poverty nor riches, and to receive the food that he needs (v. 8)—and it includes the consequences that may follow from becoming poor or rich (v. 9). Both the request and the potential consequences have connections with Agur's preceding words. The phrase "feed me my apportioned food" (*hatrifeni lekhem khuqqi*) (v. 8) is formulated with a verb (*t-r-f*) that normally refers to animals tearing their prey; it could be translated, "let me devour my apportioned food."[34] The use of a verb that brings to mind a wild animal perhaps develops the image Agur uses in v. 2, which can be translated, "I am more beast than man."[35] The prayer also demonstrates Agur's reliance on God for his everyday needs, showing that he believes the adage he quoted earlier, that God "is a shield to those who take refuge in him" (v. 5).[36]

Agur's explanation of why he does not want to become rich (v. 9) echoes several other places in his speech. First, Agur's concern not to "act deceitfully" (*vekhikhashti*)[37] complements his first request, to be

---

34. Longman translates similarly, "Allow me to devour my regular allotment of bread" (*Proverbs*, 516). On the meaning of *khuqqi* as "what is appointed for me," see Fox, *Proverbs 10–31*, 860. Many commentators have noted that this request is echoed in the Lord's Prayer: "Give us this day our daily bread" (Matt 6:11) (see O'Dowd, *Proverbs*, 405, 415; Longman, *Proverbs*, 525; Fox, *Proverbs 10–31*, 860).

35. On this translation, see above and n. 18. The verb *t-r-f* may have acquired a softened sense over time, however. The noun form of the root, *teref*, which typically means "prey," refers in three texts to food for humans, provided by God (Ps 111:5; Mal 3:10) or the matriarch of a household (Prov 31:15); see BDB, s.v. טֶרֶף. In Prov 31:15 this noun is parallel to the word "portion" ("She gives food [*teref*] to her house and a portion [*khoq*] to her maidens").

36. See similarly Fox, *Proverbs 10–31*, 859.

37. This word is often translated "deny you" in order to better fit the context and because the word is often used with this sense; see BDB, s.v. כחש. The object "you" must be supplied in this translation, however. It is notable that the same verb is used in a list of commandments in Lev 19:11–12 that has several connections with the present text: "You shall not steal, you shall not act deceitfully (*tekhakhashu*), you

kept far from falsehood and lying words, and both requests are consistent with Agur's concern about not adding to God's words, "lest you be proved a liar" (v. 6). The question "Who is Yahweh?" harks back to Agur's question "What is his name?" (v. 4) and is striking in its use of the personal divine name for the first time in this passage.[38]

Agur's concerns regarding the identity and name of God are seen again when he gives the possible consequence of becoming poor ("lest I . . . steal and profane the name of my God," v. 9). His desire not to profane the name of God appears to reflect the commandment not to take God's name "in vain" (*lashav'*) (Exod 20:7; Deut 5:11). It is notable that this commandment contains the same word that Agur uses when he asks for falsehood to be kept far from him: "Keep falsehood (*shav'*) and lying words far from me" (v. 8). Commentators have noticed that several of the Ten Commandments appear to be alluded to in Prov 30; the prayer itself makes reference to the commandments against stealing, giving false testimony, and taking God's name in vain.[39] These implicit references to the Decalogue fit well with Agur's message in vv. 5–6, especially given the allusion to Moses's address in Deut 4 in Agur's admonition "Do not add to his words" (v. 6).

Not only is Agur's prayer consistent with his earlier concerns for truth and keeping God's commandments, his appeal to live a life of moderation also flows sensibly from his preceding statements about the human condition. He is a person who is weary and worn out (v. 1), and he understands his own limitations (vv. 2–4). In light of this situation of human weakness, he does not ask to resist the impulse to steal or to misuse God's name; he asks rather not to be put in a situation that might lead to him committing these sins.[40] An analogy might be

---

shall not lie to one another. You shall not swear by my name falsely, and so profane the name of your God: I am Yahweh" (see O'Dowd, *Proverbs*, 398–99).

38. See O'Dowd, *Proverbs*, 405. Agur's question may also be intended to recall the question of Ps 18:31, "Who is Eloah except Yahweh?," reversing its force so that it denies rather than affirms the uniqueness of Yahweh.

39. See O'Dowd, *Proverbs*, 398–99.

40. Toy comes to a similar conclusion: "We might expect the prayer: 'teach me to use both poverty and riches aright'; but the writer's experience and observation have apparently impressed him with the dangers of both" (*Book of Proverbs*, 525).

Section 4: Prayers of Others

drawn with the request "Lead us not into temptation" (not, "Give us the strength to resist temptation") in the Lord's Prayer (Matt 6:13).

Agur's simple prayer, resonating in content and tone with the rest of his speech, is an appropriate resolution of the predicament that Agur expresses in vv. 1–4 and an illustration of the advice he gives in vv. 5–6. In vv. 1–4, the sage recognizes his own weaknesses and acknowledges God's power. In light of these things, he does not try to grasp things that are beyond his abilities, but rather focuses his prayer on the sphere of everyday life. Although there is a great gulf between God and humanity in terms of wisdom and power (v. 4), the prayer shows that God is nevertheless accessible to humans. Agur's prayer also complements his admonitions to trust in God and to obey God's words (vv. 5–6); the fact that he prays illustrates his trust in God, and the content of the prayer is focused on keeping God's commandments.

Not only does Agur's prayer function as an appropriate conclusion to his speech of vv. 1–6, it also works well as part of the conclusion to the book of Proverbs.[41] Agur's expression of ignorance is arresting at the end of a book intended to impart wisdom, but it functions as a prudent caution against misunderstanding the message of Proverbs. On one level, wisdom can be acquired; this is the underlying assumption of most of the book of Proverbs. On another level, however, wisdom is ultimately beyond the reach of humanity; this is Agur's message. Agur thus counsels trust in God's words as revealed in scripture, and he prays for help in living out these words in his everyday life. The process of learning wisdom should develop humility, and this is what Agur demonstrates in his statements and in his prayer. In a way, the content of the prayer is continuous with the proverbial wisdom found earlier in the book, which warns about the dangers of lies (Prov 6:16–19; 12:19; 21:28) and points out the perils of both poverty (10:15; 14:20; 19:4) and wealth (11:4, 28; 13:8; 23:4–5).[42] But the fact that the message of Prov 30:7–9 is presented in the form of a prayer adds another dimension to

---

41. Proverbs 30:1–9 is an appendix to the book (the first in a series of appendices in Prov 30 and 31), probably "intended to comment on the earlier material" (Fox, *Proverbs 10–31*, 849).

42. For a discussion of different perspectives on poverty and wealth in Proverbs, see Longman, *Proverbs*, 573–76.

the wisdom message, teaching that the counsel of Proverbs cannot be put into practice without God's help.

CONCLUSION

Agur's prayer is relevant for anyone confronted with a paradox that arises when trying to gain wisdom—the more one learns, the more one realizes how much ultimate knowledge is beyond one's grasp. This is true even when the quest for wisdom is focused on searching the Scriptures, as is shown by the placement of Agur's words toward the end of the book of Proverbs, presumably as an implicit commentary on the rest of the book.[43] This situation should not lead to intellectual nihilism or ethical malaise, however. Rather, as Agur demonstrates, a person wearied by the human predicament can turn to God, asking for help to live a life of integrity and moderation. Although divine wisdom is out of the reach of humans, divine provision extends to those who seek God in prayer.

BIBLIOGRAPHY

Barucq, André. *Le livre des Proverbes*. Sources bibliques. Paris: Gabalda, 1964.

Clifford, Richard J. *Proverbs*. OTL. Louisville: Westminster John Knox, 1999.

Crenshaw, James L. *Old Testament Wisdom: An Introduction*. Louisville: Westminster John Knox, 1981.

Fox, Michael V. *Proverbs 10–31*. AB 18B. Garden City, NY: Doubleday, 2009.

Franklyn, Paul. "The Sayings of Agur in Proverbs 30: Piety or Skepticism?" *ZAW* 95 (1983) 238–52.

Longman III, Tremper. *Proverbs*. BCOTWP. Grand Rapids: Baker Academic, 2006.

O'Dowd, Ryan P. *Proverbs*. Story of God Bible Commentary. Grand Rapids: Zondervan, 2017.

Perdue, Leo G. *Proverbs*. IBC. Louisville: John Knox, 2000.

Rendsburg, Gary A. *How the Bible Is Written*. Peabody, MA: Hendrickson, 2019.

Scott, R. B. Y. *Proverbs, Ecclesiastes*. AB 18. Garden City, NY: Doubleday, 1965.

Skehan, Patrick W. *Studies in Israelite Poetry and Wisdom*. CBQMS. Washington, DC: Catholic Biblical Association, 1991.

---

43. See n. 41 above.

Section 4: Prayers of Others

Toy, Crawford H. *The Book of Proverbs*. ICC. New York: Scribner's Sons, 1902.
Waltke, Bruce K. *Proverbs 15–31*. NICOT. Grand Rapids: Eerdmans, 2005.

Postscript

Reflections after Seven Years of Studying Prayer in the Old Testament

PHILLIP G. CAMP

THIS IS THE SECOND book I have co-edited on the theology, or theologies, of prayer in the Old Testament. Both books have followed annual sessions on the topic at academic conferences, first at the Thomas H. Olbricht Christian Scholars' Conference at Lipscomb University over three years and then at the meetings of the Institute for Biblical Research during four successive years. I detail the reason for initiating this study in the introduction to *Praying with Ancient Israel*.[1] Simply restated, Terence Fretheim remarked on the absence of prayer in Old Testament theologies.[2] Thus, from 2012 until the present, I have been regularly involved in hearing (and on a few occasions reading) papers, researching, contemplating, and writing about prayer.

However, this study has not been merely academic for me or for the participants in the two conferences and books. From the outset, we

---

1. Camp and Longman, *Praying with Ancient Israel*, 15–16.

2. Fretheim said, "In my estimation, there is far too little sustained theological reflection on such a widespread Israelite practice" (*Creation Untamed*, 124n1). About twenty years before Fretheim made his observation, Samuel Balentine noted that prayer in the OT was a theme that had attracted little scholarly attention (*Prayer in the Hebrew Bible*, 1; see also p. 226). Interestingly, the year before Fretheim's book came out, the third volume of John Goldingay's OT theology was released with a chapter of over 130 pages on prayer in the OT. (*Theology: Volume Three*, 191–322).

have approached this work with a concern that the outcomes of our study will help individual believers as well as the church at large in our prayer lives. At the close of the project, that question still stands for each one of us.

Over the last several years, I have gleaned much from the insightful work of my colleagues as each one has explored specific exegetical and theological details of select prayers from Old Testament figures. What follows here are more general reflections, threads that have come together, and things I might emphasize to my students and my church about prayer.

PRAYER IS DEEPLY RELATIONAL

This relational nature of prayer manifests itself on several levels. The foundational and always dynamic relationship is with God. Some of the biblical figures who engaged God in prayer had longstanding relationships with God; others were at the beginning stages. Moses' conversation with God at the burning bush (Exod 3–4) was the point at which Moses entered relationship with God and that initial dialogue seems to have been genuine prayer. As Solomon offered the temple dedication prayer, he anticipated that foreigners would pray to Israel's God, not because of a standing relationship with Yahweh, but because of Yahweh's reputation (1 Kgs 8:41–43; 2 Chr 6:32–33). Thus, membership in the covenant community was not a requirement for entering into a prayerful relationship with God.

In and through prayer, this relationship flourished, leading to deepened trust, devotion, and mutual joy. At the same time, challenges, anguish, uncertainty, and questions arose for many. They glorified God; they also accused God. They were persistent, even in the face of apparent hopelessness. On the basis of their genuine relationship with God, biblical figures like Abraham, Moses, Job, and Habakkuk could confront and challenge God and be confronted and challenged by God. They were meeting with the God they knew, were bound to, and loved. That fostered courage and trust when the unknowns seemed overwhelming.

On the basis of this dynamic relationship, Israel could approach God in confidence. Sometimes the motives were grand and selfless—intercession for the nation, deliverance from danger, or fulfillment of God's cosmic purposes. At other times, however, the prayers were about less grandiose matters—a woman's desire for a child (Gen 29:31–30:24; 1 Sam 1:9–11), care for a vulnerable child (Gen 21:16; 1 Kgs 17:20), healing from personal illness (2 Kgs 20:2–3), or forgiveness of one's sins (Ps 51).

Another relationship, demonstrated in intercessory prayer, is equally noteworthy: human-to-human relationships. For example, Moses stood between his God and his fellow Israelites both in the golden calf incident (Exod 32–34) and after Israel's rebellion in the wilderness (Num 13–14). Amos twice appealed to God for his fellow Israelites, who could not withstand the judgments of God (Amos 7:1–6).

For God's people today, active and intentional prayer is a primary means by which we develop our relationship with God. By engaging God in this way, we come to know better and better who God is, and who God has called us to be. We come to understand that we can truly engage God to share our joys, struggles, and doubts. We pray not only for things of national and international proportion, but we also bring our individual needs and concerns before God. In these prayers, we have confidence and hope because we do not address an aloof stranger but the One who knows us and whom we know and trust.

PRAYER IS DIALOGICAL

Communication with God is indeed dialogue back and forth with a Person. The dialogue can be initiated from either side. God started conversations through a burning bush, by calling Samuel's name in the night (1 Sam 3), with a "still small voice" (1 Kgs 19:12, KJV), an implicit invitation to intercede (Gen 18:17–21; Exod 32:9–10), a vision (Gen 15:1), and a dream (1 Kgs 3:5). Humans pleaded with God to "incline your ear" through birth and death, joy and sorrow, gratitude and need, confidence and questioning, seeking direction forward in God's will or longing for the way back to God. These powerful testimonies in the OT to hearing the voice of God continue into the NT as well (e.g., Acts 10; 2 Cor 12:8–9).

Admittedly, we may feel that we are the only ones really involved when we attempt to pray. We may never sense God initiating a conversation or responding to our words. If this is so, there might be merit in reflecting as to why we no longer expect to hear God. Perhaps we are too deeply shaped by contemporary cultural skepticism that denies the possibility of God speaking to us. Yet the OT (and NT) presentation of a God who engages in dialogue is calling us to rethink our understanding of prayer and to engage the practice with eyes to see and ears to hear.

PRAYER CALLS US TO TRUST IN THE GOD WHO ACTS

Those who prayed expected that God could and would do something. When Israelites prayed to God, it was on the basis of what they knew about their God, both his mighty acts and the prophetic promises. They trusted that God could give them food, or children, or victory over enemies, or safe travels, or healing, or justice, or forgiveness and restoration. Solomon expected that the foreigner would pray to God because he or she had heard of God's name and also what God had done through his strong hand and outstretched arm.

In some segments of the church, we hear prayer primarily described as self-realization or self-help, or we are told that we pray in order that God will change us—our attitudes or our longings. This latter perspective is true; prayer can certainly change the one who prays, prompting repentance, furthering awareness of God and God's purposes, or expanding our sense of God's power and majesty. Practicing prayer can teach us to submit to the will of God ("Thy will be done"). The psalmist prayed for radical change, "Create in me a clean heart, O God, and put a new and right spirit within me" (Ps 51:10, NRSV). Such a prayer, however, is not self-actualization. It is a recognition of our powerless to change on our own, and so we appeal to God to reach from heaven to earth to intervene for us and do what we cannot do for ourselves. It is trusting engagement with our loving and all-powerful God who acts in response to prayer.

Phillip G. Camp—*Postscript*

PRAYER LEADS US TO ENCOUNTER THE SOVEREIGNTY AND MYSTERY OF GOD

Though prayer for Israel was relational and dialogical, it was never a relationship or dialogue between equals. God invited Israelites to approach in prayer and engaged them through prayer, but God remained sovereign in the relationship. Prayer did not manipulate or force God's hand as though God were some sort of cosmic vending machine—put the right thing in and get what you want. Prayer was not magic words accompanied by rituals that could cajole the divine into doing one's will. That is how Baal's prophets prayed (1 Kgs 18:26–29). It is not how Israel was to pray.

In some instances, God did not respond in the expected way. Sometimes God explained why this was the case. Though God granted Moses' prayer to spare Israel after the golden calf incident (Exod 32:11–14; Deut 10:10–11), he did not grant Moses' personal request to enter the Promised Land (Deut 3:25–26). Moses had broken faith with God and did not uphold God's holiness before Israel at Meribah (Deut 32:51–52). God answered Elijah's prayers on Mount Carmel with fire and rain (1 Kgs 18), but he rejected Elijah's plea to take his life (1 Kgs 19:4). Instead, God re-commissioned him to anoint others (1 Kgs 19:15–16).

When God did not answer, at either the expected time or anticipated manner, God's people were reminded that they were most assuredly not on equal footing with the God they addressed. Even God's "explanations" in particular cases still left much in the realm of mystery—and that was (and is) as it should be. The paradigmatic example was Job who was privileged to experience God's majestic and overwhelming revelation. Job did not receive an explanation for his suffering. Rather, God's response left Job fully aware of the limits of his own wisdom and knowledge, but it also provided a basis for hope and trust. Coming before the mystery and sovereignty of God in prayer not only properly oriented the relationship between God and Israel, it engendered trust in the midst of baffling circumstances.

Prayers that extolled God's glory, power, wisdom, and majesty were equally important. In offering praise, Israel deepened their understanding of God's loving sovereignty. Thus, Habakkuk could pray in the midst of the injustice of Judah and in dreaded anticipation of the coming judgment through Babylon and the attendant disasters, "yet I will rejoice in the LORD, I will exult in the God of salvation" (Hab 3:18, NRSV).

As we pray, these cautions should be in the forefront. We must not view prayer as a way to manipulate God in order to produce our desired results. Instead, prayer brings us into conversation with the Maker of heaven and earth, the Redeemer of Israel, and the God who has redeemed us through his Son, whom we call "Lord." We are constantly reminded that God's ways and purposes are beyond us, except as God chooses to reveal the Divine will. As Jesus taught, we pray for God's will to be done (Matt 6:10), even as we express our own desires and concerns to God.

I have heard it said that God answers all prayers in one of three ways: yes, no, or wait. In light of prayers in the OT, we might add another option; God is doing something in response to our prayers that we cannot possibly imagine. God will respond to our prayer in a way that conforms to God's purposes and will bring about something beyond what we expect. Because God is faithful and sovereign, we can trust God "to do immeasurably more than all we ask or imagine" (cf. Eph 3:20, NIV).

PRAYER IS WITNESS

Israelites' prayers told each other and the world something about their God. In a remarkable declaration, Moses said that God's nearness to Israel when they prayed would serve as a witness to the nations (Deut 4:7). Psalms of praise declared both the power and majesty of God, and revealed God's concern for those in need—the needy on the ash heap and the barren woman (Ps 113:7–9; 1 Sam 2:5). Laments and other cries for help likewise testified to Israel's belief that their God was fundamentally a God of justice and mercy. Psalms of thanksgiving and songs of praise credited God with victory over enemies, sickness, and sin. When Ezra refused a protection detail for his return trip to Judah and instead prayed to God for safe passage, that was a testimony to both his fellow returnees and the Persian leaders of his faith in God's ability to protect them (Ezra 8:21–23). Prayers on behalf of non-Israelite kings (Gen 20:17–18; Exod 9:29; Ezra 6:10) bore witness that, in Israel's eyes, all kings of the earth fell under the sovereignty of God. Likewise, prayers of kings, whether Israelite or foreign (e.g., Nebuchadnezzar in Dan 4:34–35), demonstrated the rulers' recognition of God's sovereignty over them. Solomon asked God to hear and grant the prayers of foreigners who would come to the temple to pray so that they would know and fear God, as Israel was to do, and the temple was to become a house of prayer also for the foreigners (Isa 56:6–7).

Prayer continues to serve as a witness both for us and to the world. In prayer we are reminded that God acts on our behalf, compassionately hears our concerns, and calls us back into faithful relationship with him. Prayer testifies that we believe that God is good, just, merciful, and powerful, above any human powers. We bear witness to the world of our trust in God.

The apostle Paul shifts the temple imagery from a physical structure to individual Christians and the church, who are filled with the Spirit of God (1 Cor 3:16; 6:19). It is that same Spirit who intercedes for us (Rom 8:26–27). But in what sense, carrying over the temple imagery, do we as the church become the place where the foreigner or outsider can pray and be heard by God? In what sense is the church the house of prayer for the nations? We think of the expectation in Isa 56:3–8 that foreigners who turn to Israel's God will be included in the people of God, fulfilling the mission of Israel (Gen 12:3; Deut 4:6–8). This has been accomplished through the death and resurrection of Christ and the outpouring of the Spirit on Jews and Gentiles (Acts 2, 10). The church also extends to those still outside the community of faith a prayerful invitation into a relationship with our faithful God. That means praying earnestly against the temptations to succumb to contemporary idolatries and living such good lives that those who observe us will themselves glorify God (1 Pet 2:11–12).

BIBLIOGRAPHY

Balentine, Samuel E. *Prayer in the Hebrew Bible: The Drama of Divine-Human Dialogue.* OBT. Minneapolis: Fortress, 1993.

Camp, Phillip G., and Tremper Longman III, eds. *Praying with Ancient Israel: Exploring the Theology of Prayer in the Old Testament*. Abilene, TX: Abilene Christian University Press, 2015.

Fretheim, Terence E. *Creation Untamed: The Bible, God, and Natural Disasters*. Grand Rapids: Baker, 2010.

Goldingay, John. *Old Testament Theology: Volume Three: Israel's Life*. Downers Grove, IL: IVP Academic, 2009.

Index of Modern Authors

Alter, R., 79–80
Amar, I., 86, 96
Amzallag, N., 81, 87, 96
Arnold, B., 188, 190
Austin, J. L., 156, 161, 170

Balentine, S., 4, 18, 19, 26, 46, 56, 64, 84, 94, 96, 108, 117, 192, 205, 253, 259
Barnes, W., 71–72, 79, 80
Barucq, A., 239, 251
Beale, G., 63–64
Beaucamp, P., 123, 134
Beentjes, P., 82–83, 85–90, 92–93, 97
Ben Zvi, E., 119, 134, 136, 159, 171
Bergen, R., 182, 190
Beuken, W., 128, 132, 134
Blenkinsopp, J., 123, 127, 134, 208–9, 223
Block, D., 23–25, 44–46, 180–81, 190
Boda, M., 119–20, 130, 131, 133–35
Bonhoeffer, D., 96, 97
Brettler, M., 54–55, 64
Bridge, E., 161, 170
Bright, J., 139, 144, 146, 148, 153
Broyles, C., 200, 205
Bruckner, J., 165, 170
Brueggemann, W., 162, 170, 184–85, 190, 192, 205, 216, 223
Bush, F., 182, 190
Buss, M., 119, 135
Butterworth, M., 74, 80

Callabro, D., 214, 223
Camp, P. vii, 157, 163–64, 169–70, 176, 190, 253, 260

Campbell, E., 182, 190
Childs, B., 107, 117, 123, 131, 135, 163, 170
Chisholm, R., 158, 170
Clark, G., 231, 237
Clifford, R., 239, 241, 244, 251
Cogan, M., 69, 71, 79–80, 215, 223
Cohn, R., 68, 80
Cooper, D., 73, 80
Crenshaw, J., 239, 251
Cudworth, T., 84–85, 97

Davies, P., 93, 97
DeClaissé-Walford, N., 175, 190
Delitszch, F., 109, 117
DeVries, S., 57, 64, 107–9, 117
Dharamraj, H., 106, 112, 117
Dietrich, J., 88, 97
Dijk-Hemmes, F., 176, 190
Dillard, R., 82–83, 86, 97
Dobbs-Allsopp, F., 130, 135

Endres, J., 83–84, 97
Eskanazi, T., 219, 223
Evans, M., 183, 190

Firth, D., 184, 190, 193, 200, 204–5
Fishbane, M., 227, 237
Floyd, M., 119, 134
Foster, B., 23, 47
Fox, M., 239, 241–44, 247–48, 250–51
Franklyn, P., 239, 241, 247, 251
Fretheim, T., 73, 79–80, 116–17, 158, 170, 180, 185, 190, 253, 260
Friedman, R., 230, 237
Fritz, V., 79–80

Index of Modern Authors

Glueck, N., 231, 237
Goldingay, J., 5, 7, 19, 120, 123, 129–30, 132, 135, 158, 170, 175, 190, 253, 260
Grayson, A. K., 67, 80
Greßmann, H., 123, 135

Haemig, M., 96–97
Hall, S., 198, 205
Hanhart, R., 212, 223
Hasel, G., 133, 135
Hawkins, R., 109, 117
Hays, R., 226–27, 237
Heffelfinger, K., 130, 135
Heschel, A. J., 140, 153
Hill, A., 86, 97
Hobbs, T. R., 76, 79–80
Holladay, W., 144–45, 153
Hollander, J., 227, 237
Hoyt, J., 167, 170
Hubbard, R., 181–82, 190
Hundley, M., 53–54, 57, 64
Hurowitz, V., 52–53, 64–65

Jacobson, R., 130, 135
Janzen, D., 207, 223
Japhet, S., 82–83, 85–86, 90, 92, 97, 218, 223
Jebasingh, J., 95, 97
Johnson, D., 130, 135
Jones, G.H., 69, 71, 79–80
Jones, P., 113, 116–17

Kalimi, I., 82, 97
Kang, J., 54, 65
Keil, C. F., 109, 117
Kibbe, M., 25, 47
Kim, B., 182, 190
Kiuchi, N., 105–6, 117
Klein, B., 82–83, 86–87, 92, 97
Kloner, A., 212, 223
Knoppers, G., 82, 87–88, 90–91, 94, 97–98
Kuntzmann, R., 84, 87–89, 92, 98

Lamb, D., 67–68, 74, 80
Leithart, P., 71, 79–80
Levenson, J., 55, 60, 65
Limburgh, J., 168, 170

Lister, J., 61, 65
Loete, J., 128, 136
Lohrmann, J., 73, 80
Long, B., 54, 65
Longman, T., vii, 196, 205, 219, 223, 241, 248, 250–51, 253, 260
Luckenbill, D., 67, 80
Lundbom, J., 160, 170
Lynch, M., 85, 98
Lyons, W., 159, 161–62, 171

MacDonald, N., 159, 162, 171
Mandolfo, C., 130, 136
Mann, S., 154–55, 157, 167, 171
Mathewson, D., 63, 65
McKenzie, S., 82, 98
McKnight, S., 115, 117
Mendenhall, G., 87, 98
Merrill, E., 35, 47
Mettinger, T., 57, 65, 123, 132, 136
Meyers, C., 179, 190
Middleton, R., 112, 118
Miller, P., 29, 32–33, 36, 42, 47, 162, 164, 168, 171, 175, 177, 187, 190, 192, 205
Mitchell, G., 202, 206
Moberly, R., 26, 47
Montgomery, J., 105, 118
Morrow, W., 204, 206
Motyer, J. A., 128–29, 136
Myers, J., 210, 223, 226, 237

Nelson, R., 109, 112, 117–18
Nurmela, R., 133, 136

O'Brien, J., 207, 223
O'Dowd, R., 240, 241, 243–45, 248–49, 251
Oswalt, J., 120, 128, 132, 136

Pan, C., 143, 153
Parker, I., 52, 65
Paul, S., 165, 171
Payne, D., 123, 135
Payne, J. B., 87, 98
Pellikan, K., 73
Perdue, L., 240, 251
Perrin, N., 63, 65
Propp, W., 164, 171

Index of Modern Authors

Rad, G. von, 102, 111, 113, 118
Rainey, A., 82, 98
Redditt, P., 210, 223
Reid, D., 196, 205
Rendsburg, G., 242, 251
Richter, S., 57, 61, 65
Rösell, C., 86–87, 90, 94, 96, 98

Sakenfeld, K., 181, 190, 231, 237
Sarna, N., 176, 191
Schultz, R., 227, 237
Scott, R. B. Y., 239, 241, 251
Searle, J., 155–56, 171
Seitz, C., 129, 131, 136, 139, 140, 147, 152–53
Shin, D., 196, 206
Simon, U., 167, 171
Singer, I., 23, 47
Skehan, P., 245, 251
Smith, G., 132, 136
Smith-Christopher, D., 219, 223
Southwood, K., 211, 223
Steck, O., 126, 136
Stipe, N., 119, 135
Strawn, B., 215, 223
Strübind, K., 92, 98
Sugimoto, T., 82, 98
Sweeney, M., 79–80, 105, 118–19, 130, 136
Surls, A., 36, 47

Tadmor, H., 69, 71, 79–80
Thiel, W., 111, 118
Thompson, J. A., 82, 98, 139, 142, 144, 153
Throntveit, M., 54, 65, 209, 210, 212, 224
Tischler, N., 176, 191

Toffelmire, C., 119, 136
Torrey, C. C., 208, 224
Toy, C. H., 239, 244, 247, 249, 252

Vanderveken, D., 156, 171
Van der Toorn, K., 212, 224

Walsh, J., 56, 65
Waltke, B., 113, 118, 239, 241–42, 245, 247, 252
Walton, J., 63, 65
Way, R., 92, 98
Webb, B., 180, 191
Wenham, G., 188, 191
Wenham, J., 194, 206
Werline, R., 102, 118
Westermann, C., 120, 123, 127, 136
Wheeler, S., 61, 65
Whybray, R. N., 125, 136
Widmer, M., 8, 11, 19, 103, 107, 113, 118, 141, 143, 147, 151–53, 230, 237
Wieringen, A., 130, 133, 136
Williams, D., 52, 65
Williamson, H. G. M., 83, 92, 98, 129, 131–32, 136
Wilson, I., 61, 65
Winther-Nielsen, N., 194, 206
Wiseman, D., 68, 73, 79–80
Wolff, H., 129, 137
Wray-Beal, L., 71, 79–80, 109, 118
Würthwein, E., 210, 219, 224

Yu, C., 113, 118

Zwingli, U., 73

Index of Ancient Sources

OLD TESTAMENT

Genesis

Reference	Pages
1	167–68
9:9–11	168
12:3	259
12:7	41
15	19, 186
15:1	255
15:5	176
16:6	176
16:7–14	176–77
16:9	176, 187
16:10	176
16:11	176, 188
16:13	188
17:7	31
17:15–21	186
18:16–33	25, 155
18:16–21	157–63
18:16	158
18:17–21	255
18:17	104, 158, 159
18:18–19	158
18:18	158–59
18:19	158
18:20–21	158
18:20	159
18:21	159
18:22	158, 159
18:22–33	116
18:22–32	157–63
18:22–23	103
18:22	158
18:23–32	160
18:23–24	158, 160
18:23	160
18:23b	160
18:24b	160
18:25	158, 160
18:25b	160
18:26–32	158, 161
18:27	161
18:28ab	160
18:30	161
18:31	161
19:12–16	163
20:7	25, 30
20:17–18	259
21:12–13	187
21:16–19	177
21:16–17	175
21:16	177, 255
21:17	177
24:67	74
25:21–23	17
25:21	186, 187
25:22–23	177–78
25:22	175
29–30	178
29:31—30:4	255
29:31	179, 187
29:32–33	178
29:35	175, 178
30:2	179, 187
30:6	178
30:14–18	178
30:17–18	178
30:17	188
30:22–24	178

Genesis (continued)

30:22	179, 187, 188
30:23	179
30:24	175
32:9–12	30
32:9	36, 41
32:22–32	19
32:24–32	6
32:28	108
35:16–20	178
36:8	82
37:34	196

Exodus

2	78
2:23–25	94
2:24	77
2:25	78
3–4	25, 30, 254
3:1—4:17	7
3:6–10	37
3:7	78
3:8	33, 37
3:12	33
3:18	33
4:23	33
5:1	33
5:3	33
5:17	33
5:22–23	116
6:2–9	37
6:2–8	36
6:2–7	31
6:6–8	33
6:6	62
6:7	31
7:3	43
7:16	33
8:1	33
8:7	33
8:20	33
8:27–28	33
8:28–32	8
9:1	33
9:13	33
9:27–35	8
9:29	259
10:3	33
10:7–8	33
10:11	33
10:16–20	8
10:24	33
10:26	33
12:31	33
12:35–36	210
12:36	209
14:11–12	33
14:13–14	81
14:15	27
15	179, 207
15:1–18	179
15:1	179
15:13	180
15:21	175, 179–80
15:25	27
18:15	188
19–24	107
19:3–25	25
19:3	25
19:6	25, 139
19:9	25
19:16–25	112
19:19–21	25
20:1–2	103
20:3	106
20:7	249
20:18–21	25
20:32–34	103
22:20	110
24:3–4	139
24:18	111
28:30	16
32–34	8, 140, 152, 226, 235, 255
32	46, 163–65, 228, 234–35
32:1–4	234
32:1	31
32:7–14	104, 155
32:7b–10	163–64
32:7ba	163
32:7bb–9	163
32:9–14	188
32:9–10	255
32:10aa	163
32:10ab–10b	164
32:11–14	27, 29, 257

Index of Ancient Sources

32:11–13	26, 27–28	14	46
32:11	30, 235	14:9	210
32:11b–13	163–64	14:13–25	164
32:11b–12a	164	14:13–20	27
32:11ba	163	14:13–19	27–29
32:11bb	163	14:14–16	33
32:12	33	14:14	30
32:12aa	163	14:19	29
32:12ab	164	14:20	29, 74, 75
32:12b–13	164	20:1–13	43
32:13	32, 230	20:1–12	35
32:14	27, 29, 34, 75	20:12	38, 42
32:30–34	41, 188	20:14–21	89
32:31–33	228	21:7–9	27
32:32–33	232	21:7	30
33:11	230	23:19	74
33:12–13	205	24:3	241
33:19—34:7	111	24:4	241
33:20	112	24:15	241
34	230, 231, 235	24:16	241
34:5–9	112	27:12–14	35
34:5–6	112		
34:6–7	36, 39, 140, 228, 230, 231, 232		
34:28	111		
40	54		

Deuteronomy

1:6	38
1:9–12	42
1:37	41
2:3	38
2:4–5	88–89
2:5	82
2:7	25
2:9	88–89
2:19	88–89
3:23–29	25, 34–38, 39–40
3:23	36
3:24	35, 41, 45
3:25–26	257
3:25	35, 38
3:26–28	38
3:26	35, 41
3:27	43
4	247
4:1–40	55
4:1–2	139
4:1	62
4:2	43, 246
4:3–4	42
4:6–8	33, 46, 259

Leviticus

8–9	54
9:24	109
17:11	105
19:11–12	248–49
21:1–3	105
25:55	32
26:40–45	148

Numbers

6:24–26	16
9:6–7	105
10:33–36	197
11:2	27
11:15	111
12:1	180
12:3	44
12:13–14	27
13–14	198, 255

Deuteronomy (continued)

Reference	Page
4:6–7	24
4:7–8	24
4:7	24, 36, 55, 94, 258
4:9–13	24
4:20	31, 55
4:21	41
4:25–31	55
4:25	26
4:28	24
4:29	6, 55
4:31	30
4:32–40	33, 37, 42, 45
4:34	43, 59, 62
4:37	32, 33
4:39	55
5:1	62
5:2–5	42
5:6	24
5:7–9	106
5:11	249
5:22–33	25, 43
5:23–29	188
5:28–31	140
6:4–5	115
6:10–15	6
6:10–11	42
6:14–15	115
6:20–25	24, 37, 42
6:21	36
6:22	43
6:23	42
7	220
7:1–3	211
7:1	209, 212
7:3	217
7:6–11	42
7:6–10	34
7:6–9	33
7:9	231, 235
7:12–16	42
7:16	31
7:19	43
8:1–5	42
8:2	25
8:4	25
8:7–14	42
8:7–10	37
8:11–20	6
8:12–13	42
8:15–16	42
8:17–18	34
9	38, 46
9:1–24	34
9:3	87
9:4–5	32
9:7–8	27
9:9	26, 32
9:13	32
9:14	26, 40
9:15–17	26
9:18–19	25–27, 30, 39–40
9:18	41, 45
9:18a	29
9:18b	26, 29
9:19	27, 34, 29
9:20	26
9:21	26
9:22–24	27
9:25—10:11	39–40
9:25–29	25, 26, 27–30
9:25	41, 45
9:25a–26a	29
9:26–29	28–29
9:26	30–32, 35, 41, 45
9:26b–29	29, 30
9:27a	32, 30
9:27b	30, 32–34
9:29	31
10:1–5	29, 34
10:8–9	34
10:8	55
10:10–11	257
10:10	34, 111
10:11	34, 42
10:12	116
10:15	42
11:2–4	42
11:9–12	37, 42
11:13–15	42
12:11	54
12:15–16	42
12:20–25	42
12:28—13:18	43
12:32	43, 246
13:2	43

Index of Ancient Sources

13:3	43	31:26	55
13:5	110	32:8–9	31
13:13–18	110	32:39	106
13:12–18	202	32:48–52	41, 42
14:2	31	32:49–52	42
15:9	24	32:49	43
17:2–7	110	32:51–52	257
17:14–20	42, 44	32:51	43, 44
17:14	67	32:52	43
17:19–20	71	33:1	43
18:9–22	25	34:1–11	43
18:9–19	25	34:1	38
18:15–22	8, 24, 43, 140	34:4	43
18:20–22	25	34:5–12	34
18:20	43	34:10–12	8, 44
23	220	34:10	24, 230
23:3–6	90		
23:3	211		
23:6	217	**Joshua**	
23:7–8	212	1:1—5:12	193, 196
23:7	212	1:1–9	198
24:1–15	24	1:5	198, 200, 202
24:19–21	105	2	194
26:5–9	37	2:10	199
26:5–8	42	2:11	195
26:8	59	3:7–17	197
26:9	42	5:1	195, 199
26:18	31	5:13—11:23	193
28	55, 59	5:13–15	13
28:1–14	42	6:6	197
28:22	55	6:18	194
28:23–24	55	7	196, 204, 205
28:25	55	7:1–6	193–95
28:36	55	7:1	193, 201, 202
28:42	55	7:5	199
28:64	55	7:6–13	13
28:68	36	7:6–9	192, 193, 195–200
29:5	25	7:6	196
29:24	55	7:7–9	197
30	226, 235	7:7	198, 202
30:1–4	228, 233–35	7:7a	198
30:1	232, 233	7:8	198, 199, 202
30:4	233	7:9	198, 199, 203
30:6	109	7:10–15	193, 200–203
30:11–14	24	7:10–12	201
31:9–13	139	7:11–12	202
31:9	55	7:11	202
31:25	55	7:12	202

269

Joshua (continued)

7:13–15	201
7:15	202
8	194–95
8:1–3	194
8:27	194
8:30–35	197
8:33	197
9:1–2	195, 199
9:14	13
10:1–5	195, 199
10:12–14	13, 192
10:14	81
11:1–5	195, 199
21:44–45	58
22:4–5	58
22:16	199
23–24	210
23:1	58
23:14	58

Judges

1:1	13
4	180
4:3	13
5:1–31	175, 180–81
5:2	180
5:3	180
5:4–5	180
5:7	180
5:9	180
5:12–15	180
5:20	180
5:24–27	180
5:31	180
6:6–7	13
6:11–23	13
6:36–40	13
10:10–15	13
11:17	90
11:30–31	13
13:8	17
13:9	17
16:28	13
20:18–28	13
21:1–3	13
21:18	13

Ruth

1:8–9	175, 181
2:20	181
4:14	175, 182
4:15	182

1 Samuel

1:5	183
1:6–8	183
1:6	183
1:9–11	255
1:10–16	17, 182, 183
1:10	30, 175, 182, 183
1:11	183, 188
1:12	182
1:15	183
1:16	183
1:12–15	175
1:12–13	183
1:17	17
1:19	183
1:26–27	182
2:1–10	17, 175, 182, 183–84
2:1	182, 183
2:2	183, 184
2:3	14
2:4–8	183
2:4	184
2:5	258
2:6–8	184
2:9	184
2:10	184
2:21	183
3	255
3:1–14	9
5:1–4	197
7:3–12	107
7:5–9	9, 188
7:5	30
7:6	5
8:5	67
8:6–9	9
8:11–17	162
9:5–10	188
9:6–9	188
12:18–25	9

Index of Ancient Sources

12:22–23	151
13	7
14:24–45	14
15:11	9
15:29	74
16:1–3	9
22:6–23	14
23:1–12	14
28:6	14

2 Samuel

1:17–27	5
2:1	14
3:35	14
5:19–25	14
6–7	54
7:3–5	72
7:3–4	72
7:18–29	14
7:18–24	36
7:22	55, 57
7:27	30
12:16–23	186
12:16–20	14
12:16	92
12:21–23	92
12:24–25	184
12:25	56
13:31	196
13:39	74
18:29	36
18:32	246
21:1	14
21:2–14	14
22:31	246
23:1	241
24:10	14
24:14–25	14
24:16	75

1 Kings

1–11	52, 56
1–2	56
1:6	56
2:1–12	70
2:1	70
2:12	111
3–8	15
3:1	213, 219, 220
3:5–12	68
3:5	255
3:7	58
3:9–11	185
3:16–28	56
3:28	185
4:29–34	56
5–9	52, 53
5:1—9:10	56
5	56
5:3–5	52
5:6–18	53
6:1–38	53
7:8	213, 220
7:13–51	53
7:18–24	36
8	18, 51, 54, 55, 207, 208, 213, 214, 220–21, 222
8:1–13	52
8:1–11	53
8:1	55, 60
8:2–4	54
8:6	55
8:9	58, 59
8:10–13	54
8:10–11	61
8:12–61	53
8:12–13	57, 61
8:13	59
8:14–21	52
8:14	52, 60
8:15–26	58
8:15–21	57, 61
8:15	36, 55, 56, 59, 62
8:16–20	61
8:16–18	57
8:16	55, 58, 59
8:17–19	54
8:17	55, 56
8:19	56, 57, 58
8:20–21	57
8:20	55, 56, 57, 59
8:21	58, 59
8:22–53	52, 208
8:22–30	52

1 Kings (continued)

Ref	Pages
8:22	52, 60, 214, 215, 220
8:23–52	55
8:23	55, 57
8:24–26	56, 57, 58
8:25–26	57, 59, 68, 217
8:25	54, 55
8:26	217
8:27	54, 58
8:28–30	58, 214
8:28–29	61
8:28	60
8:29	57, 60, 61, 62, 68
8:30–59	59
8:30	30, 59, 60, 62, 64, 215
8:31–51	52, 58, 59
8:31–32	59
8:31	57
8:32	59, 62
8:33–34	59
8:33	35, 57, 60, 62
8:34	59, 60, 62, 64
8:35–36	59, 64
8:35	30, 57, 60, 62, 64
8:36	59, 60, 62
8:37–40	59
8:38	57, 60, 214
8:39	59, 60, 62
8:40	60
8:41–43	15, 59, 61, 217–18, 254
8:41	57
8:42	30, 57, 60, 62
8:43–44	57
8:43	59, 60, 61, 62
8:44–45	59
8:44	30, 54, 57, 59, 60, 61
8:45	59, 60, 62
8:46–53	216
8:46–51	59
8:46	60, 62
8:47–49	60
8:47–48	55, 60
8:47	35, 60
8:48	30, 54, 55, 57, 59, 61, 216
8:49	59, 62
8:50	60, 64, 216
8:51	55, 58, 59, 60
8:52–53	52
8:52	55, 58, 60, 62
8:53	58, 59, 60, 218
8:54–61	52
8:54–55	52, 60
8:54	215, 220
8:56–61	58, 61
8:56	58, 59
8:57	61
8:58	63
8:59	35, 60, 61, 62
8:60	55, 57, 64, 185
8:62—9:9	52
8:62–66	53, 61
8:64	61
8:65	54, 61
8:66	57, 60
9	15, 51
9:1–9	53, 216
9:3	35, 57, 61, 62, 68
9:4–5	57, 58
9:4	56
9:5	54, 57, 59
9:6–9	58
9:6	57
9:8	55
9:9	55, 64
9:24	218, 221
10	56
10:9	175, 184–85
11:1–8	217
11:1–2	213
11:1	212, 213, 220
11:3–9	218
11:6	68, 69
11:11	68
11:31–33	68
13:6	68
14:9	69
16:30	69
16:31–33	102
16:33—17:1	110
17	101, 103, 106
17:1	101, 103, 112, 150
17:3–5	103
17:8–10	103
17:13–14	104
17:14	101, 103
17:17–24	115

Index of Ancient Sources

17:18–20	104	19:15–17	7
17:18	104	19:15–16	257
17:19–24	9	19:15	113
17:20–21	104, 116	19:17–19	113–14
17:20	255	19:17	113
17:21–22	101	19:18	113
17:21	111	19:19–21	102
17:22	106	19:19	114
17:24	102	21:27–29	69
18	101, 257	22	15, 81
18:1–2	103	22:6	113
18:1	103, 110, 115		
18:4	113		
18:10–40	116		

2 Kings

18:13	106, 113, 116	1	114
18:15	103, 112, 150	1:10–14	114
18:18	110	1:10	109
18:21	106, 107	1:12	109
18:22	106	2:1–18	114
18:23–24	107	2:12	111
18:24	106, 107	3:9–20	4
18:26–29	257	3:14	150
18:26	107	4:32–36	104
18:27	107	4:33	68
18:29	107	4:34	105
18:30–32	107, 113	5:16	150
18:36–38	114	6:17–20	9
18:36–37	7, 9, 108–9	6:17	68
18:36	68, 103, 107	6:18	68
18:37–38	115	9–10	113
18:37	106, 108, 109, 116	13:2	69
18:38	109	13:4	68
18:39	102, 109, 113	13:23	228
18:40	109	17:24–29	211
18:41–46	101	18–19	67
18:42	110, 115	18:3–6	76
18:44	110	19	71, 72
19:1	109, 110	19:1–14	15
19:2	113	19:1	72
19:3–4	101	19:14–19	68
19:4	68, 110–11, 117, 257	19:15–19	15, 30
19:7–8	111	19:15	36
19:9–18	9	19:15b–19	30, 41
19:9–15	111–13	19:20–34	15, 68
19:9–14	7	19:37	67
19:10	111, 117	20	69, 70, 72, 74
19:12	10, 255	20:1–7	105
19:13–14	117	20:1–6	69, 70–72

2 Kings (continued)

20:1	66, 70, 72
20:2–3	15, 66, 255
20:2	70
20:3	71, 76, 79
20:4–11	15
20:4	69
20:5	69, 70, 72, 76–79
20:6	70, 76, 77
20:19	71
20:21—21:1	72
21	114
22–23	141
22	144, 145
22:12	36
22:13–20	16, 188
22:13	68
22:19	68, 71
23:25	142
23:26–27	142
23:31–35	144
25:8	36
25:26	59

1 Chronicles

4:9–10	6
4:41	82
5:20	91
10:12	92
13–26	14
21:15	75
21:16–17	5
22:8–9	57
22:8	14
28:20	81
29:10–19	30, 85, 92
29:11–13	41
29:11–12	84–85
29:18	84–85

2 Chronicles

1–9	92
2:12–13	56
3:1	14
6–7	15
6	54
6:3	91
6:12–13	91
6:14–42	90
6:21	91
6:25	91
6:27	91
6:28–30	90–92
6:30	91
6:31	61
6:32–33	254
6:34–35	90
6:34	91
6:39	91
7:14	30, 92, 94
7:15	92
8:11	218, 221
9:8	184
14:11	86–87, 93
16:7–9	15
17–20	81
17:14–19	87
18:31	91
20	92, 94
20:1–30	81
20:1	82
20:5	83
20:6–12	81, 82–84
20:6	83, 84–85, 95
20:7	83, 87–88, 93, 95
20:8–9	83
20:8	91
20:9	90–92, 95
20:10–11	83–84, 88–90
20:10	82, 90
20:11	95
20:12	84, 86–87, 93, 96
20:13	84
20:14–17	81
20:15–30	95
20:22–23	82
26:7	82
30:9	228
32:20	151
32:24	15, 69
33:1–20	15
33:10–17	142
34	141
34:3–7	144

34:8	144	1:6ab	229
34:19–28	188	1:6b–7a	232
34:20	36	1:6c	229
34:21–28	16	1:6cd–7	229
		1:7–9	228, 232
Ezra		1:7d	229
		1:8–9	229
1	54	1:8	227, 233
1:2	230	1:8a	229
1:6	209, 210	1:8b–9	232–33, 234
3–6	209	1:10	229, 234
3:3	210	1:11	235
3:4	210	1:11a	229
4:2	211	1:11b	229
4:4	211	1:11c	229
6	54	2:4	230
6:10	259	2:20	230
8:21–23	258	4:4–5	16
9–10	207, 208, 210, 212, 219, 221	4:4	232
9	204, 207, 208, 213, 214, 215, 220–21, 222	4:5	228
		4:9	16
9:1	208, 209, 211, 220	5:19	16
9:3—10:6	5, 16	6:9	16
9:3	213	6:14	16
9:5	214	7:73b—8:18	208, 209
9:6	215	8–10	210
9:8–10	216	9	16, 207, 235
9:8	215, 216	9:1–2	92
9:9	215, 216	9:10	43
9:10–12	218	9:17	228, 232
9:10	216, 218	9:31	228
9:11–12	218	10:28–39	16
9:12	217	11:7	241–42
9:13–15	215	13:14	16
9:15	216	13:26	213
9:24	218	13:31	16
10	208, 217–21		
10:8	209	**Job**	
Nehemiah		6:4	187
		7:11–21	187
1:4–5	16	9:13–18	187
1:4	230	28	239, 244
1:5–11	225, 226	38–42	244
1:5	228, 229, 230	38:5	244
1:5a	231	42:8	30
1:6a	229		

Index of Ancient Sources

Psalms

7:1–6	4
18	247
18:30	246
18:31	246, 249
22:1	187
22:15	187
30:8	35
35:13	5, 69
36:1	241
42–43	133
44	200
44:9–22	200
50:22	246
51	255
51:10	256
73	239, 241
78:43	43
86:15	228
88	5
102:14	18
103:8–10	228
104:29	106
106:6	55, 60
106:45	75
109	18
109:21–24	69
110:4	74
111:4	228
111:5	248
113:7–9	258
114:7	246
115	142
115:2–8	24
116:5	228
122	18
131	175
135:9	43
139:19	246
139:23	61
141:2	16
145:8	228

Proverbs

1:2	244
3:5	244
3:29	245
3:31–32	245
3:35–36	245
6:16–19	250
9:10	242
10:15	250
11:1–7	244
11:2	244
11:4	250
11:28	250
12:19	250
13:8	250
14:20	250
19:4	250
21:28	250
23:4–5	250
30:1–9	239, 240, 242, 250
30:1–6	250
30:1–4	243, 246, 247, 250
30:1–3	244, 245
30:1	238, 239, 240–42, 243, 249
30:2–4	239, 242–45, 249
30:2–3	240, 242, 243, 244, 245
30:2	242, 248
30:3	243
30:4	244, 245, 249, 250
30:5–9	239
30:5–6	239, 243, 245–47, 248, 250
30:5	246, 248
30:6	240, 246, 247, 249
30:7–9	6, 238, 239, 240, 247–51
30:7	240, 247
30:8	240, 247, 248, 249
30:8b–9	240
30:9	240, 248, 249
30:10–33	240
30:10	239
30:11–14	239
30:15–33	239
30:15–31	240
30:15–16	240
30:18	240
30:23	240
30:28	240
31:1	239
31:15	248

Index of Ancient Sources

Ecclesiastes

3:11	244
7:23–24	244
8:17	244
12:12	244

Song of Songs

8:11–12	219

Isaiah

1–39	127, 139
6–12	133
6	10, 119, 131, 133
6:3	133
6:5	133
6:11	133
7–12	131
7–11	131, 132
8	131
8:18	131
10	151
11:11–16	133
11:11	133
11:16	133
12	10, 17, 130–33
12:1–2	131, 132
12:1	130, 131
12:1a	130
12:1b–2	130, 131
12:2–3	132
12:3–4a	130
12:3–6	131, 132
12:3	130, 132
12:4–5	132
12:4	130, 131
12:4a	130
12:4b–5	130, 132
12:6	130
13–27	132
21:1–4	129
24–27	127–30, 132, 133
24:1–13	129
24:4	128
24:7	128
24:8	128
24:11	128
24:12–13	128
24:13	128, 133
24:14–16a	128, 133
24:16	128, 129
24:16b	128
24:17–23	128, 129
24:17	128
25:1–9	132
25:1–5	6, 10, 17, 129, 132
25:6–8	132
25:9–10a	132
25:9	129
26	129
26:1–3	6, 10, 17
26:7–15	10
26:17–19	17
30:9–11	133
30:19	10, 17
32–34	126
33:2–4	10, 17
35	125–26, 133
35:1–2	125–26
35:8–10	126
35:10	125
37:1–14	15
37:4	151
37:15–20	15
37:21–35	15
38	69, 70, 74
38:1–6	69
38:2–3	15
38:2	70
38:4–8	15
38:5	70
40–66	127, 131, 132, 133
40–55	120–25, 126, 127, 129, 130, 131, 132, 133
40	119, 126, 131
40:1–11	130
40:1	120, 127
40:19	120
40:27—49:13	132
40:27—49:12	121
40:27	120, 125
41:8	87–88, 93
41:10–12	88
41:18	125
41:19	125

Index of Ancient Sources

Isaiah (continued)

Reference	Page
41:29	107
42:10–12	121, 123
43:18–21	124–25, 133
44–45	142
44:23	122, 123, 127
45:8	123
48:20–21	123
48:20	122, 133
49	119
49:1–12	120
49:3	120, 127
49:10–12	125
49:13–14	124, 129
49:13	120–21, 122, 123, 124, 130
49:14—54:17	121, 132
49:14	120, 124, 125
51:1	133
51:2	122
51:3	123, 125
51:9–10	4, 10
51:11	125
52:7–12	133
52:7–10	122–23
52:9–10	123
54:1–3	123
54:1	120, 121, 123, 124
54:8	10
55:6–7	10
55:12	123, 124, 133
56–66	126–27, 130
56:3–8	259
56:6–8	208
56:6–7	259
56:7	10, 60, 218
57:17	10
57:18–19	126
58:9	10
59:2	10
60–62	126
60	127
60:21	127
61	127
61:1–3	127, 133
61:3	127
62	127
62:6–7	6
62:10–12	126
65:18–19	126
66:10	127

Jeremiah

Reference	Page
1–15	146
1:1–2	144
1:4–10	7
2:30	146
3:6–10	146
3:16	55
3:22–25	146
4:1–8	146
4:2–3	167
4:10	10, 143
4:19–22	143
5:1–3	146
5:3	142
5:27	142
5:30–31	142
5:31	141
6:6	146
6:11	143
6:13–15	142
6:13	141
6:16–19	146
6:20	147
6:25	146
6:26	146
6:28	147
7	145, 146
7:1–15	146
7:4–10	142
7:8–11	147
7:12–15	147
7:13	143, 147
7:16–28	10
7:16	138, 143, 147
7:17–19	147
7:18	17, 142
7:20–29	147
7:22–26	142
7:24	143
7:31	142
8:10–12	142
8:10	141
8:19	18, 142
9:13	142

Index of Ancient Sources

9:14	142	20:7–18	10, 143
10:1–16	142	20:7–10	187
10:17	148	21:1–11	145
10:23–25	148	21:4	55
11:2–10	148	21:5	59
11:3	55	22:1–2	145
11:4	55	22:6	145
11:7–8	142	23:9–40	142
11:11–14	10	23:11	141
11:11	148	23:18	25
11:13	142	23:21–22	25
11:14	138, 148	23:33–34	141
11:17	142	25:3	152
12:1–2	116	26	145
12:7	149	26:1–11	117
12:15	149	26:3	75
13:12	55	26:7–16	141
13:13	141	26:13	75
14:1–6	149	26:19	75
14:7–9	149	27:18	145
14:10–12	149	28	142
14:11–12	10, 69, 138, 149	29:1–10	141
14:11	145	29:10–14	152
14:13	150	29:12–13	6
14:14–16	142, 150	30–31	152
14:17–18	150	30:17	233
14:17	143	31:18	109
14:20–22	150	31:20	143
15:1–4	138, 150	32:6–25	151
15:1	103, 150	32:18	228
15:4	142, 151	32:19	61
15:6	75	32:21	59
15:10–21	205	32:23	55
15:15–18	10, 151	36:1–3	149
15:16	151	36:1	145, 149
15:19–21	10, 113, 151	36:2	145
17:10	60–61	36:4–5	145
17:14–18	151	36:6	149
17:19–20	144	36:7	149
18:8	75	36:9	149
18:10	75	36:10	145
18:19—19:3	113	36:15	145
18:19–23	151	36:32	145
19:3–4	144–45	37:3–17	151
19:13	145	37:3	148
19:14–15	145, 146	40:12	233
20:1–6	146	42:1—43:7	17, 151
20:1–2	145	42:2	148

Jeremiah (continued)

42:10	75
42:20	148
43:1–7	152
43:5	233
44:17–19	17
44:25	17
45:1	145, 149
49:5	233
49:36	233

Ezekiel

3:14	11
4:14	11
9:8	11
11:13	11
14:1–8	11
20:1–3	11
20:30–31	11
20:33–34	59
22:30–31	141
27:30	196

Daniel

2:20–23	11
4:34–35	259
6:10–13	11
6:18	69
7	11
8	11
9	18
9:1–19	11, 30
9:3	5, 69
9:4	30, 36, 41
9:20–23	11
10:1–3	69

Hosea

11:8–9	166

Joel

1:1–14	149
1:13–15	69
1:13–14	11
2:12–17	11
2:13–14	75
2:13	228
2:15–17	92
2:18–19	129
2:32	11

Amos

3:2	165
3:7	104
5	6, 11
7:1–9	12
7:1–6	155, 165–66, 255
7:2b	165
7:5b	165
7:3	75
7:6	75

Jonah

1:1–2	166
1:3	166
2	207
2:1–9	12, 167
3–4	46
3:1–4	167
3:5–8	5
3:6–9	12
3:9–10	75
3:10	167
4	166–68
4:1–11	12, 155
4:2	75, 167, 228
4:3	111
4:4	167
4:6–7	167
4:8	111
4:9	167
4:11	166, 167

Micah

3:4	12
7:18–20	12, 228
7:18	231

Index of Ancient Sources

Nahum

1:3	228

Habakkuk

1–2	12
1:2–4	204
3	12
3:16–19	205
3:18	258

Zephaniah

1:14–18	12
2:3	6, 12
3:9	12

Zechariah

1:12–13	12

Malachi

3:6	74
3:10	248
4:5–6	114

APOCRYPHA

Tobit

3:10–17	175
8:4–7	175

Judith

8:31	175
9	175
12:8	175
13:7	175
13:14	175
16:1–17	175

Additions to the Book of Esther

14:3–19	175

Sirach

48:1–14	115
48:1	101

Baruch

3	245
3:29—4:1	239

1 Esdras

8:66	212

2 Esdras

7:109	115

Susanna

13:42–45	175

NEW TESTAMENT

Matthew

5:10–12	117
5:13–16	170
6:7	108
6:9–13	63, 236
6:9	258
6:11	248
6:13	250
6:24	116
6:31–32	116
16:13–14	152
21:13	60

Mark

11:17	218, 222

Index of Ancient Sources

Luke

1:16–17	114
4:14–30	114
5:8	104
7:11–17	114
7:13	105
9:52–54	114
12:48	44
23:34	114

John

2:19–22	63
17:14	222

Acts

2	259
10	255, 259
12:5–17	46

Romans

8:26–27	259
9:3	105

1 Corinthians

3:16–17	63
3:16	259
6:19	63, 259

2 Corinthians

12:8–9	255

Galatians

1:6–9	43
3:13	106

Ephesians

2:19–22	223
3:20	258

2 Timothy

3:12	95
3:16	102

James

5:16–18	101, 114
5:16	27, 45, 76
5:17–18	103, 114
5:17	102, 115

1 Peter

2:11–12	259
4:12–19	95

2 Peter

2:6–8	163

Revelation

6:10	204
21:22	63, 95

JOSEPHUS

Ant.

14.22	115

RABBINIC WRITINGS

m. Ta'anit

2.4	115
3.7	115

www.ingramcontent.com/pod-product-compliance
Lightning Source LLC
Chambersburg PA
CBHW071238230426
43668CB00011B/1498